SELF-IDENTITY AND EVERYDAY LIFE

'Identity' and 'selfhood' are terms routinely used throughout the human sciences that seek to analyze and describe the character of everyday life and experience. Yet these terms are seldom defined or used with any precision, and scant regard is paid to the historical and cultural context in which they arose, or to which they are applied.

This innovative book provides fresh historical insights in terms of the emergence, development, and interrelationship of specific and varied notions of identity and selfhood, and outlines a new sociological framework for analysing it.

This is the first historical/sociological framework for discussion of issues which have until now, generally been treated as 'philosophy' or 'psychology', and as such it is essential reading for those undergraduates and postgraduates of sociology, philosophy, history and cultural studies interested in the concepts of identity and self. It covers a broader range of material than is usual in this style of text, and includes a survey of relevant literature and precise analysis of key concepts written in a student-friendly style.

Harvie Ferguson is a sociologist with wide-ranging interests in historical, cultural, and existential aspects of the development of modern society. His recent work includes studies of warfare, the development of modern Japanese society and phenomenology. He is currently Professor of Sociology at the University of Glasgow, Scotland.

THE NEW SOCIOLOGY

SERIES EDITOR: ANTHONY ELLIOTT, FLINDERS UNIVERSITY, AUSTRALIA

The New Sociology is a book series designed to introduce students to new issues and themes in social sciences today. What makes the series distinctive, as compared with other competing introductory textbooks, is a strong emphasis not just on key concepts and ideas but on how these play out in everyday life – on how theories and concepts are lived at the level of selfhood can cultural identities, how they are embedded in interpersonal relationships, and how they are shaped by, and shape, broader social processes.

Titles in the series:

Religion and Everyday Life
STEPHEN HUNT (2005)

Culture and Everyday Life
DAVID INGLIS (2005)

Community and Everyday Life
GRAHAM DAY (2005)

Consumption and Everyday Life
MARK W. D. PATERSON (2005)

Ethnicity and Everyday Life
CHRISTIAN KARNER (2007)

Globalization and Everyday Life
LARRY RAY (2007)

Self-Identity and Everyday Life
HARVIE FERGUSON (2009)

Gender and Everyday Life
MARY HOLMES (2008)

Forthcoming titles in the series:

Cities and Everyday Life
DAVID PARKER (2009)

Nationalism and Everyday Life
JANE HINDLEY (2009)

The Body and Everyday Life
HELEN THOMAS (2009)

Media and Everyday Life
ELLIS CASHMORE (2009)

Risk, Vulnerability and Everyday Life
IAIN WILKINSON (2009)

SELF-IDENTITY AND EVERYDAY LIFE

HARVIE FERGUSON

Routledge
Taylor & Francis Group

LONDON AND NEW YORK

**For an inspiring new generation,
Oscar, Olivia, Hannah,
Maya, Cleo**

First published 2009
by Routledge
2 Park Square, Milton Park, Abingdon, Oxon, OX14 4RN

Simultaneously published in the USA and Canada
by Routledge
270 Madison Avenue, New York, NY 10016

*Routledge is an imprint of the Taylor & Francis Group,
an informa business*
© 2009 Harvie Ferguson

Typeset in Garamond and Scala by
Swales & Willis Ltd, Exeter, Devon
Printed and bound in Great Britain
by TJ International Ltd, Padstow, Cornwall

British Library Cataloguing in Publication Data
A catalogue record for this book is available from the British Library

Library of Congress Cataloging in Publication Data
Ferguson, Harvie.
Self-identity and everyday life/Harvie Ferguson.
p. cm.
1. Self. 2. Identity (Psychology) I. Title.
BF697.F447 2009
155.2—dc22
2008046088

ISBN 10: 0–415–35509–5(hbk)
ISBN 10: 0–415–35508–7 (pbk)
ISBN 10: 0–203–00177–X (ebk)

ISBN 13: 978–0–415–35509–4 (hbk)
ISBN 13: 978–0–415–35508–7 (pbk)
ISBN 13: 978–0–203–00177–6 (ebk)

CONTENTS

SERIES EDITOR'S FOREWORD

'The New Sociology' is a Series that takes its cue from massive social transformations currently sweeping the globe. Globalization, new information technologies, the techno-industrialization of warfare and terrorism, the privatization of public resources, the dominance of consumerist values: these developments involve major change to the ways people live their personal and social lives today. Moreover, such developments impact considerably on the tasks of sociology, and the social sciences more generally. Yet, for the most part, the ways in which global institutional transformations are influencing the subject-matter and focus of sociology have been discussed only in the more advanced, specialized literature of the discipline. I was prompted to develop this Series, therefore, in order to introduce students – as well as general readers who are seeking to come to terms with the practical circumstances of their daily lives – to the various ways in which sociology reflects the transformed conditions and axes of our globalizing world.

Perhaps the central claim of the Series is that sociology is fundamentally linked to the practical and moral concerns of everyday life. The authors in this Series – examining topics all the way from the body to globalization, from self-identity to consumption – seek to demonstrate the complex, contradictory ways in which sociology is a necessary and very practical aspect of our personal and public lives. From one angle, this may seem uncontroversial. After all, many classical sociological analysts as well as those associated with the classics of social theory emphasized the practical basis of human knowledge, notably Émile Durkheim, Karl

Marx, Max Weber, Sigmund Freud, and Georg Simmel, among many others. And yet there are major respects in which the professionalization of academic sociology during the latter period of the twentieth century led to a retreat from the everyday issues and moral basis of sociology itself. (For an excellent discussion of the changing relations between practical and professional sociologies see Charles Lemert, *Sociology After the Crisis*, second edition, Boulder: Paradigm, 2004). As worrying as such a retreat from the practical and moral grounds of the discipline is, one of the main consequences of recent global transformations in the field of sociology has been a renewed emphasis on the mediation of everyday events and experiences by distant social forces, the intermeshing of the local and global in the production of social practices, and on ethics and moral responsibility at both the individual and collective levels. 'The New Sociology' Series traces out these concerns across the terrain of various themes and thematics, situating everyday social practices in the broader context of life in a globalizing world.

Against this backdrop of large-scale institutional transformations, no piece of progressive social criticism of the last 10–15 years has appeared complete without reference to the ways in which identity, selfhood and personhood are changing, and changing very fast. It is true that identity has proved to be one of the most vexing and vexed topics in the social sciences and humanities, from classical sociology through to contemporary philosophy, and this looks set to continue and possibly intensify in our own age of do-it-yourself identities, identity-politics and therapeutic selves. Yet is a paradox of our times that, just as the world beyond academia becomes more sociologically-minded in its thinking of large-scale social problems such as global warming, international drug smuggling and Internet pornography, so the professional practice of sociologists has turned – and with renewed energy – to consider identity and its more lethal brands of fundamentalist identity-politics. This has meant, among other things, that if current social change has a threatening or menacing quality to it, then this is because the social system goes all the way down – right into the inner textures of experience, at once depleting and displacing the energies of individuals in their traffic with others and the wider world. In this sense, identity is a sociological problem and not simply a psychological category. Indeed, as Harvie Ferguson demonstrates in this beautifully crafted introduction to the topic of identity, contemporary women and men are always and everywhere – and perhaps increasingly so – called upon to negotiate the complex demands of inner life, interpersonal relationships and social demands within the usually tedious, though sometimes exhilarating, fabric of everyday life.

Much talk, in recent years has been about identity: identity and its problems, the transformation of identity, and, perhaps most fashionably, the end or death of the 'human subject.' In terms of sociology, notions of identity seem inevitably to capsize into either modern or postmodern forms of theorizing. In modern theorizing, the catchword for identity is that of 'project'; in postmodern theorizing, it's that of 'fragmentation'. The 'project' of modern identity is that of identity building. By identity building, sociologists refer to the building up of conceptions of oneself, of one's personal and social location, of one's position in an order of things. One particular strength of *Self-Identity and Everyday Life* is that the author reviews an enormous range of scholarship pertaining to the self that extends beyond narrow, mundane accounts of western self-experience. Whereas most accounts of identity simply presume the context of modern western society, Ferguson demonstrates that important insights can be gained by adopting a broader comparative framework which reckons into account a number of different kinds of modern and non-modern societies.

Nevertheless, identity is generally regarded as becoming disconnected from the power of traditions and the influence of customs in modern times, and so is now a kind of self-propelling or self-reflexive entity. Identity, in conditions of modernity, becomes in a sense *radicalized*. Modernity, it might be said, is much preoccupied with identity as an end in itself: people are free to choose the kind of life they wish to live, but the imperative is to "get on" with the task and achieve. Perhaps the most comprehensive analysis to date that we have of this modern conception of identity building has been provided by the British sociologist Anthony Giddens, who lists 'reflexivity' as a core defining feature of modern identity. By reflexivity of identity, Giddens seeks to underscore the complex, contradictory ways in which women and men are called upon to monitor, track and trace the production and reproduction of their selfhood in negotiation with other people in settings of daily life. How such reflexivity of identity has risen to prominence in contemporary social conditions is investigated with great insight by Ferguson, who reviews social theories for their insights into identity from Max Weber to Erving Goffman and Paul Riceour. He examines how identity always presupposes others, cultures, contexts, systems – indeed, the production of the identity of self is fundamentally bound up with the ordering of predictable social contexts and their relatively risk-free repetition.

Harvie Ferguson's *Self-Identity and Everyday Life* is a remarkably readable, clear and stylish guide to the complex sociological debates over identity - both classical and contemporary. It is very ambitious in scope, but always drawing the reader in and along on the twists and turns of identity transformations. As Ferguson makes clear, everyday life is not just the setting of identity; rather, everyday life is where identity is constituted to its roots - made, remade and transformed. This book rewrites the critique of everyday life through the paradigm of identity-studies. It is a most welcome addition to 'The New Sociology'.

Anthony Elliott
Adelaide, 2008

INTERRUPTION 1: STORY

Begin, Muse, when the two first broke and clashed,
Agamemnon lord of men and brilliant Achilles.

(Homer)

As a young person born after the war (at that time the Second World War was known simply as 'the war'), and brought up in the protected environment of a small seaside town, the author during his teenage years felt entitled to an 'identity crisis'.

Why not? After all, in London, or Paris, or New York a period of youthful uncertainty and personal doubt was an obligatory feature of growing up. Or so he believed. Haphazard exposure to contemporary literary works convinced him that there, at least, a self-imposed *rite de passage*, rich in juvenile anxiety and indecision, was no longer the privilege of a few well educated and precociously talented souls but had become essential even for those, conscious of modest gifts and faltering resolve. Unadventurous and compliant as he was, he nonetheless felt obliged to experience an identity crisis 'of his very own'. (It was some years later before he appreciated the paradox of claiming as his 'very own' the absence of a definite self-identity).

Admittedly the small town in the west of Scotland where he lived offered little by way of encouragement to a nascent interest in cultural experimentation and nothing in terms of opportunity for direct contact with an existential *avant garde*. In fact, the breaking wave of a popular culture, which in hindsight he claimed as his inspiration, hardly registered against the background of activities and interests grown prematurely dull; no more than a vague succession of dislocated sounds and images that bore no relation to his actual or imagined life. 'Surely', he thought 'there must be something more to life!' And, sure enough, by way of uncritical reading and rejection (from timidity), of the few available forms of illicit excitement open to his acquaintances, the unremarkable difficulties of a provincial teenage life became charged with obscure metaphysical longing. Life, 'real life', was elsewhere and something quite different, he thought, to both the stultifying routine that his parents and teachers found so gratifying, and the mindless release in which his friends occasionally indulged. However, he could not prevent the scepticism that exposed the shallowness of life around him from applying equally to himself, and effectively undermined his own conviction of a higher destiny. He felt the weight of local expectations drawing him irresistibly into a predictable and, above all, respectable world.

The author's half-hearted identity crisis, in other words, amounted to little more than envy of those he imagined struggling with the 'real thing', and self reproach for his lack of courage in failing so miserably to join them in their decisive project of liberation. Too fearful simply to set off for London or New York where, he still believed, an uncertain but brilliant future awaited him, he withdrew into himself, became bookishly clever, and went to university. This unplanned but ingenious compromise allowed him to prolong his much-loved adolescent 'crisis' while simultaneously giving every appearance of settling down to a mature and responsible task.

The study of sociology, which he excused on the grounds of its modernity and relevance to the future, did not offer his parents the immediate gratification and known trajectory of medicine or law but promised, nonetheless, an assured and prosperous future; a professional career in which they could take pride. This misunderstanding, and the enormous prestige in their eyes of an ancient university, allowed him painlessly to free himself of their world.

Or so he thought. He had expected a sudden transformation in himself; a veritable metamorphosis in which a wholly new person would awaken to a world altered in its innermost character. But the superficial novelties of student life quickly adapted themselves to the routines of a familiar and anxious existence. Nothing, after all, had changed. The alluring worlds opened to him in innumerable books remained stubbornly out of reach. He could not enter into and share the life he imagined they described and analyzed. Everything vital was remote and imaginary while all that was real remained dull and unexciting.

He reached the obvious conclusion; or, rather, the unspectacular claims of routine obligations took hold of him and he 'grew up'. Without reflecting or deciding upon the matter he began to recall his own past with mature condescension, and saw that it was his imagination alone that had endowed other people's lives with the glamour he felt to be absent from his own. In reality the mundane world he was reluctant to embrace was the only reality there was. Elsewhere was no different; nothing stood out against the ubiquitous indifference of the present. And although this realization implied the abandonment of an unfulfilled wish for something (anything) more perfect, it also meant that other people's lives, after all, were no more or less interesting, or valuable, or real than his own. He quickly learned to feign a sophisticated disdain for the identity crisis to which he had recently aspired. Adolescent *angst*, long before he knew the meaning of the term, was consigned to a past he claimed to have outgrown. In any event he became much too busy to worry over pointless and ultimately trivial questions. 'Who was he?' 'How should he live?' 'To what should he devote his talents?' These were meaningless questions that had been out of date long before they had briefly, and unwisely, been revived by Tolstoy, who should have known better (had known better!) than to take them seriously. Fashionable cynicism replaced fashionable existentialism as his ready-made account of contemporary experience.

After a period of academic research and teaching concerned primarily with historical and cultural aspects of the development of modern society the author returned, but in quite a new context, to issues of identity. His own past life, now transformed by changing interests, the accumulation of (fruitless) literary endeavour, and the work of memory offered itself as an exemplary instance of a particular social-historical type of experience rather than a personal narrative. The indeterminate and self-absorbing inward struggle that had at one time imparted a peculiar tension to every event and activity could now be viewed in a broader context as characteristic of an entire period, age cohort, and gender. And, at the same time, this typical form could be contrasted with other characteristic types of experience, each of which developed meaningfully in relation to a specific historical and social context. The differences among such typical experiences could, in turn, be grasped in relation to large-scale distinctions of nation, class, community, religion, ethnicity and so forth.

Like many academics he was readily tempted into projects made compelling by prior experience that had, in fact, done little to prepare him for the task. Intrigued and alarmed in equal measure he found himself committed to writing a book called *Self-Identity and Everyday Life*.

These remarks are not intended as an authorial preface. They do not fall into any of the varied paratextual conceits designed to satisfy the author's urge to self-advertisement (Genette 1997). Nor do they bear kinship with the frequently displayed and equally superfluous photograph displayed on the back cover of many books. The intention, rather, is to raise at once and in a direct manner the central themes of the following discussion. Properly to grasp the meaning of identity and the character of selfhood in contemporary society involves a surprisingly wide-ranging exploration of many subjects that, at first, appear remote from the actual experience of contemporary life that is both its point of departure and its only justification. Thus, before embarking on these necessarily eccentric considerations, it is all the more essential to begin with reality immediately as it is; to begin, that is, with ourselves; *begin*.

Or, rather, it is important to begin *before* the beginning. Prior to identity, in the shadowy beginning that lies before the beginning, is the story. Story gives birth to identity as the distinctiveness of a beginning; the emergence, that is to say, of a 'something' that only in hindsight and through recollection takes on a definite form. Story is nothing but beginning; it is eternal beginning, birth. Schoolchildren are wrongly advised that all stories have a beginning, middle and end. This confuses story with plot. Story is ceaseless emergence; it is the *interruption* in which is put forward the possibility of experience, and it is through the repetition of stories that life takes form as reality. The story impulse 'is inherent in the emergence of humanity' (Crossley 2008: 11), and it is this rupture that is invoked in every bold announcement of 'once upon a time'. The story has no antecedent. The first stories (myths), thus, tell of the inexplicable origin of the world and the differentiation of its various orders, species, forms, and relations. And modern stories, likewise, begin before the beginning of modernity by telling what does not yet exist, but which, through telling, takes shape as self-identity.

The story of self-identity, in other words, foreshadows the development of a particular kind of world and serves as an appropriate introduction to a sociological account of that world. It serves, above all, to draw attention to the equivocal character of its reality. If self-identity begins with a story (a story about itself), then the existential, as well as the logical and metaphysical, status of self-identity is called into question. Is self-identity 'just' a story? Or is its being a story just what gives self-identity its significance as an indubitable reality?

It is important to begin in this way because, otherwise, there seems to be little that is difficult or puzzling here. The world, including ourselves, commonly appears in a non-problematic way as a vast assembly of things that lie *outside* us. 'We' are constituted, in contrast, internally; both as the effortless stream of conscious life that is always 'here' and 'now' and as the recollected past and imagined future of an experiencing subject. 'We' appear with our own past; both an emerging moment of experience and as an image of that moment preserved and projected in time. We are so accustomed to experiencing reality in this way that we find it difficult to reflect upon it; indeed, we rarely feel any need to reflect upon what seems obvious, self-evident, and natural.

At least that is how we *talk* about our experience. But this is often misleading and obscures many of the most striking characteristics of *lived* experience. Without any special effort of reflection and, rather, taking things as they at first appear to us, we frequently orient ourselves to the world and ourselves in a different and more equivocal fashion. Only rarely, in fact, do the objects that fill our world present themselves as uniformly remote from, or wholly exterior to, us; few things are experienced as 'dead' matter. Things that 'belong' to us share, to differing degrees, in the spontaneous stream of life that animates us. 'My' clothes, 'my' books, 'my' furniture, and 'my' car, are related to me in a special, intimate way. We recognize in a gift some aspect of the human character of the giver. And, more generally, beyond such personal relational properties, many different kinds of things possess their own 'subjective' characteristics. Musical instruments, for example, have a different 'nature' to tools, or cooking utensils; a watch or a fountain pen, in addition to its functional character, may be endowed with valued cultural qualities; toys seem to enjoy a life of their own.

Nor is experience 'all of a piece'. While 'I' frequently distinguish myself from 'we' in an automatic and thoughtless manner, both the 'I' and the 'we' may refer to quite different realities. The 'I' that stumbles from bed in the morning is not the 'I' that delivers a lecture, or buys fish for dinner. And the 'I' that identifies itself as part of one group rather than another does so in a variety of continually changing ways; with deliberation, casually, hopefully, reluctantly, and so on. Equally, the 'we' to which 'I' belong, or of which I am a part, is a varied and shifting form. The 'we' that is my family is not just distinct in terms of its members from the 'we' that is my working colleagues but constitutes a different kind of relationship and a different kind of identity. The membership of either group is variable and may be more or less extended depending on the circumstances. At a funeral, for example, one comes across relatives and colleagues previously unknown or rarely encountered. My colleagues may be constituted by members of 'my' department in the university, or members of all the departments in the faculty, or all the academic staff of the university, or British sociologists with similar academic interests, or academics throughout the world, past and present, whose work is significant for my research, and so on, depending upon the context. We are soon led to wonder if 'I' and 'we' are nothing more than common ways of speaking that hardly bear the weight of significance thus thrust upon them.

Furthermore, we frequently experience the world as dissolving, indistinct, and indeterminate. We become fatigued and sleepy, we suffer pain, we get drunk, we fall in love, we forget; in such states and in a variety of ways the 'ordinary' world of objects fade and alter in the most radical fashion. These transformations of exterior reality are, simultaneously, fundamental changes within, and of, the experiencing subject. In ordinary life, that is to say, we are conscious of the most profound changes affecting not only the content of our experience but the very forms of experience itself.

Any account of ordinary experience, such as the opening story, is bound to render events, feelings, memories, and so on, in a relatively neat and comprehensible form. The original messiness of experience is tidied up in innumerable ways; much of what was lived through as a series of disjunctive and even contradictory events becomes reorganized and recollected as a single, uninterrupted story in which the 'self' is the central character. In retrospect, and in prospect, selfhood plays a regulative role in ordering experience. More than that, it constitutes a world as the 'stuff' of experience.

This is rather puzzling. Selfhood is constructed from experience while, at the same time, it gives experience its characteristic form. It is both the possibility and consequence of experience. Furthermore, selfhood is not a fixed relation or structure through which, as it were, experience passes; it is an historical form of life. Selfhood, that is to say, not only changes over time in terms of its characteristic content, it emerges as that which we experience as the 'self' in a particular period. Outside of a particular historical and cultural context, experience is not constituted as selfhood at all, nor, indeed, is the world constituted as experience. It seems that even if we begin with a simple story and try to stick to the bare essentials we are soon forced into a consideration of larger conceptual as well as historical issues.

Beginning with a straightforward account of normal experience, that is to say, turns out to be much more difficult than might at first be imagined. There is no way adequately to communicate the strange complexity and variable texture of immediate experience; and every attempt to do so generates a particular image of events, and tells the story in one way rather than another. In the brief opening passage, for example, much is obviously omitted. The mode of expression is oddly distancing and ironic. Why does the author refer to himself in the third person? And why does he present himself in such an unflattering light? Is the author referred to, in fact, Harvie Ferguson? Is he identical to the Harvie Ferguson whose name appears on the front of this book? And does this name refer to the same person listed in the bibliography as the author of a number of sociological works? Is he also responsible for the novel *Driscoll's Folly* (2000), a story of disintegrating selfhood and failing identities?

How can we gain some essential insight into the apparently shifting character of selfhood and its changing identity-relationships? And what have these various relations and misrelations to do with everyday life in contemporary society? How, in short, are we to grasp the most immediate realities of life and relate them to those large dynamic, historical processes in which they are implicated? This is the task undertaken in the following pages. The first chapter deals with major conceptual issues. What is meant by the terms identity, selfhood, and everyday life? How can they be defined and how should they be used? These and related concepts were developed and widely used throughout the modern period prior to the development of sociology as a discipline. To understand the current sociological usage of such terms, therefore, it is important to locate them in a broad interdisciplinary perspective focused on the thematic development of modernity. This will involve some discussion of philosophical, literary and scientific work, and artistic movements, but discussion of these developments will be touched upon only so far as they are helpful in gaining an adequate understanding of the sociological issues involved.

The conceptual discussion cannot be separated from substantive, historical issues of identity formation, which will be taken up in Chapter 2. Whereas most accounts of self-identity assume the context of modern western society, important insights can be gained by adopting a broader framework that allows comparisons among a number of different kinds of modern and non-modern societies.

Chapters 3 and 4 pursue central issues for any understanding of identity. How is the experience of *unity* and the unity of *experience*, constituted and how are they related to self-identity? How are unities, whatever their origin and foundation, combined and connected to form *totalities*? Or should totality be grasped as a reality *sui generis* from which unity and self-identity emerge through processes of differentiation? This discussion provides insight into the wide-ranging implications of the, often unacknowledged, social character of self-identity at every level of experience.

Chapter 5 takes up the question of everyday life in the context of contemporary society in a more critical mood, and suggests a variety of ways in which existing sociological accounts of self-identity should be revised to take account of the fragmentary character of ordinary experience.

Conventional sociological thought argues that throughout the development of modern society self, identity, and everyday life constituted an intimately interrelated structure. According to the argument advanced here, this is no longer the case; now self, identity, and everyday life are best seen as unrelated, or even antagonistic, processes. It is just the radical *disconnection* of what hitherto had been regarded as essentially interrelated aspects of experience that gives contemporary life its distinctive, overwhelming quality.

Parallel with the sequence of chapters, a parallel series of *Interruptions* present sceptical commentaries on the text, critical reflections on related issues of method, and suggest connections with a variety of contemporary issues. The result, like everyday life, makes no pretence to systematic or descriptive completeness, but aims, rather, to present a report on the confusion and incoherence as well as the dreamlike clarity of the present.

1

CONCEPTS

Each of the key terms in the title of this book is ambiguous, obscure and subject to a variety of common as well as academic usages. While it is not possible and would not be desirable, to constrain such prodigality in the use of words and although the intention of the following discussion is substantive rather than analytical, it is helpful to establish at the outset what is meant (here if nowhere else), by these central concepts. In an academic book there is nothing surprising in such an opening observation. However, for a *sociological* account of these matters, this is neither a preliminary nor a pedantic exercise and is worth a brief justification.

The words identity and self are part of ordinary language and, as such, seemingly refer to and communicate appropriately meaningful content without the need for further elaboration. Equally, everyday life seems so obvious and self-evident a term as hardly to require comment; it is simply the living context in which language is embedded. Academics, of course, are free to adopt these words and specify a more precise and contextually delimited meaning for them; that is, to use them as *concepts*. Mathematicians, for example, use the term identity, grammarians refer to self and some philosophers discuss everyday or ordinary experience, in quite particular ways. While these precise usages are (or at one time were) related to everyday language, their mathematical, grammatical, or philosophical meanings depend upon their location within a more or less extensive network of related, disciplinary concepts. A sociological understanding of identity and self, however (to say nothing of self-identity), cannot wholly free itself from the imprecision of common language. It is just the aim of sociology, in fact, to elucidate, rather than usurp, these usages and, thus, to clarify and account for the experience of everyday life. Sociologists, in fact, are well advised to resist the temptation to construct formally impressive but abstract and insubstantial concepts that become increasingly remote from and incapable of adequately characterizing the actual content of peoples' lives (Wright Mills 2000). In a sociological perspective it would be fruitless to define in advance the meaning of terms that are justified academically only to the extent that they help to provide insight into the *experience* that is its fundamental object of study.

Sociology, that is to say, must remain in close interrelation with its subject; humanly as well as intellectually. At the same time, a sociological perspective is not automatically given as a part or an aspect of social life. It begins when we ask ourselves (and each other) awkward questions about all those characteristic experiences of life that are normally taken-for-granted. Rather than assert or deny something about our identities, or ourselves, in other words, we ask why and under what circumstances people assert such things and with what implications and consequences.

Thus, to begin by outlining *sociological* concepts is to begin *doing* sociology. It is already a step in the process of reflecting on the variety and ambiguity of actual human experience; not with the aim of tidying-up the confusion of everyday speech, eliminating its contradictions and setting out what identity, self and everyday life *should* mean, but to grasp and understand that complexity as part of the larger task of understanding society.

IDENTITY

Identity commonly refers to that which makes, or is thought to make, something just what it is.

Forms of identity

Identity is manifest in an astonishingly broad range of diverse forms, which includes, among many others, several that are frequently paired as opposites; particular and categorical, singular and plural, objective and subjective.

Particular and categorical

We commonly identify objects as the *particular* things we daily encounter and use: the pen the author bought in Kyoto, a favourite shirt, the DVD rented the previous evening and due to be returned, a lottery ticket bearing a 'lucky' numbers and so on. There may be many similar objects but what is referred to here is just *this* object and no other. Frequently we deal with more complex, but still easily identifiable, objects; the house of a friend, the office building in which the author works, the train on which we have booked seats, a foreign city in which we have newly arrived and many other equally recognizable complex unities. Particulars may be objects, people, events, times, places, sensations, feelings, or whatever and are always unique. There is only one pen that the author bought in Kyoto (and if there were more than one he could still identify unambiguously the particular one that is on his desk at the moment), only one city of Copenhagen, just one lottery ticket, though it bears the identical number to several, previously discarded tickets.

Particulars are identified primarily by their turning up where and when we expect them and being recognized as part of the familiar, everyday world. The author's house appears when he returns from shopping, or from the office, just where he left it. If it were not there he would be bewildered and anxious; he would demand an explanation. Has it been bombed and the rubble already removed? Did he take a wrong turning on his way home and wander into a nearby, similar, but not identical, street? Is it there just as usual but somehow and alarmingly, he cannot see it? Equally, he would be thrown into confusion if he were to recognize as his house a building that was nowhere near where he lived. He would immediately suppose himself mistaken; it is not, surely, *his* house, in which he normally lives, miraculously transported to a new location. It is, perhaps, one that looks very like it.

What makes *this* pen particular in an identifiable way for the author is inherently connected with the accident of his selecting it, rather than any other, from several hundred on display in a famous Kyoto bookshop. Particular identities, that is to say, are inseparable from the history of our relationship to them and are defined through this relational history.

But what makes this particular pen a pen, rather than, say, a pencil, or a brush, or any other writing instrument is another matter. The *penness* of the pen does not depend on the contingent fact of its ownership but on its manner of functioning. In practice it is often very difficult to specify precisely the characteristics of different kinds of functionally related objects; is a fountain pen in some sense more fully pen-like than a roller-ball? Is a quill a pen?

These trivial examples raise some important issues that will be more fully explored in later chapters in relation to non-trivial identity disputes. The significant initial point is simply to draw attention to two quite distinct notions of identity. Both *particular* things and *kinds* of things are what they are by virtue of their identity. There is an important difference, in other words, between the identity that is *my* pen and the identity that is my *pen*. Particulars and sorts are interrelated in interesting ways. *My* pen is a unique object but is one of a kind that includes, among other things, *my* wristwatch, *my* wallet, *my* spectacles and *my* mobile phone; a sort that has the identity 'small personal objects that I carry around with me;' an identity that might be expanded to 'and without which I feel ill at ease'. And my *pen* is an instance of a kind that includes my *pencil*, my *notebook*, my *laptop* and my *PC*, having the identity 'my writing equipment'.

What sorts there are and what counts as one sort rather than another, does not depend on the contingencies of a personal kind but, more generally, on the history and culture that produces and uses them. This includes, importantly, the sorts of things we think of as belonging independently to 'nature' (Latour 2004). The social construction of categories raises large issues that will be explored, in different ways, throughout this book.

Singular and plural

In relation both to particulars and to sorts of things identity refers to individuals *and* collectivities. Identity may be singular or plural. Singular identities are not necessarily particular, in fact most individuals are instances of sorts rather than uniquely particular. My *pen* is just *one* of a common sort, a Pilot Ball Point, which is an identity it shares with thousands of other individual pens of the same sort; only its *myness* makes it particular. Notice that I am free to treat it in either way; as a unique object that is part of my life, or as an instance of a multiplicity.

Essence and accident

It is also worth noting here that for particularities *essence* and *accident* are united; what makes something particular is a contingent fact of its history in relation to myself. For sorts of things, however, essence and accident are distinct. Accidental qualities can be altered without affecting the functional unity and coherence of the object and, therefore, its categorical identity. For example, the colour, location and ownership of a pen do not affect its penness and it may be used to write a shopping list or a poem. But, for *me*, of course, its accidental qualities may be importantly connected with its ultimate use. In recent years many sociologists have cast suspicion on the term essence on the grounds that it unreasonably imputes qualities of permanence and universality to what are, in fact, socioculturally constructed and therefore contingent and changing, relations. In fact there is nothing wrong with the everyday notion that identity manifests something essential about an object, person, or event. In fact, it is just because objects are always *socially* defined that we can talk about their identity at all. To claim, or contest, what it is that makes something what (some) people take it to be, does not imply that in some other, non-social or 'natural' way, it 'really' is so. Someone might be regarded as 'essentially Scottish', for example, by virtue of parentage, birthplace and residence. Equally, it might be argued that the same person is not essentially Scottish because of their failure to support the national football team, their dislike of porridge, and evident friendliness towards English people. The issue is just to decide what 'being Scottish' really means. Arguments over essentialism are usually disagreements over what constitutes specific identities.

Object and subject

People are not things. In contemporary sociology, as in everyday language, however, one common way of identifying human individuals and groups is by reference to thing-like characteristics and properties. Another approach, however, grasps human identity in terms of processes of forming and expressing inner-states of feeling and sentiment. The first approach, which identifies people through externally observable characteristics such as age, nationality, gender, and occupation (information normally available from official records), is often thought of as *objective*. The second approach, which identifies people in terms of states of mind and sentiment such as belief, attitude, and opinion (judgements normally inferred from spontaneous or elicited statements), is usually considered to be *subjective*. A good deal of contemporary sociology consists in relating one to the other. Once again, however, we should be wary of jumping to unwarranted conclusions. Objective data is frequently unreliable; the use of documents to establish identity is far from unambiguous and straight-forward (Groebner 2007; Cole 2001) and, worse, often does not tell us what we most want to know. Furthermore, expressions of opinion or feeling may only hint at forms of meaning and significance that can and should, also be studied independently through written sources and their traditions of commentary, interpretation and scholarship. Max Weber, for example, elucidated the subjective identity of, amongst other groups, seventeenth-century Puritans through a careful, contextually sophisticated reading of original documents and related historical works; that is by consulting objective data.

Recent discussions, in quite different ways, have sought to connect these distinctive approaches. To take just one example, Manuel Castells defines identity as 'people's source of meaning and experience;' and elaborates as follows:

> By identity, as it refers to social actors, I understand the process of con-struction of meaning on the basis of a cultural attribute, or related set of cul-tural attributes, that is/are given priority over other sources of meaning. For a given individual, or for a collective actor, there may be a plurality of identi-ties. Yet, such a plurality is a source of stress and contradiction in both self-representation and social action.
>
> (Castells 1997: 6–7)

Here, 'meaning' and 'attribute' are brought together in an attempt to include both subjective and objective criteria under the singular term 'identity' which, as a result, assumes the dignity of being something pri-mordial. Identity, thus defined, is fundamental and constitutive of reality; it carries explanatory weight for the sociologist as well as existential sig-nificance for the subject. The relation between meaning and attribute, however, remains contingent, unpredictable, and opaque.

A broader and more philosophically oriented discussion (but one still friendly to historical sociology) can be found in the work of Paul Ricoeur. Although focusing exclusively on individual, personal identity, Ricoeur makes an important distinction between two characteristic forms in which it appears in modern society; the identity of *sameness* and the iden-tity of *selfhood* (Ricoeur 1992). The first involves a notion of permanence; an unchanging set of features that unambiguously designate an object. The second refers to the continuity of character and felt self-presence of the subject. The first, in spite of the typical language through which it is construed, is an essentially spatial concept, while the second is a temporal notion of identity. In a sophisticated treatment Ricoeur points to a series of contradictions inherent in both views and, going beyond the scope of most sociological discussions, proposes a notion of *narrative* identity as both a resolution of the internal difficulties within each perspective and a bridge over the abyss which separates them.

Form and substance

But there is already a danger of falling into the trap of over-elaborating formal distinctions at the expense of substantive considerations. Of course form and substance are intimately related and the changing character of this relation will be discussed at length in following chapters. But for the moment the temptation to investigate puzzling aspects of identity at a purely conceptual level is best resisted. It is quite sufficient to establish as a point of departure that the concept of identity, in the most general sense and in ways that are readily exemplified with reference to everyday experiences, is simply 'what makes anything the thing that it is'. Identities commonly define particulars and categories of things, singular and plural things and, in the case of human identities, may be objective or subjective. These distinctions are neither comprehensive nor logically rigorous but, often as one sided and undefended assumptions about identity, remain significant in many sociological investigations.

Social identities

All identities are social identities, but in the context of everyday life, rather than academic discourse, how are the personal and social characteristics deployed in the process of identification to be characterized? In a remarkable way, notions of identity that emerge here are constituted as relations rather than entities. In the context of everyday life, identities describe how people and things are interconnected. The question of how one thing, person, or group is related to another takes precedence over the issue of what makes something the thing that it is, or what defines a category and so on. Everyday understanding of reality, in this regard, is sociologically more adequate than many philosophically sophisticated discussions and has to be taken seriously. And, unconstrained by logical embarrassment, identity here refers to sameness *and* difference, reality *and* appearance, permanence *and* change.

It is convenient briefly to distinguish three common identity-relations in contemporary everyday life; sameness, difference and empathy.

Sameness

The first common relationship of identity in modern society is sameness. This expresses the *equivalence* of two related objects, events, persons, and so on; the idea of sameness is that one item from a group can be substituted for another without altering the structure or functioning of the group. If two items can be interchanged they are, by definition, equivalent.

Sameness defines the individual being as the instance of a type. This means that the individual is considered exclusively in terms of the characteristics that define the category and all other particular characteristics are suppressed as inessential and secondary. The singular being is defined as the unitary member of an ideal collection or set of all other such objects. It is an identity in which the relation between the individual object and the set of objects is viewed as determinate. All members of the group are identical in the sense that, ultimately, they are interchangeable and can be distinguished from one another only by the contingent fact of spatial separation. This notion is vividly exemplified by the collection of identical, unmarked headstones in a large war cemetery, or in the identification of school pupils by the position of their desks in a classroom, prisoners by their cell, factory workers by their location on a production line, soldiers by their number, and so on.

This everyday notion of identity-relation rose to prominence in the early modern period and is coterminous with large-scale social processes of assembling and ordering both nature and society (Smith 1994; Meyerson 1930; Foucault 1977).

Difference

Identity-relations also proclaim the significance of difference; of what distinguishes one object from another, one person or group from another. As Amin Maalouf nicely puts it 'My identity is what prevents me from being identical to anybody else' (Maalouf 2000: 10). This conception of identity finds its most significant modern voice in European Romanticism and the various philosophical schools of idealism that developed around it. Human self-identity is here viewed in the context of a psychology of interior experience, feeling, and meaning; a tradition most influentially represented by Rousseau, whose *Confessions*, first published in 1782, proposed a radically new form of self-understanding (Gusdorf 1948). In this perspective human identity is conceived as an organic and continuously developing process in which each individual becomes increasingly differentiated, internally and externally, from every other.

Empathy

In the context of contemporary everyday life what is meant by identity is not something fixed and permanent or even continuous and changing but, rather, fragmentary and periodic assertions of sameness and difference. It is striking that, for all the analytic reflection and empirical research across the social sciences (Castells and Ricoeur can again be cited as exemplary), little attention has been paid to what is probably the most common mode of identification in contemporary everyday life; that is transient *empathy*. It would be misleading to dismiss such fleeting states as insignificant or unimportant in comparison with what has generally been taken to be fundamental, or even essential, forms of identity (Hankiss 2001). It is just the character of contemporary life, in fact, increasingly to make a host of identities once thought to be permanent, fundamental, and exclusive (nationality, gender, ideology and so on), available in a casual, empathic mode. To take a deceptively simple example (all such examples, by definition, appear trivial), one can eat Italian food one night and Chinese or Thai the next and, in an unserious but meaningful way, experience in turn a sense of 'belonging' to the distinctive traditions and cultures of which that cuisine is an aspect. The question of identity here is not so much 'who are we?' but 'who are we like?' or, 'who would we like to be like?' Similarly, clothing styles, tastes in art, religious beliefs and practices, even languages, can periodically be 'borrowed' for relatively brief periods to experience 'at first hand' one, then another, of the identities that circulate through modern society. It is just for this reason that many people find an appealing aspect of foreign travel in the possibilities of identity excursions that it seems to offer.

Empathic identities are usually short-lived, imaginative bonds with individuals or groups conceived as other than (rather than different to) ourselves. Such bonds are, in principle, unlimited in terms of time and space and may involve actual or fictive objects. Wilhelm Dilthey (1988) and Max Weber (1947, 1975) made the term empathy significant for sociology primarily as a methodological principle of historical understanding; a descriptive term for the peculiar capacity to enter imaginatively into the situation other people, often quite distant socially and culturally from ourselves (O'Hear 1996). Empathy should not be confused with what Adam Smith called sympathy, or what Max Scheler later called fellow feeling, both of which invoke the notion of *shared* experience, rather than a distinctive power of identification with someone *other* than ourselves.

In the present context, it is the multiplicity, diversity and ceaseless flow of mundane and apparently insignificant identifications that should be stressed. These features become evident in the proliferation of fictional worlds that is characteristic of modern society. In an unprecedented step the modern novel, for example, simply asserts itself and its own world, as a free creation into which the reader may enter by a simple act of surrender. Empathic identification is immediate; it is framed by the act of reading or viewing and not by the accumulation of factual detail that might allow readers or viewers to generalize from some aspect of their own experience to the lives unfolding in the fictional world. An initial suspension of the actual in favour of an imaginary world, in advance of knowing anything about it, characterizes empathic identity (Iser 1993). The novelist simply presents the fictional world for the reader and provides access to it as a series of new experiences. A character need not initially be named, described, or contextualized to be the object of identification. The radical freedom of empathic identification is evident, for example, in the stunning opening sentence of Franz Kafka's *Metamorphosis*; 'As Gregor Samsa awoke one morning from uneasy dreams he found himself transformed in his bed into a giant insect' (Kafka 1999). Not only do we effortlessly identify with Gregor, we identify with him *as an insect*.

Sameness, difference and *empathy,* are all fundamentally modern forms of identity-formation. The same individuals and groups in a variety of different social contexts successively invoke them and each plays a significant part in different aspects of everyday life. To appreciate more fully the significance of these forms of identification requires a consideration of the broader comparative and historical context that will be outlined in the next chapter.

Defining feature and family resemblance

There is no single, overriding concept of identity current in sociology or implicit in everyday language. Many academic disputes, as many arguments in everyday life, however, revolve around (usually unacknowledged) differences in the *concept* rather than the content of identity. Such disputes and the seemingly unregulated conceptual space they indicate, encourages the abandonment of the use of the term at all. While such an outright rejection of the idea of identity would be premature, it is appropriate at this point to introduce an important modification relevant to all the procedures noted above.

The notion of identity is usually approached in terms of isolating and defining a key feature through which something is determined as the very thing that it is. However, as the philosopher Ludwig Wittgenstein observed, there may not be any such feature. What we recognize as an identity is something much looser; a network of resemblances rather than the strict presence or absence of a critical defining feature. It seems obvious that eating pasta or attending opera does not make anyone Italian; the question, however, is whether *any* single characteristic or attribute of a person would necessarily make them Italian. Italian birthplace, parentage, tax liability, voting rights, social security number, passport and so on, taken singly or in combination are closely associated with 'being Italian' but do not unambiguously allocate individuals to such a collective. Wittgenstein, therefore, prefers the notion of family resemblance to that of identity. From a series of photographs of family members we can usually detect resemblances among them, but they do not all share the same features. A particular shape of nose, eye colour, hairline and so on does not invariably appear in every case. Rather, an unpredictable combination of features tends to be repeated. In an influential discussion Wittgenstein illustrates the point more fully by considering the identity of games (1968: 31–33). We recognize a complex series of distinct activities as similar in the sense that they constitute games. It is not possible, however, to specify a single defining feature of such activities. Rather, a range of characteristics is relevant to the identity of games, which appear singly or in various combinations in a frankly bewildering manner. It may well be helpful to approach personal and social identity in these terms and a fuller exploration of this possibility will be developed at a later point. The idea has an immediate relevance, however, to the second key concept; self.

SELF

The concept of self is closely related to the idea of identity. Self, it seems, is just what makes us who we are. The term is frequently given in a definite form; *the* self, or selfhood, which is unfortunately suggestive of a particular kind of *entity* and a form of thing-like identity that precludes an adequate grasp of the ongoing active process to which the term properly refers (Harré 1998: 3–4). Self is, first of all, a *relation* rather than a simple unity. The self-relation arises in the continuous possibility of becoming aware of the world as ongoing, past and future potential experience. That is to say, in experiencing the world, we are aware not only of that world in all its richness and complexity, but also of ourselves as having, or undergoing, that experience. We are both conscious and self-conscious; we are *reflexive* beings. In a curious way we are continually open to the possibility of attending to and reflecting upon the ongoing stream of life; and, rather than being immediately aware of the objects of consciousness, become conscious of ourselves as experiencing subjects interrelated with other people, times, and places.

Self arises in a long history and it is only the characteristically modern variant that is immediately familiar to us (Taylor 1989; Siegel 2005). Modern self (what seems to us to be *the* self), transposes all experience into an inner stream of consciousness; a continuous flow of content as thoughts, perceptions, feelings, images, hopes, etcetera, which is identified as *my* experience, *my* life and *my* world. Just as there is a critical identificatory difference between *my* pen and my *pen*, the same kind of difference pertains between *my* world and my *world*; *my* family and my *family*, *my* country and my *country* and so on. That is to say, the modern *form* of self deals in particularities and, given the pre-eminence of self as *the* experiential reality of modern life, seeks to grasp everything in terms of its own content. There is an almost irresistible tendency, as a result, to regard our own limited experience as made up of general or even universal phenomena and to be convinced we are in possession of 'self-evident' truth. The experiential priority of self, which has become 'second nature' for us, is also the most compelling evidence for, and the inner conviction of, the unity and coherence of the world, including ourselves. This has important implications; not least it indicates that prejudice and a widespread tendency to overgeneralize on the basis of our own limited and fragmentary experience and interpret other lives in terms of the meaningfulness and emotional flux we find in our own is, in part at least, a condition of experience rather than a wilful attitude or the result simply of ignorance. *If* experience comes to us in this form, we suppose, it *must* do so because it is perfectly conformed to the reality it conveys. What underpins the overwhelming certainty that the world we see is the same as the one we touch and hear, what links the perception of this world with the recollection of its past, how the 'I' that intends to act is recognized by the 'I' that has just fallen in love, or brushed up against the absolute, is just what we call self; a higher order unity of the disparate manifold of experience.

Having begun with the notion of identity it makes sense to approach the idea of self by asking 'what is the identity of self?' What makes self, self; rather than anything else? And, following from the initial delineation of forms of identity this question can be specified in terms of a range of sameness and difference in relation to which self emerges as an identifiable unity. This procedure, however, in one vital respect may prove to be misleading. In asking about the identity of the self we at once assume there is such a 'unity of experience' that corresponds to the term. And this should not be assumed. Nevertheless, in order to develop the argument, it is necessary to introduce the idea as if it were 'real'. In subsequent sections the idea (and actuality) of self will be more critically scrutinized (as will the apparently obvious aspects of identity that have just been outlined). Whatever can be said initially about self, nothing will be ventured at this stage as to its *existence* as an empirical entity.

Identities of self

Self is *like* and often identified with, *soul, person, subject, individual,* and *role*; overlapping terms that, indeed, bear a distinctive family resemblance one to another and, collectively, might be thought of as constituting the larger identity of 'human being' or, more precisely 'historical western human being'.

Soul

The notion of the soul appears in Classical Antiquity to describe and account for a developing sense of the inner coherence and unity of life experiences (Martin and Barresi 2006). The chaotic, emotionally mobile and passionate world of the Homeric epic, whose protagonists are open to competing and contrary passions that come, unbidden, from the gods and in relation to which they are helpless, is transformed into a morally compelling demand for inner unity under the control and guidance of the soul. The Greek *psyche* (soul) had originally been described as a cloudy substance, or shadow, released from the body at death and played no part in the organization of living matter and the consciousness associated with it. Throughout the cultural development of classical Greek civilization *psyche* underwent significant development and was ultimately transformed into a resident, internal monitor and agency of consciousness. The soul acted, so to speak, in its own interest to gain ever more secure control over the inner life and experience of people; indeed, it began the long process of constituting all experience as an inner-world and in doing so simultaneously established the precarious coherence and unity of the body as something outer (Rohde 1925; Vernant 1991; Sorabji 2000). The creation of the soul, that is to say, was simultaneously the creation of the body as a unified structure and the establishment of continuous interrelations between them.

The soul was subsequently Christianized and progressively divested of its lingering bodily associations (Brown 1988). The idea of the soul became central to the development of the complex religious psychology that dominated the interpretation and understanding of human behaviour in the medieval west. Soul, on the one hand, animated and organized the human body and gave it the capacity to act responsibly and, on the other hand, internally mirrored both the divine creator and His creation. The soul was made 'in the image and likeness' of God and thus, to a degree and in spite of its fall into sin, participated in His absolute identity (Gurevich 1985; Kleinschmidt 2000).

The language of soul has decayed and most academics are uncomfortable with the word. But many of the characteristics of modern self are clearly continuous with an older history of soul. Self is like soul in terms of its propensity to rise upward, in other words to develop, to achieve its potential, and to become *authentic*. And in these terms soul is taken up and given renewed and characteristic expression in both Renaissance Humanism and modern European Romanticism (Richards 2002; Gusdorf 1993).

Person

Self and person also have a long interrelated history and are linked primarily in the notion of moral unity and integrity. In an important essay Marcel Mauss (1979) gives striking expression to the historical character of the person. The notion of the person appears first as the Latin *persona* or mask (Benveniste 1964). And, Mauss points out, only the slave has no *persona* because he does not own his body. *Persona* anticipates, in its ambiguity and variety of meanings, the complex subsequent history of the person that Mauss sketches for us. But only in the modern period does person become self; a category 'Far from being a primordial, innate idea clearly inscribed since Adam in the deepest part of our being, we find it still being slowly erected, clarified, specified and identified with self-knowledge, with psychological consciousness, almost into our own time' (Mauss 1979: 87).

The person is that aspect of the soul that makes and responds to ethical demands and is, therefore, essentially interactive and intersubjective. Person is the conscience of the psyche and the responsibility of agency. In a modern sense and pre-eminently in the writings of Immanuel Kant, the idea of person is grasped in a distinctively secular form as a self-imposed imperative; to act in relation to others as ends, not means. To become fully a person, therefore, requires that we recognize others, equally, as persons. Indeed, we only gain autonomy as persons through appropriate social relations (Schneewind 1998; Ameriks 2000) Thus person and self remain closely identified in the notions of dignity, respect, and character; all of which develop in the context of modern civil society (Taylor 1989; Siegel 2005; Sennett 2004). In more recent times the notion of person, which had been viewed as a universally valid form of human self-realization, has been transformed into the quite different idea of personality as a property of the individual. A particular individual *is* a person, but *has* a personality. Personality manifests itself as a concrete and unique combination of characteristic traits that 'belong' to the individual; an idea crucial to the development of the modern 'psychological' understanding of self (Dilthey 1996; Ginzburg 1991; Carrithers *et al.* 1985).

Subject

In a somewhat different way self is also related to subject. The idea of the subject is decidedly modern and is used to express two, often contradictory, historical tendencies that characterized the social transformation of the early modern period (from approximately the last quarter of the sixteenth century to the end of the seventeenth century). Subject refers to both subjugation and to liberation. The subject is both a subject of and subjected to, the absolute power of the ruler (Foucault 1977; Marin 1988). But, at the same time the subject of the ruler is accorded a legal identity; a status to which rights as well as obligations may be attached. To be subject to the ruler meant to be freed from the local ties and conventions of small communities in which most people's lives had previously been lived out (Poggi 1978).

This dual aspect of power, subjugation under the ruler and the exercise of rights guaranteed by the same ruler, also characterizes the notion of modern subjectivity. Self is subject *to* the relentless stream of experience (its own experience!) and in the face of which it is powerless; self is, first of all, passive receptivity. And self is the subject *of* experience, freely creating and forming according to its own limitless resources of imagination. The double-sidedness of self as subject is now frequently obscured in favour of an over simplifying approach in which self is understood as subjectivity (rather than subject) and identified with the immediate character of experience as expressed in interview responses and other research instruments.

Individual

The likeness of self to individual is also a distinctively modern theme (Heller *et al.* 1986; Lukes 1973). Since Jacob Burckhardt's (1990) classic work in the Italian Renaissance, first published in 1867, it has become commonplace to characterize modern culture in terms of the progressive freeing of individuals from constraining traditions. The guiding notion of individual here involves the gaining of control over and taking responsibility for, your own life. It was modelled first of all on the powerful princes and aristocratic courtiers among whom new forms of personal conduct and bearing developed. A formalized system of etiquette regulated the social life of courtly society throughout the seventeenth century and subsequently, through the establishment of new institutional structures of the state and the market which extended the possibilities of individuation to much larger and growing numbers of people, served as a model for the formation of bourgeois manners (Elias 2000; Bumke 1991; Becker 1988). The individualizing tendency in Renaissance *decorum* was explored by and became a central theme, for its greatest writers. In Shakespeare's drama and Montaigne's *Essays* (1991) the possibilities, limitations and paradoxes of modern self as individual are fully exposed. The identifiable likeness of self to the modern individual hinges on two linked ideas. Firstly, the sense in which each individual is not only distinct from any other but is constituted primarily through a stream of conscious experience that is, in principle and ineluctably, separate from any other. And, secondly, the growing awareness that, as individuals, people could and should become responsible for themselves, not only in terms of observable features of *decorum* but, more significantly, in relation to the inner psychological reality of their experience. Taken together these amounted to new possibilities of *self-fashioning*, that is, for the first time on a significant scale people became aware of themselves through creating and maintaining a particular kind of self, or self-image (Greenblatt 1980).

Role

Self is also likened to role in a theatrical sense. Rousseau made this notion central to his autobiographical critique of modern culture and it has become a staple of contemporary sociology through the symbolic interactionist school and laterally in the well known work of Erving Goffman. The role is always less than the person, a part more or less consciously played out in relation to the expectations of all those involved in the action. Self, in this perspective, is a fugitive presence; viewed alternatively as the relational totality of roles, psychic independence from roles, or a sense of continuity among roles. From the pioneering work of William James, Charles Horton Cooley, and George Herbery Mead this has been one of the central themes of American psychology and sociology (Joas 1993).

Self, that is to say, may be identified through a network of affinities, which also locates its development within a particular historical and cultural tradition, frequently if imprecisely referred to as Judeo-Christian and/or western and modern. In subsequent chapters this context will be more fully examined, but for this preliminary discussion it is sufficient to introduce the important idea that self is a many-sided historical phenomenon and not a simple, fixed and unchanging identity in some peculiar way lodged within and inseparable from an individual body.

Self-identities

The identity of self is established through a network of differences as well as similarities and affinities.

Different/other/alien

The distinction of self from other, similar selves is a relative and continually shifting boundary. Such distinctions, however, frequently become the focus of a more general characterization of a person or group as another self. Thus, for example, a distinction of accent or dress may be interpreted as a reliable indication of a whole range of related and possibly significant, features of the person or group. A distinguishing difference is taken to be a general criterion of classification. Someone wearing a dress and high-heeled shoes is taken to be a woman and this assumption guides our behaviour towards 'her'. Such generalizations, interpreting difference in some specific dimension of variation to indicate a whole series of 'corresponding' differences, is frequently an enabling assumption for many practices of everyday life. It also leads to embarrassing and prejudicial mistakes that, unsurprisingly, generate hostility. Nonetheless, it would be tedious and disruptive to approach every interaction with a completely open mind. Everyday life 'works' on the basis of many such assumptions and general characterizations. Differences of self become differences among selves; marks of distinction become handy tools for classifying people into significant categories and groups.

In surprising and historically important ways the development of self within modern society has been accompanied by and to a large extent constituted through, the continuous and simultaneous production of an extraordinary variety of *others*. For self to become fully conscious of itself, to become authentically self-identical, it required a negative image against which to test itself. Self is *not* this or that particular appearance, this or that sort of person, this or that mode of being. Modernity, as a result, became a huge repository of *otherness*; paradoxically filled with just those identities it claimed to have outgrown. Generally speaking, the more strenuously self sought to establish itself as an identity, the more conscious it became of difference and, ultimately, the more difficult it became to sustain its claims to exclusivity.

The other is still another self, but self defines itself also and more radically in relation to what is absolutely outside itself. In some challenging and influential accounts of contemporary life, self can only realize its full potential as self through an encounter with its radical or absolute other; that is to say not with another (stranger) self, but that which is other than a self (alien) (Theunissen 1984). This idea is difficult to grasp. If self is simply the ongoing synthesis of experience what can there be *other* than, or *other* to, self? Difficulty notwithstanding, this idea has become central to many of the most interesting current discussions of self (Derrida 2008).

Assimilation

Self, in modern society, is inherently unstable and its ambiguity becomes prominent in the astonishing way in which it comes to resemble all the differences generated in its striving for identity. Self, that is to say, is not only like itself it resembles its varied others.

If self resembles soul, person, subject, individual, and role (and this list could be extended), then it would seem obvious that self distinguishes itself from what is frequently regarded as opposite to those terms; that is, from body, creature, object, and collectivity. The identification of self with person, for example, seems to indicate a non-identity of self with living creatures other than persons, or non-living functional unities such as machines. Self has almost always been regarded as species specific. And, equally, self has been viewed as non-identical to objects, as something other than a 'thing' or a thing like entity. In relation to the distinction between individual and collectivity, however, a strong counter-intuitive view has emerged. The whole development of sociology and related disciplines insists not only on the collective as well as individual character of self, but argues strenuously that, in relation to self-identity, the distinction between individual and collective is misguided. It cannot be over-emphasized that *both* the collective *and* the individual are thoroughly social. It is, in fact, the relational character of *both* individual and collective social phenomena that allows us to identify each as self and self in both. This sociological insight owes most to the work of Émile Durkheim (1984, 1995, 2002) whose writings, in particular *Suicide* (2002) and *The Division of Labour in Society* (1984), argue vigorously that it is only in advanced and complex societies, with a highly differentiated and interdependent division of labour, that it is possible for an individual experience of the world to become at all common.

The paradoxical character of self is more immediately evident in terms of its identification with role. Where role is self 'playing a part', self might seem more properly to be identified with authenticity or transparency; that is, with an expressive form that directly reveals the inner truth of and bears witness to, self presence. And it might well be suspected that self can, equally, be identified with the antithetical term to all the historic members of its conceptual family circle. Recent writing across a broad range of human and social sciences suggests that this, indeed, is the case, or is becoming the case. A century after the key works of Sigmund Freud (1990, 1991) it finally seems obvious that self is body as well as soul. Significantly, for contemporary culture, body that is identified as, or with, self is not confined to our own body. Other bodies, bodies of other species, are to an increasing degree being accorded the status of selves. The very possibility of, for example, proclaiming and defending animal 'rights', as well as much current concern over animal 'welfare', to say nothing of literary, philosophical, and psychological reflection is predicated on the assumption that humans and many types of animals, in some sense, share a life together (Santner 2006; Agamben 2004; Gaita 2004; Coetzee 1999; Gray 2002).

Or, to take another apparent antithesis, the categorical difference between persons (selves) and machines (non-selves) is daily challenged, not only by the developing sophistication of prosthetic devices, computer software, and biotechnologies, but, more significantly, in the everyday use of objects as having 'a mind of their own'. Certainly, it is only for the abstract sciences that objects are denied selfhood; in the everyday world *my* pen is part of *my* world; part of *myself*. Selves and partial selves inhabit objects, things, places, events, memories, and so on. Many objects are 'personalised' through ownership, some more easily than others (Appadurai 1986). The ordinary experience of life is not an interaction between a 'living' subject with 'dead' matter; self, rather, to varying degrees characterizes *both* and makes the world a place of continuous negotiation, persuasion, and anxiety (Harman 2002).

Contrary to many orthodox academic and everyday conceptions of self as a distinct from, the essential character self-identity as reflexivity emerges only through identity-relations with its *other*. Difference turns out to be *internal* to self and, what is more baffling, what is *other* to self is *also* self (Ricoeur 1992).

Mediation and synthesis

The peculiar capacity for reflexivity, for self-consciousness and the radical identificatory freedom of selves, implies an important distinction between any possible identity of self and the notion of self-identity. Self, consequently, has to be grasped in terms of new emergent relations and in this respect can be understood as a process either of *mediation* or *synthesis* of apparently opposed terms.

Mediation should not be understood as standing between polarized terms, neither fully one nor fully the other, but, rather, inclusively, as being *both* fully one and *fully* the other; soul *and* body, individual *and* collective, and so on. Self is a relation that holds these distinctions and oppositions in a continuous, unresolved tension. This view of self became highly significant towards the end of the eighteenth century and has continued to be influential in a variety of contexts to the present.

Equally influential, however, is a view of self is the synthetic unity of experience in which all conceptual contradiction and discontinuity is finally resolved as the streaming consciousness of 'being present'. At its simplest, self is *noticing* that we are alive as distinct from just being alive. The most compelling and influential account of self in these terms and one, which, at the same time grasps self in its fundamentally historical in character, is to be found in the work of the German philosopher Hegel. His *Phenomenology of Spirit*, published in 1807, was written in the aftermath of the French Revolution and powerfully conveys a sense of the dynamism embodied in, and released by, that sequence of events (Hegel 1977). Nothing is left untouched by the restless, transformative spirit of the times. The revolutionary drama of modernity is played out in Hegel's text, where it takes form as a universal history of self-identity (Nancy 2002). What Hegel refers to as spirit, the development of which he describes as a movement from simple consciousness to self-consciousness, is the (frequently rejected) philosophical progenitor of contemporary sociological and psychological notions of self and an important point of transition from older, Pagan and Christian, traditions to modern secular conceptualizations (Hegel 1977).

What is important to grasp at this stage is less the detail of his argument or even the manner in which a narrative of self-identity unfolds through it, as the radical character of Hegel's approach. Self (spirit) is a synthesis and its history, therefore, must be grasped in its own terms. No real understanding of human historical development comes from the practice, widespread in Hegel's time and even more prevalent today, of seeking its explanation by reducing its complex, interactive and mutually transforming relations to a single continuously acting 'cause', or, what is little better, by analyzing the whole into a series of judiciously weighted 'factors'. Self is a synthesis, so its transformation and development is the *self-movement* of this synthesis. Hegel grasps this process as one in which self comes to be more and more self-like; to become increasingly self-identical. Self gathers into its own field of self-consciousness and self-activity, all the previously scattered and dissociated elements of its own life and increasingly brings them together in a higher self-conscious unity.

In spite of the challenging difficulty of Hegel's work and the obscurity of its language, the notion of spirit as the self-moving and developing historical synthesis of human experience proved to be enormously influential. It provides the immediate context for the writings of two of his most important and creative critics, Karl Marx and the Danish religious writer

Søren Kierkegaard and played a decisive role in the formation of later nineteenth-century thought (Löwith 1964). His notion of spirit has been continually renewed and revived in the historical and cultural sciences. It is prominent in the writings of Friedrich Nietzsche (1986, 1999, 2008) and in the impressive historical sociology of Wilhelm Dilthey (1988), both of whom were influential in the formation of Max Weber's thought. It appears also in the modern phenomenological approach in philosophy; from its beginnings in Edmund Husserl, to its divergent interpretations in Martin Heidegger and the emergence of existentialism, to the hermeneutics of Hans-Georg Gadamer, Paul Ricoeur and others and, not least, animates contemporary exercises in deconstruction, most notably in the work of Jacques Derrida and Jean-Luc Nancy. This rich literature is mentioned at this point to draw attention to the centrality of the idea of self for every form of reflection on human experience. As a *concept* self does not belong to sociology (or psychology) alone and sociologists are well advised to situate their work and their own contribution to contemporary self-understanding in as broad a framework as possible. Questions of self-identity cannot properly be grasped, far less answered, without continuous reference to and interrelation with, philosophical and literary as well as historical studies.

EVERYDAY LIFE

The notion of everyday life has recently gained currency in sociology and cultural studies. The influential work of, amongst others, the outstanding French historian Fernand Braudel (1974, 1981) and other leading French academics including Henri Lefebvre (2008) and Michel de Certeau (1984; de Certeau *et al.* 1998), American and British sociologists influenced particularly by the writings of Erving Goffman (1959) and social historians whose intention is to write history 'from below' and deal, therefore, with the experience of ordinary people, albeit it often in extraordinary times (Lüdtke 1995), have contributed to a general reorientation of contemporary social thought (Highmore 2002). In a somewhat broader perspective, indeed, it might well be argued that the current prominence of everyday life in political, cultural, and historical writing is a long overdue recognition of one of the central theme in the development of modern society and the discourses that reflected upon it.

As a result of this new interest, many novel research topics have emerged. The broader forms of history from below and in particular studies of working class life that grew out of the earliest social surveys (Halsey 2004) have been extended; histories of women (Duby 1992–1994), private life (Duby and Ariès 1985–1987), childhood (Ariès 1996), and old age (de Beauvoir 1976), are the most obvious and have already achieved the status of classics. Now there are histories of the senses (Jütte 2004; Smith 2007), the body (Corbin 2006), of health and illness (Porter 1999), reading (Saenger 1997), media (Mattelart 1994), the home (Sarti 2002), domestic technology (Giedion 1948; Kern 1990), clothing (Roche 1996), furniture (Auslander 1996), feelings and emotions (Reddy 2001), food and eating (Mennell 1985; Flandrin and Montanari 1999; Fernández-Armesto 2002), friendship, conversations (Zeldin 1995) and, of course in addition to much else, the self and its vicissitudes (Foucault 2005; Rose 1999).

Where classical sociology and the historical and cultural disciplines of the eighteenth and nineteenth centuries which are its immediate predecessors, focused on the large-scale historical-institutional transformations of societies and with those social groups and institutional complexes that seemed strategic to the task of explaining such change, the more recent focus on everyday life restores the immediate experience of society to the mainstream of historical understanding. Everyday life has now become a serious topic of academic study (Stearns 2006) and ranks alongside such staples of sociological inquiry as the state, the market, industrialization, urbanization, warfare, science, religion, and art as significant for any comprehensive account of the emergence and development of contemporary society. More than that, having been discovered, the notion of everyday life has become a universal theme and appears, often uncritically, as the organizing principle for an enormous variety of works devoted to the understanding of very different societies. Extensive, scholarly and popular series on 'daily life in …' and 'everyday life in …', for example, Ancient Greece and Rome, Ancient Egypt, premodern China, India, Japan, Persia and so on, have sprung up in recent years and continue to expand. The notion of everyday life, furthermore, provides the meaningful context for and background to, many innovative trends in contemporary scholarship. Serious historical, literary and sociological work on almost any aspect of contemporary society (such as gender, sexuality, illness and health, belief) cannot afford to neglect the dimension of everyday life and, more often than not, treat it as the most significant level of analysis for research material. The concept of everyday life is now, in fact, implicitly if not explicitly, the most general and important focus for understanding society.

And not just everyday life; it is the everyday life of *ordinary* people that, overwhelmingly, has become the privileged theme of contemporary historiography and our chosen means of making the past real and bringing it to life. Of course, members of social elites, powerful individuals and groups, and all kinds of celebrities also experience an everyday life. But many sociologists have now become sceptical of the extent to which the study of elites and the formal institutional framework of society that they inhabit and operate, illuminates the development of modern society in terms of how it actually works (Te Brake 1998). In this new perspective, the daily life of ordinary people emerges as both the primary *locus* and the source, of the characteristic dynamism of modern society.

For the vast majority of people, including many sociologists, that is to say, the society described and analyzed by previous generations of historians and sociologists, seems remote and incomprehensible. A new interest in everyday life, therefore, promises a welcome focus on the concrete, practical and readily graspable details of actual experience. However, the chaotic proliferation of thematic interests in everyday life and its history already makes it impractical to survey the entire range of such studies as a series of linked topics, far less as a coherent enterprise. The idea of everyday life, newly discovered and assuming the dignity of its own discourse, almost at once dissolved into a confused and obscure series of increasingly specialized, overlapping, and ill-defined special areas. Having set out to challenge the conceptual abstraction and remoteness of academic philosophical accounts of social life, the very diversity and arbitrariness of such studies has, in fact, encouraged fresh attempts to grasp everyday life in a theoretically coherent way; that is as a *concept*. Consequently, the title 'everyday life', far from indicating immediately accessible accounts of modern society, has become the emblem of treatises of daunting abstraction and conceptual sophistication (Lefebvre 2008; Sheringham 2006; Elias 1998).

Orientations to the everyday

But how can the everyday be grasped conceptually? What, in other words, is the identity of everyday life? Two approaches, rooted in divergent tendencies in contemporary social and historical thought, have been widely canvassed. Fernand Braudel's global history of material culture, on the one hand and, on the other, Alfred Schutz's phenomenology of the 'taken-for-granted' reality of social life, suggest alternative frameworks through which the elusive character of the everyday might be grasped.

As the most general region of human experience, everyday life becomes visible, so to speak, only in terms either of the largest historical and sociological perspectives or in the minutiae of immediate social interaction. It is through comparison with other societies and in the context of what the French *Annales* school of social history term the *longue durée* of western history, that the contours of everydayness appear (Braudel 1981). And it is through the painstaking description of personal experience in the light of that comparative history that its peculiar quality springs to life (Zeldin 1995).

Thus, for example, Braudel characterizes as everyday or material life the simplest and most basic level of social existence: the immediate relationships and activities involved directly with food and shelter; dealing with appetite, and need and the entire social world that develops routinely around this.

In quite a different way, the overarching contextual presence of everyday life becomes the central preoccupation of phenomenological sociology, which has its roots in modern European philosophy and has inspired a distinctive style of sociological analysis and research (Schutz 1967; Berger and Luckmann 1967; Ferguson 2006). In this perspective, society takes root in the cultural assumptions that make possible the practices of everyday life, rather than in these practices directly. The everyday world is enabled and sustained primarily through beliefs about the nature of reality; implicit concepts that are uncritically accepted as obvious or natural. Our everyday behaviour does not call for explanation, it is simply what we do, what we 'get on with'.

It would be misleading, however, to draw too sharp a distinction between a 'material' and a 'cultural' approach here. Everyday life is constituted without regard to such distinctions. People do not live first materially and then culturally, or vice versa; as if, in any case, material life was in any way not cultural, or culture could exist other than through material forms. The immediate experience of everyday life is prior to such a distinction and is the reality into which that distinction finally dissolves.

The identity of everyday life, like that of self, cannot be given directly. These approaches, nonetheless, have been influential and will reappear in later chapters. For the present, proceeding on the basis of the analysis of self, it might be expected that everyday life would yield to conceptualization in terms of its preferred identificatory elements, or as the mediation, or synthesis of antithetical terms to which it bears some kind of resemblance? This tempting procedure is, however, likely to be of limited value.

Self lends itself to historical conceptualization just because it develops as a felt unity; as something that stands out from the confusion of immediate experience. Everyday life, by contrast, *is* confused immediate experience; the very background from which both concept and self arises as something definite. Everyday life, in other words, might be thought of as an 'anti-concept;' as an ill-defined region into which all concepts finally dissolve. Any attempt, therefore, positively to identify everyday life by isolating its key characteristic, or by cataloguing its family resemblances, will create an unreal theoretical object. Everyday life, rather, has to be grasped negatively; it is the *non-identical*. This is difficult to understand and harder to describe.

Once again, however, there is a danger of rushing too quickly towards a conclusion. An initial orientation within this confused region can be gained by reviewing the notion of everyday life in relation to some well known sociological concepts that might suggest themselves as evidently, if obscurely, connected to it. Everyday life might very well be thought of as related to some of the major thematic developments of modern society as reflected in classical sociological theory and its contemporary extensions; themes emerging from the framing contrast between premodern *gemeinschaft* (community, small-scale, traditional social relations among persons living and working together) and modern *gesellschaft* (society, large-scale, impersonal, highly differentiated, limited and contractual relations among strangers) (Tönnies 1955). The most immediately suggestive contrasts are between the sacred and the profane (Durkheim 1995), the religious and the secular (Weber 2001) and the public and the private (Weber 1947; Habermas 1989). The particular points of contact between these large themes and the notion of everyday life can briefly be considered under general descriptive headings; *mundane, obscure and unbounded*.

The mundane

One way of trying to identify the everyday is in terms of Durkheim's famous distinction between the sacred and the profane. It seems possible to characterize the everyday as profane rather than sacred. To see the limitations of such a view it is important to understand the claim he advanced in his last major work *The Elementary Forms of Religious Life* (Durkheim 1995) that religion is a universal phenomenon and the foundation of society. Durkheim defines religion through the crucial distinction that it establishes between the sacred and the profane. By the sacred he referred to anything and everything that a community set apart and treated in a special way. The sacred was 'above' the profane and its distinctness was established and maintained through the proliferation of special rules and conventions. It was the realm of spirits and of powers over which human beings had no direct control. The sacred, in other words, was kept separate from and, in important respects, was formed in opposition to, the profane world. The profane was 'everyday;' everything that constituted the practical world of routine tasks and had, literally, to be attended to on a daily basis. The profane world of practical social life arose in response to recurrent human needs. However, Durkheim argued, in order that it could arise and its conventional arrangements sustained it was necessary, first of all, to establish the *possibility* of making such arrangements at all; the possibility, that is, of creating society. The sacred does just that. By treating some things, times, and places as 'special' and effectively removing them from the sphere of practical life a foundational convention was established upon which the arrangements essential to the profane world could be built. If Durkheim were justified in his claims, then the notion of everyday life might well be understood as a historically specific version of the universal category of the profane.

A number of difficulties arise in Durkheim's analysis, however, which, aside from their consequences for his theory of religion, compromises the identification of everyday life with the profane. Durkheim's important insight was that society was nothing other than a conventional order. That is, there was no natural necessity underlying society, which came into existence only through the possibility of acting according to humanly instituted and ultimately arbitrary norms. If this were not the case then all societies would be more or less the same, which clearly they are not. The sacred is pure conventionality; rules without purpose other than the creation of a rule. There is nothing about these objects, empirically, that suggests their sacredness. Anything can be sacred; the quality of sacredness inheres in the acceptance of the conventions that separate such objects from all others.

Durkheim went on to account for the sacred as the pre-eminent collective representation of society as a whole. The sacred is the symbol of society. However, the profane is also and in an equally pre-eminent sense, social; it cannot be anything else. So the division with which he began has a tendency to collapse and this leaves the distinction between the sense of ordinariness and extraordinariness unexplained.

The profane, furthermore and for other writers, is not a residue of ordinariness but, rather, a *transgression* of the sacred (Bataille 1994, Girard 2005). Profanation is equally as extraordinary as the sacred, so that both run counter to the unremarkable character of everydayness (Agamben 2007). And, finally, yet other scholars have suggested the primary world of early humans and of simpler, undeveloped societies is best understood as wholly sacred; the sacred cosmos is all-inclusive (Eliade 1959). For such societies the everyday *is* the sacred world.

Far from offering a useful conceptual hold on the confused world of the everyday Durkheim's dichotomy raises more problems than it solves. The everyday, it seems, can be either sacred or profane, but does not adequately correspond to either. More precisely we are inclined now to call the everyday *mundane* rather than sacred or profane. But this new term is related directly to contemporary experience and cannot be used to characterize the everyday as a universal category. The mundane is a particular kind of everydayness; it is the banality of contemporary life that includes everything in itself. The mundane is neither sacred nor profane, nor is it the sacred and the profane; it is outside such a distinction.

The obscure

For Max Weber a contrast between the religious and magical, on the one hand and the secular, on the other, helps to identify the specific character of everyday life in modern society as the locus of the most general forms of rationalization and *disenchantment*. For Weber, modern society is *secular* rather than either magical or religious and in his famous essay on the spirit of capitalism he views the Reformation as the culmination within the religious tradition of a process of *rationalization*. Whatever significance we attach to the religious origins of modernity, Weber insists that modern society has freed itself from the religious impulse and is now driven by wholly rational processes. He describes modernity as the 'disenchantment of the world' and, thus, opens the way for a new understanding of the importance of everyday life (Weber 2001; Kalberg 1994; Schluchter 1996).

In Weber's view the 'disenchantment of the world' that is characteristic of modernity has two primary aspects both of which are linked to the process of rationalization which is the long-term tendency of western society towards the normative standard of calculative social action. That is to say, rather than act directly in relation to non-rational ends, such as transcendental religious values, or persist in irrational traditions and magical practices, social life is more and more completely organized in terms of conscious calculation. Completely rational and scientifically validated procedures of comparison and judgement now determine almost all aspects of social life, which is continually transformed through the application of the most effective means available to attain concrete, empirically verifiable goals. Consequently, everyday life is no longer suffused with transcendental significance and meaning, nor is it shrouded in mystery. In principle the human world has become wholly clarified and subject to universal standards of knowledge and judgement (Brubaker 1984).

Weber's work, however, remains an equivocal commentary on the character of modern *everyday* life. Weber himself noted the extent to which the religious values and irrational practices progressively suppressed and excised from the institutional world of modern society continue to play a significant role in the *private* world of individuals (Weber 1947). And in his most general work on the sociology of religion he views the entire process of rationalization and its encounter with religious values not, so to speak, as a direct confrontation and conflict, but as different forms of an indirect challenge to the magical practices that most directly answer to the arbitrary, unpredictable, and immediately pressing issue of everyday life. Ultimately, however, neither can wholly succeed, so that everyday life, in its unpredictable incoherence, cannot ever become wholly disenchanted. And, of course, irrational magical practices, as well as religious beliefs of the most varied sorts remain prominent in the everyday life of contemporary society (Latour 1993).

It is against the relentless pressure of demands that have their origin obscurely in everyday life that the institutional and ideological structure of western society has developed. Everyday life does not enter directly into Weber's historical sociology; it remains an unclarified background to his schematic narrative. Everyday life is neither enchanted nor disenchanted, nor is it both enchanted and disenchanted; it remains obscure.

The unbounded

The distinction between public and private is also suggestive for a sociologically adequate characterization of everyday life. The everyday translates rather readily into the private and this, perhaps, is the common way in which it is now understood (Duby and Ariès 1985–1987). The everyday is a vast, diffuse region of activity and experience that is not directly the responsibility of the state, or the product of organized labour, or made meaningful through higher culture. It is an *immediate* life that is not anyone else's business; or so it seems. However the distinction between public and private is not, itself, immediately obvious. The notion arises, as Habermas (1989) reminds us, as a 'category of bourgeois society' (Zaretsky 1976). The private is not strictly the domestic (family life), or life, so to speak, withdrawn from large-scale participatory forms of modern society. It refers, rather, to the non-official world; to those social relations in which people participate, first of all, in terms of their personal attributes rather than anonymously, or in terms of their position within a formal organization.

Of course these spheres are not always clearly demarcated and continually interact. Crucially, the private economic interests of the owners of capital were the effective (if hidden) organizing principle for the public life of society as a whole. But throughout the development of modern society the private sphere became more clearly defined, ideally separated from public life, and was organized around intimate social relations. Family life became its normative model but always, in fact, displayed wide variations in practice. A critical issue here is the extent to which personal and intimate relations (the private), is a region where people interact as 'whole personalities'. That is, while public life demands the performance of specific and limited roles according to set criteria of adequacy, which may require highly specialized training and skill, private life, which is 'functionally specialized' to provide and organize emotional expression and support, engages the whole person. The 'person' rather than the 'role' is the elementary unit of private life (Luhmann 1998; Unger 1984; Giddens 1995).

This view, in its current form, owes most to the sociology of Talcott Parsons (Parsons 1952) and while recent reformulations have added considerably to its historical plausibility, it is not without difficulties. The private also involves limited, role specific performances and quite what 'the whole personality' means in the context of contemporary society requires a good deal of elaboration. Equally, public roles often make purely personal demands and large organizations, to an increasing degree, require personal 'commitment' as well as technical competence in the performance of tasks. In any event the distinction is not generally relevant to the designation of everyday life. The public, as well as the private, has its everyday aspect. Indeed it might well be argued that it is the public sphere with its highly rationalized repertoire of conventional and predictable behaviour that is more typically everyday in its monotonous familiarity, while private life, which is the locus for rich experiences of spontaneous affection, hatred, love, birth, death and grief, is the sphere, above all, of the exceptional, extraordinary and non-everyday.

However unsystematically, an intuition of different kinds of social space underlies the distinction between public and private; the difference, approximately, between the open and the closed. The everyday, by contrast, is *unbounded*. The everyday is 'here' and 'now;' it is the immediate experience of society. Lefebvre, in fact, defines everyday life as a specific 'level of analysis;' the most fundamental and general level at which society is formed (Lefebvre 2008). The everyday, thus, is not bound to a pre-structured location but, as it were, forms its own space appropriately in terms of ongoing social relations. In literary as well as sociological writing this is recognized in the characterization of everyday life in terms of currents of energy, waves of sentiment and the stream of consciousness and subject to moods, tones and colours; all terms of indefinite and changing location. The space of the everyday is continually improvised, but always in such a way as to establish a predominant feeling-tone of *familiarity*. The everyday is not either public or private, nor is it both public and private; it is unbounded.

Henri Lefebvre nicely captures the conceptual unruliness and practical significance of the term; 'In one sense there is nothing more simple and obvious than everyday life. How do people live? The question may be difficult to answer, but that does not make it any less clear. In another sense nothing could be more superficial: it is banality, triviality, *repetitiveness*. And in yet another sense nothing could be more profound. It is existence and the "lived", revealed as they are before speculative thought has transcribed them: what must be changed and what is the hardest of all to change' (2008, vol 2: 7).

The everyday is shadowy presence; it is not an identity, it has no identity, not even as other. It is the unbounded, obscure and mundane background from which identities arise and in relation to which the self-synthesis of experience is formed.

SELF-IDENTITY AND EVERYDAY LIFE

As concepts, identity is used in a bewildering number of different ways, self is almost ungraspable in its paradoxical elusiveness, and everyday life effortlessly confounds any of its suggested representations. How can three such ambiguous and opaque terms be placed in interrelation in such a way as to illuminate contemporary social life? In fact, and quite surprisingly, linking together these damaged concepts brings into focus not only the actual character of contemporary experience, but suggests fruitful historical and cultural comparisons through which it can be more adequately understood. The impasse which blocks further conceptual analysis is not an insurmountable obstacle to a deeper understanding of the real world; it is, rather, the fruitful starting point for a different kind of investigation which will be taken up in the next chapter.

The conceptual discussion suggests the core idea of self-identity in modern western society might be expressed in the idea that self-identity is the coherence of everyday life. Where Immanuel Kant enquired philosophically into the conditions of possibility of any experience, more modestly, it might be suggested that, for modern society, at least, the sociological answer seems to be self-identity. Experience presupposes the experiencing subject and, as it were, arrives conformed to that peculiar sociocultural form. Self-identity is both the receptive and active agency of experience and the form of experience itself. This does not imply an individualistic approach to understanding modernity; far from it. Self-identity is a social form, at both collective and individual levels. The self-identity of the historical subject is collective, as well as reflexive, distinctive, interactive, and so on. It is the aim of the chapters that follow to show such an idea is both incoherent and implausible and that other approaches to grasping contemporary social reality are now required. While it is obviously dangerous to begin with errors and then seek to modify and correct mistaken ideas, there is little alternative to such a procedure.

INTERRUPTION 2: THEORY

Every body continues in its state of rest, or of uniform motion in a right line, unless it is compelled to change that state by forces impressed upon it.

The change of motion is proportional to the motive force impressed; and is made in the direction of the right line in which that force is impressed.

To every action there is always opposed an equal reaction: or, the mutual actions of two bodies upon each other are always equal, and directed to contrary parts.

(Sir Isaac Newton, *Principia*)

In these terms Newton states his famous Laws of Motion. From these axiomatic statements he proceeds to a complex and systematic elaboration of their implications, providing a wealth of examples, illustrations, and problems which he was able to deal with in a manner consistent with these initial statements. The entire work constitutes a deductive system that emulated Euclid in clarity and rigour. The *Principia*, in fact, looked like a text on geometry, but where Euclid's interest lay in the demonstration of pure mathematical relations, Newton's points and lines represented actual bodies, with real mass, moving in space. Here, for the first time in a truly comprehensive and compelling fashion, the operation of nature was adequately revealed through a system of pure mathematical reasoning. The result was so successful that mechanics became the normative standard, not just for the physical sciences, but for both the natural and social sciences as they developed during the following 300 years. Newton's *Principia* was cited, often by those who had never studied its contents, as a triumphant vindication of theoretical thinking (see Newton 1999).

The subsequent development of the sciences rarely achieved the consistency and integration of their theoretical model, but this served only to heighten the prestige of the original. In fact, the sciences increasingly departed from the norm of theoretical thinking and, to varying degrees, addressed practical considerations and the understandable wish to explain specific phenomena. Theory was enlisted to explain, with a view to controlling, the contingencies of everyday life. The extraordinary success of Newtonian mechanics was due primarily to its focus on astronomical data which, however large in scale, constituted a relatively very simple and isolated physical system. The movement of planets around the sun could be described quite accurately by his mathematical method because the physical reality, over a lengthy period of time from a human perspective, was, in fact, a kind of simple geometry involving very few interacting bodies. The relative position of the planets was overwhelmingly dependent on simple, measurable, and mathematically representable variables; mass, distance, and time. Accounting successfully for specific terrestrial events, however, such as an earthquake, involved the interaction of so many variables that theoretical thinking was led either into incalculable complexity or oversimplification.

Theory failed; but this was primarily a failure to grasp what theory is, and what it is for. Theory does not explain *empirical* events. Theory is an account of reality purified of actual events; it is what the world would be like if nothing ever happened. Theory is an interrelation of concepts. 'What is involved is not just the simplification of abstraction; it is the tendency to transform a relation into a thing in order to see conserved, not only the laws, but also the object' (Meyerson 1930: 22).

Galileo's pathbreaking science thus begins with a daring act of negation. He imagines a body falling freely in space, or a frictionless inclined plane. Theory demands this radical break with the everyday world and places it in a new context of understanding. Galileo is able to analyze the forces acting on a freely falling body simply by ignoring the always present and actual effects of such variables as air pressure, temperature, humidity, and the friction of the air. In practice, for example in carrying out an experiment to 'test' his theory, these variables cannot be eliminated and are not negligible in their effects. The result of any test, therefore, is expected to depart somewhat from the expectation of theory alone. In many cases the departure from a theoretical account may be quite large; but theory retains the advantage of being systematic and comprehensible, whereas a purely empirical approach to explaining actual events (effects) by actual antecedent conditions (causes) can never reach the satisfactory clarity of mathematical demonstration. Galileo's theoretical world is not just idealized, it is impossible (Koyré 1978).

The natural sciences in the modern period are not the only theoretical discourse that began in a radical rejection of the everyday world. Philosophy also, and in an unexpected way, anticipated the dislodging of understanding from experience. Descartes, in the early seventeenth century, freed philosophical thought from the authority of the past, especially of the church, and insisted that the only things he could know with certainty arose directly in his own experience. The problem was that the only thing arising in his own experience was himself, so that self-certainty, far from illuminating the world with fresh philosophical insight, kept itself to itself. Descartes found all immediate experience of the world, as distinct from the ongoing self-consciousness in which this experience was registered, to be doubtful. We could not have certainty about the world, primarily because, as self-conscious human beings, we did not directly experience the world; the only experience that came to us was already conformed to and transformed by the self-presence of the human subject. We were forced, therefore, to gain knowledge of the world through a system of representations which we supposed in some, philosophically unjustified, way reflected its real character. Philosophy, which considered the world exclusively in terms of its certainty or doubtfulness (as distinct from Galileo's science, which considered it exclusively in terms of its mass and motion), radically rejected everyday reality and ordinary experience as doubtful, against the immediate experience of the world and its assumption that things were, indeed, just as they seemed.

The hostility of theory to everyday common sense stemmed from the emergence of a modern understanding of its task. Theory became a specialized and even esoteric pursuit. In this regard it was no different to any other aspect of life; modern society institutionalized distinct and specialized institutional structures and everyday practices concerned with particular aspects of human activities. In the early seventeenth century it was not only science and philosophy that emerged with distinctive theoretical agendas, the modern world took shape through an extensive series of social differentiations of all sorts. Human activities were split up and treated according to the particular requirements of task rather than being absorbed into a context which was directly lived through. The exchange of goods, for example, became an economic phenomenon, warfare was conducted by way of specialized armies of fighting men, government was carried out by administrative staff, domestic life was organized as a family matter, and so on. This occurred over a lengthy period and unevenly. Theory was in the forefront of this process of differentiation, defining itself in terms of specific intellectual tasks which included that of providing a general understanding of a world that was rapidly fragmenting, so that one of the special tasks of theory was in a sense to preserve the sense of unity and coherence that modernity seemed to threaten, and act in some way against the spirit of the age, in seeking some more holistic and integrated view of the world; to rejoin what was breaking up.

The regulatory principle of theory, wherever it was deployed and whatever its subject matter, was reason; and reason was the universal and essential identity of human being. Reason was what made human being human, and distinguished human being unambiguously from every other kind of being. However difficult it might be to gain a genuine theoretical insight, once gained it became available to everyone. And the major difficulty, in fact, turned out to be effectively throwing off the assumptions of everyday life and the authority of tradition each of which, in different ways, polluted the mind with prejudice and irrational fear.

More specifically reality was understood, from a theoretical standpoint, as a systematic totality of formally identical, elementary units in continuous motion. To understand the world it had first of all to be deprived of contingency and grasped exclusively in terms of its essential identities. Here the principle of reason was translated into both a physical and a social theory. Matter, experientially complex, highly differentiated in form, appearance, and function was analyzed into particles that fell into one or another of very few types distinguished by shape, mass, and motion. Particles could be adequately represented in the rational system of mechanics by points and, inexplicably, resulting numerical and geometrical relations could be manipulated logically and mathematically in a manner than simulated natural processes. Nature was a rational system and human reason, which involved the application of spatial logic to experiential qualities, uncannily modelled its ideal equilibrium.

Theory, that is to say, grasped nature in its systematic unity as a rational system; it was an actual mechanism that could be *thought*. Theory was successful to the extent that it adequately represented the essential identity of the elementary constituents of nature. Modern social theory likewise began by seeking to characterize the essential identity of the fundamental constituents of society. The elementary particles of society, rather than being dead matter to which motion had mysteriously been added, appeared to be none other than the self-identical, active subjects familiarly present in everyday life as individual human beings. This assumption, which seemed to bring theory suspiciously close to the everyday world from which the natural sciences had triumphantly liberated themselves, was justified by very similar thought experiments to those suggested by Galileo and Newton. The isolated individual was conceptualized as a natural unity whose essential identity gave rise to just those characteristics necessary for the spontaneous generation of a completed interactive system of the type actualized in modern society. And, where the natural scientist had been forced to add motion to the system of nature, as it were, from the outside, social theory had the advantage of including motion, or the inherent tendency to motion (will, intention, desire), within the individual as its 'nature.'

The assumptions that founded social theory were assumptions about identity, about the self-identity of the human subject. However unjustified such assumptions turned out to be, and they were compromised just to the extent that they were insufficiently radical in their rejection of everyday experience, their persistence, in spite of strenuous criticism, attests to the centrality of the problem of identity for modern society. Identity was *the* problem for modern society because the coherence of experience, the very possibility of experience at all, seemed to depend upon it. Social life of any sort, let alone the more perfect order promised in the unprecedented dynamism and power of modern productive techniques, was seemingly founded on the inherent characteristics of its individual members. And first among these characteristics was the reflexive character of self. It was the identity of individuals as self-identical that made modern society actually possible as well as rationally comprehensible.

Much of the critical sociological commentary on what remains the standard theoretical model of society (an interactive unity founded on the individual impulses of formally equivalent individuals, endowed essentially with reason, and a capacity to feel want and pleasure), has been less coherent than the theory it has criticized. What counts as theoretical thinking in contemporary sociology has centred on the complaint that the standard model fails to account for the actual character of modern life.

And this apparent shortcoming is merged with social criticism. Modern society, that is to say, *ought* to be free, liberal, egalitarian, and rational but is conspicuously otherwise. Society should be more like the theory of society.

Story anticipates identity by asserting something; mysteriously drawing itself from oblivion. Theory begins by annihilating the everyday world so that it can ideally reconstruct its essential nature. There is an immediate tension between theory and everyday life, just as there is between the story and the everyday life from which it departs. Story asserts identity as singularity; its world is absolute and it leaves it up to us, its readers, to do likewise and generate from the incoherence of everyday life a living identity that is not just in the 'real world' but is so as something necessary. Theory, on the other hand, resists positing any kind of existence and establishes identity in the pure mental space of thought. Story and theory, in different ways, grasp fundamental reality in terms of identity, and both do so by distancing themselves from everyday life, which is accidental and incoherent; the non-identical.

2

CONTEXTS

A purely conceptual discussion of self-identity and everyday life, is important and highlights variety, ambiguity, and inconsistency in the use of the terms. It also points to widespread misunderstandings and misuse as, for example, the tendency to attribute identity through a property rather an essence. There is an important difference, thus, between the notion of 'a disabled person' and 'a person with a disability', just as there is between someone who *is* Scottish, female, old, rich, and so on and a *person* who displays any of those characteristics as attributes. However, it quickly emerges that the initial formulation of the thesis which concludes the conceptual discussion (the possibility of society is given in the essential identity of its individual members as self-identical), not only requires some modification if it is to be useful as a general proposal for the investigation of any society but, more surprisingly, requires radical rethinking if it is to prove useful in the limited task of grasping our own experience.

Even as concepts the terms outlined in the first chapter need to be related to each other within a broader framework if they are to be fully clarified and it is important at this point to take up more specific historical, contextual issues. To grasp the connection of self-identity as a phenomenon, ideas about self-identity and the developing practices of everyday life to a larger social context is particularly difficult if the analysis is confined to one kind of society. So far the discussion has assumed a context of what is generally and somewhat confusingly, termed 'modern western society'. A comparative approach makes more evident aspects of self-identity that, often taken to be universal characteristics of human beings, are inextricably tied to particular conditions of life in our own society. The aim here is not to consider all societies, or even a large number of different kinds of society. An extensive and inclusive approach invites unmanageable empirical complexity or theoretical abstraction, so a very limited comparison will be undertaken. Practices and ideas related to self and identity in three closely related societies, premodern western society, modern Japanese society and modern western society; will be outlined briefly. A further comparison will be introduced at a later stage through a discussion of self and identity in postmodern, global society.

Though a small sample, chosen deliberately to restrict the range of variation, such a comparison presents a dauntingly complex and demanding field of investigation that no single academic can hope adequately to cover. It is, nevertheless, worth proceeding inadequately rather than not at all. Yet more awkward is the suspicion that thus to select, in advance and without prior justification, comparators that are named and characterized as 'types' of society is to assume just what needs to be demonstrated. Is 'Japanese society' or 'premodern' society a different kind of society, or just a society that displays some distinctive and perhaps not very consequential, property? This may well be a case of overgeneralization on the doubtful assumption that a distinctive property is, in fact, a key variable or, even, an essential identity.

Methodological difficulties notwithstanding, this comparative perspective suggests that the form of self-identity familiar from everyday life is neither a necessary nor general mode of experience and reality construction. Self-identity is firmly located in a particular society such that, even those that might be thought to be most closely related to it (either modern or western, but not modern western) display radically different characteristics. For premodern western society, reality is given as 'selfless identity', and modern Japanese society the world consists of 'non-identical selves'.

SELFLESS IDENTITY: PREMODERN WESTERN SOCIETY

Most sociological accounts of premodern western society are conditioned by a particular view of 'medieval' Western Europe following the withdrawal of Roman Imperial occupation as characteristically 'feudal'. The term feudal is not a neutral descriptive term but is inextricably bound up with *modern western* ideas about the past. Feudalism, a term introduced by French legal theorists in the post-Revolutionary period, was developed as a self-conscious contrast between newly established constitutional safeguards to individual liberty, on the one hand, and a society for which law was the personal prerogative and political weapon of a small aristocracy, social relations among elites were organized in terms of reciprocal personal relations, and the mass of people lived in closed, tradition bound communities on the other. In fact, the historical and geographical limits of feudalism were more restricted than was often assumed; in its fully developed form it characterized rural society in what is now west and northern France, Belgium, Holland, and England, for a period of about 500 years from around the ninth to fourteenth centuries (Bloch 1989). A related understanding of the premodern west, though a no less vague and contentious term, Christendom, has often been interrelated with feudalism to describe the socio-cultural composition of post-Roman societies that coalesced in response to the rapid spread of Islam in the seventh century C.E. (Pirenne 1939; Herrin 1989). This image of premodern western society was highly selective, ignored the significance of 'barbarian' tribal societies, non-feudal social relations, and underestimated the importance of Arabic, Jewish and Oriental traditions (Goody 2004, 2006).

Given an initial understanding of self-identity in conceptual terms as reflexive difference (self-conscious grasp of our own distinctiveness individually and collectively) how was this understanding contextualized in an historical account of the emergence and development of our own society? What was the critical difference, in other words, between us (moderns) and people in the premodern west? The answer was not given in terms of a different self-identity, but of the difference between a society for which self-identity was the given form of experience and a different, now strange and incomprehensible world for which reality was not conformed to self-identity at all. Any radical understanding of the modern as genuinely new required some such account of the past. It was not just a matter of acknowledging that people in premodern western society had a different experience of life; it was not the same kind of life, not the same kind of being that constituted the person, and not the same kind of reality that we grasped in and as experience.

The difference from the past was profound and, thus, difficult to describe and understand. A helpful approach is to contrast the most taken-for-granted aspects of modern experience with corresponding 'categories' of medieval culture. The categories of medieval culture were as distinctive of their world as were those certified by Immanuel Kant as the normative standard of reason for modern culture (Gurevich 1985).

Thus, the social meaning and forms of organizing space and time were quite distinct. For medieval culture space is not empty, uniform extension; at both a theoretical and a practical level, space is divided and interrelated according to the characteristic qualities of *place*. Medieval society is one in which everyone 'knows their place', or, better, they are determined by the place they are in. Person, group, community, corporation, court, are all spatial terms and manifest specific forms, qualities and attributes by virtue of 'belonging' to an appropriate place. Human qualities are not distributed randomly among people who were then allocated in some way to the place where such qualities are most appropriately deployed. Human beings and all other beings, are not distinct and separable from their location. Space, that is to say, is itself ordered according to socially meaningful differences. This effectively 'keeps people in their place'.

Movement, thus, implies an actual transformation of the person. It is not just a matter of constraining the mass of the population to a variety of closed communities; the hierarchical order of medieval society in principle is guaranteed by the differentiation of space itself. If people were able to break out of their enclosed worlds they would, as a result, cease to be the kind of person they were. To move from place to place was to undergo an essential change; a metamorphosis (Bynum 2005). The metamorphosis of being inherent in all change of location was also the effective mechanism of pilgrimage. Travel to the Holy Land, or to any of the many sites of holy relics scattered throughout Christendom, transformed the soul of the traveller, purifying and elevating by virtue simply of drawing close to the earthly location of sacred objects and events. Of course, the return journey was a 'fall', but, the pilgrim continued for some time at least to benefit from release from the heavy weight of previously accumulated sin. Qualitative change not only affected people moving from place to place; all change, was understood as the 'intension and remission' of qualities.

Space was not distinct from the substance of things located in a particular place. And distinct places were organized in a *cosmos* that was the singular, whole, hierarchical order of creation. Everything found its place in a schema that manifest, in its various orders, differing degrees of perfection. Every created being *depended* for its existence on a higher and more perfect being to which it was linked; a being which, in its turn, depended on one yet more perfect. Creation extended as a ladder or Great Chain of

Being that linked simple lifeless matter, through more complex forms, to sentient beings and beyond to supraterrestrial angelic beings. The Ladder of Creation ultimately terminated in the absolute perfection of the Divine Being. God was the Being, as St Anselm expressed it, 'than none greater could be thought'.

Within a feudal society, that is to say, it was obviously the case that everything was ordered according to 'degrees of greatness' or perfection. Everything depended, ultimately, on the person, the will, of the Supreme Being; that is, on the monarch and the monarch made absolute as God. Feudal relationships were organized at two levels. For the minority, who were members of superior political elites accorded individual legal status, dependence on the ruler was expressed in a muted form through a, notionally free and voluntary, oath of allegiance. Becoming a vassal to a great lord or ruler was not, in fact, acceptance of a wholly dependent state but, rather, an unequal exchange (an exchange of incommensurable goods), in which the vassal received rights of possession in a specified domain or fief, as a kind of compensation for the, in principle unlimited, military services that he was required to undertake on the lord's behalf. And for the masses of, legally dependent, peasants, retainers of many kinds and household servants, serfdom was a relation of evident and one-sided dependence. This was not a matter of what in modern society would be understood as inequality. It was not even a combination of different kinds of inequality, reinforcing each other. It was, rather, a relation in which the subordinate was subsumed within the *person* of the superior. And the superior did not possess the serf in a modern sense of holding property rights over them; they became responsible for their domain, including its serfs and could not divest themselves of that responsibility. The lord was not free to sell or transfer his rights. The serf, thus, was not accorded a legal, political, or social 'identity'. Identity was a distinguishing characteristic of higher beings that flowed downwards, such that the subordinate appeared to be a less perfect version of the superior. Each person was 'the man of another man', or the member of a community whose collective identity was permanently fixed as a place to which each person was bound and without which any person ceased to be identifiable.

This, of course, is a sketch of an ideal that rarely corresponded to actual social practices. But as an ideal it had a rhetorical significance and was invoked in justification of some at least of the wide variety of institutional arrangements characteristic of medieval western society (Bloch 1989).

The cosmological model of medieval society was important as a justification for feudal social practices but, given that justification was always secondary to the threat and actual use of force, was more significant as a comprehensive and intellectually compelling account of the world as a whole. It is in terms of a world view that feudal social relations, themselves uncertain, impermanent, and insecure, were realized as the Great Chain of Being in which everything found its place. In the present perspective the key idea expressed in this cosmological scheme is the singularity of identity. The medieval world view is fundamentally theological; God uniquely constituted identity. This is expressed simply in the declaration; God *is*. The 'isness' of God (*ipseity*), is absolute, unchanging and perfect Being. This means, in fact, that God does not exist in the familiar, empirical, spatio-temporal world. Identity is *transcendental*. Ultimacy rested with God;

> When medieval thinkers turned their attention to the study of the beautiful, it was inevitable that such study should turn upon comprehension of God – the creator of all visible forms, which do not exist in themselves but only as a means to comprehension of the divine reason. In exactly the same way, history did not present itself to the medieval mind as an independent process, spontaneously generated by its own immanent laws: this stream of events, unrolling, developing, in time acquired meaning and significance only in the light of eternity and the fulfilment of God's design ... Philosophy was "the handmaiden of theology" ... Theology represented the highest generalisation of medieval man's social behavior; it provided a general semiological system in terms of which the members of a feudal society apprehended themselves and saw their world both motivated and explained.
>
> (Gurevich 1985: 8–9)

Everything in the mundane world, by contrast, is subject to change, corruption, decay, and the cycle of rebirth. For the medieval west this powerful conception of identity was given a specifically religious interpretation. God was God; the perfect identity. What then was the mundane world? It was made up of a vast range of imperfectly identical beings. However, in so far as every being manifest in its existence some, temporarily formed substance, every being displayed a propensity towards, and partial actualization of, an identity of a lesser sort. All entities, that is to say, were temporary, partial identities. Each substantial form, cosmologically distinct from every other, could only come into existence at all and could persist only so long as, it was sustained by the being of a higher form. The social and political imperative of hierarchy was made necessary for the medieval world view in terms of its religious presuppositions. God, the perfect identity, was moved to create the world. This much was evident; but creation posed a real theological problem for medieval thinkers. If God was perfect why should He need to create anything? It was inconceivable that He created for no reason at all, that He acted, so to speak, on a whim? And worse, having created the world, He had necessarily created something less than Himself; something non-identical to the Absolute and, thus, imperfect. But how could God have created anything imperfect? The theological issue proper is less significant here than its implication for any, practical as well as theoretical, grasp of identity in the everyday life of medieval society (Gilson 1990).

On the one hand, as created forms, each being was essentially distinct and was readily identifiable by appearance and location. Peasants were not simply inferior to aristocratic landholders, or clerics; they were essentially different beings. There were no 'human' beings in a general sense; only human beings differentiated according to qualitatively distinct, inherent characteristics. On the other hand, all beings depended for their existence upon the Being who created and sustained them and were, thus, linked together in the Divine Order; and shared, in some sense, in the singular Identity. The manner of finite beings participation in Identity was baffling and highly contentious. The orthodox view, developed over a lengthy period, relied on the idea that all created substance formed into determinate beings were *symbols*; that is to say, their appearance and form ware directly related to and part of a larger, non-material, cosmos. Empirical existence was viewed, thus, as an abbreviated, or condensed, version of and stood for, a larger, whole and perfectly identical reality; just as the Lord's Prayer, or a splinter from the Cross, was a symbol of Christianity in its completeness and Truth. It is in this non-arbitrary and substantial sense of symbol that appearance was understood as bodying forth the real qualities of things. And the human body itself was the master symbol; the *microcosm*, that was both part and structural replica of the *macrocosm*. Human beings, as genuine *microcosmic* beings made in the 'image and likeness', analogically created objects that also served as symbols of Divine Order. The cathedral, thus, was a structure 'designed as a replica in every detail of the cosmic order: its interior, with its dome, altar and side chapels, was meant to give the beholder a complete representation of the structure of the universe' (Gurevich 1985: 71).

And this is why appearance was carefully regulated. The different orders of human beings symbolized the hierarchical social order and bore the evidence of their differences in bodily form and bearing, in clothing and all the paraphernalia of daily life. Rich and colourful fabrics adorned feudal superiors; their costumes were not simply splendid decoration; their colour and vibrant texture were an essential expression of nobility (Pastoureau 2004). Sumptuary regulation ensured that food, clothing, equipment, and so on were carefully controlled and bundled together for the use of the appropriate social group and community. Daily life for a monk, for example, was vastly different to that of a member of the nobility, or a townsman; and this was not a matter of economic resources alone but was an obligatory aspect of differentiated social orders (Duby 1980; Le Goff 1980).

For medieval society, thus, the entire world, including the world of human beings, was highly differentiated into essentially distinct, substantial forms and, at the same time, each form, by virtue of its sharing, to varying degrees, in the singular, absolute Being of the Creator, served as symbol of the same, unique Identity. In medieval society there were many differences but just one identity.

The interplay between multiple difference and singular identity is exemplified in the figure of the monster. Each being was essentially different to any other, but the substantial, qualitative character of place meant that metamorphosis was an ever present possibility (Cohen 2003; Bynum 2005). It was all too easy to fall into the form of another; to become ill-formed and monstrous. All movement was dangerous and straying into wild places, having the opposite effect to the spiritual elevation of the pilgrimage, was productive of physical corruption. The outcast, literally, became monstrous; and deformed, diseased and wasted bodies revealed those who had strayed, physically and morally, from their proper place. The terrible fate of metamorphosis was, nonetheless and in a different way, evidence of the cosmological order that had been breached, but yet included deformity and monstrosity within its catalogue of possibilities and, thus, asserted Identity above all else. Even the monstrous could not come into existence as an extraneous and uncreated essence.

And if the created order was more fluid and less stable than, from a modern perspective, is often assumed the characteristics included within different forms and species were often strikingly at odds with modern systems of classification. There was no general notion of humanity in the sense that what was deemed to be essential to and characterized all, human beings differentiated them collectively from any other species or kind of being. What moderns regard as distinctively human capacities and attributes were shared across species because, to some degree, all creatures shared Identity. Animals, thus, could be held responsible for crimes, prosecuted and made to stand trial (Pastoureau 2004). Nature, as well as Man, was tainted with sin and subject to the cycle of death and rebirth.

The problem of identity in medieval society is to account simultaneously for difference and unity; it is not an issue of self, or self-identity. This follows directly on the practical and conceptual organization of social life. Medieval people lived in communities, corporate bodies, and closed institutions; in terms of daily life people were immediately recognizable and familiar in a variety of different contexts. People rarely met and interacted anonymously as strangers. Even feudal lords were known in person and demanded compliance on the basis of personal allegiance and loyalty. The routines of everyday life were well established and sanctified by immemorial tradition. There was, thus, little sense of playing a role and no need to demonstrate to people who were unfamiliar, the intentions behind any particular action. Consequently there was little need, or foundation, for a separate sense of self standing apart from, or behind, the varied and linked interaction of ordinary life. The reflexive character of self hardly arises where there is no need to reflect on any particular situation, make choices from a range of possibilities, or exercise a sense of inner freedom in projecting a particular self-image. Where appearance is linked essentially to substantial forms, every form is ultimately rooted in a singular identity, and all live in the same God-centred cosmos; reflection turns outwards as contemplation of the Divine Order, rather than focusing inward on subjective processes of self-formation.

NON-IDENTICAL SELVES: JAPANESE MODERNITY

Premodern western society may be characterized in terms of selfless, singular, transcendental identity; modern Japanese society, by contrast, through the non-identity of immanent, multiple selves.

Japanese everyday life is experienced in terms of transition; it is, above all, a dynamic flux within which nothing remains fixed and unchanging. Nothing remains identical with itself; everything passes away. This includes the experiencing subject, or self, which, far from standing apart from the fluidity of its own experience, is wholly absorbed in its transitions. Self has a purely contextual reality, neither standing out against the obscurity of an ill-defined background of everyday activities, nor preserving itself in the security of inner reflection.

This situation is well expressed by Augustin Berque (1997), one of the most perceptive of European students of Japanese society and culture:

> ... there is a link between, on the one hand, the imprecision even the redundancy of the grammatical subject in the Japanese language and, on the other, the tendency to base the subject in its environment, to glorify the identification of humans with things, to favour other idioms over verbal communication, to value sensibility more than reasoning, to magnify nature, the natural, the mood, the ambience and the milieu, the tendency, basically, to condemn the individuation of the person and to celebrate the communal identity, which Japanese culture has always done.
>
> (Berque 1997: 229)

Berque's view is closely related to and explicitly relies on, the writings of the modern Japanese philosopher, Watsuji Tetsuro. The latter's book on climatic culture (*Fudo*) is easily misunderstood by European readers who, implicitly interpreting his views in the light of western assumptions about the separation of environment from the human subject, have read it as an example of geographical determinism. Berque's corrective draws attention to the subtle complexity of Watsuji's writings and emphasizes the interactive and mobile nature of his central notion of *milieu*, which is close to the now widespread sociological term *habitus* and which Berque (1997) reformulates as *mediance*. For Japanese scholars, generally, any plausible account of experience is sensitive not only to the multiplicity and variety of interaction between people, but also between the present and the past, the human and the non-human, the immediate, always transforming situation and a wider framework of more distant, mediated actions and events.

The social organization of space in Japan is distinctive. The social interaction that creates and sustains spatial distinctions is a primary constituting process of the Japanese cultural world. Space in Japan is neither an abstract continuity, as in the modern west, nor the qualitatively defined substantial form of *place* that characterized premodern western society, but, rather, is continually formed and reformed according to the character of the *performance* taking place. The primary significance of space is not to locate the subject, but to establish the aspect of subjectivity most relevant to the situation. Space imparts a certain ritual tone to whatever is taking place. But where, in the medieval west, the qualitative aspect of space is essentially related to the cosmological position of the objects located there, for Japan spatial boundaries define relations and performances rather than objects; hence the importance, throughout Japan, of bounded and enclosed spaces, such as gardens, theatres and, above all, the home. Everything in Japan is enclosed. From walled gardens to boxed lunches, everything is wrapped. Times and events, as well as objects, are carefully framed and demarcated. Wrapping is a process that confers value on the simplest object. The rituals of gift giving and, receiving and returning involve to an extraordinary degree precise forms of wrapping and presentation. The *furoshiki*, a cloth used for wrapping, is often of more monetary worth than and is not part of, the gift itself (Hendry 1993). The inside is never predictable from the wrapping, wall, fence, or cover. The most exquisite gardens are enclosed in dull, uniform walls.

Significantly the world inside is not simply distinct from, but incommensurable with, the world outside. There is no contrast here because the boundary does not separate two zones, but defines the boundary of a particular interactive unity. There is no space in the sense of continuous extension; the multiplicity of enclosures are not related together in terms of some general, overall plan. Separate spaces are not located in relation one to another but exist, as it were, in themselves. The cityscape, thus, often appears incoherent, adjacent buildings bear no relation to each other, areas fold into each other in unpredictable ways. Space, in Japan, is formed ideally into what the eighteenth-century European philosopher Leibniz termed *monads*, separate and distinct worlds hermetically sealed from one another. Of course, this ideal is never actualized, any more than reality for the premodern west was, even in its own terms, a perfectly formed Great Chain of Being. The assumption of discontinuity, however, is important for any understanding of the distinctive features of modern Japanese culture. As distinct from western forms, Japanese culture is 'lococentric' rather than 'logocentric' (Lebra 2005).

The first division of space is between inside and outside. This is not only an important division between private space and public space; the internal organization of the home, in particular provides a rich texture of spatial divisions that also find meaningful expression as social relations. Lebra insightfully suggests a fourfold schema rather than a simple inside/outside distinction organizes socio-spatial relations. *Omote* (front) is the public interface and ritually guarded boundary between inside and outside; the performance criteria of this region involve precise and elaborate forms of courtesy relations. *Uchi* (interior) is a restricted zone governed by, equally precise and codified, forms of intimacy. *Soto* (outside) characterizes relations with strangers and includes anomic and disruptive forms of behaviour. *Ura* (back) is the hidden interior of secretive relations, including domestic abuse (Lebra 2005: 39). The ternary, rather than binary, system offers possibilities of ambiguity, multiplicity, indeterminateness, merging and complex, shifting contextualization.

The juxtaposition of incommensurable and unconnected spaces, however, is counteracted by the in principle unbounded character of spiritual contact with, and participation in, the world of transient experience. Reflexivity is expressed spatially rather than in terms of immediate self-awareness and self-modification. In the west subjectivity was generated as 'mental space;' in Japan subjectivity is a primary characteristic of the world. And as subjectivity is not locked inside the person there is no inherent barrier between human beings and any other being, or between human beings and the natural world. That is to say, the human is not an identity, and subjectivity spreads throughout the world. The Japanese term for 'person' *ningen*, for example, means *between* human beings (Yuasa 1987). Originally a Buddhist term, humanness always implies 'betweenness' (*aidagara*). Thus for Watsuji and many other contemporary Japanese thinkers the everyday is taken as a point of departure, not the self-identical consciousness (Kant), but the betweenness of relational activity. Thus, 'Whereas in the modern Western view self and environment are opposing terms, in Japan they are seen as interactive; the self melds with the environment by identifying with patterns of nature which are, nonetheless, culturally constructed' (Rosenberger 1992: 93). Enclosed space forms and reforms according to particular performance criteria and momentarily exists as entire and self-sufficient worlds; at the same time the open space of self awareness is unlimited and absolutely inclusive.

Spatial terms characterize forms of subjectivity as well as classify social relations and performances. Space, rather than self-identity, is the fundamental experiential form of Japanese culture; 'The contingent subject, terminologically multiple, unfixed and spatially extended, does not appear as an "agent," as the English *I* so sharply implies' (Lebra 2005: 23–24; Gottlieb 2005). As distinct from the subject-predicate structure of English sentence is the topic – comment structure. The avoidance of personal pronouns and subject identification in speech and writing is one of the most striking features of Japanese life for any western observer. In language: 'Japanese has no single first-person pronoun *I* as it exists in English, a generalized or transcendental term for self regardless of who is self and who is other. Rather, Japanese first-person indicators are variable, in terms of (a) gender; (b) self's relation to the listener by age, seniority, status and familiarity; and (c) the given interactive situation, such as formal or informal. These contexts dictate how the self term "unfolds"' (Lebra 2005: 20). Additionally, to accommodate the rich contextualization of speech, 'Japanese often resort to other, nonpronomial words'. By contrast it is worth noting the rarity of relational third person term such as 'uncle', 'father', 'boss', and so on in everyday English, particularly in referring to self. And its occasional written use, as, for example, self-reference to 'the author', appears affected. The characteristic I-form in European languages, however, is relatively modern and seems to be largely absent from ancient and early medieval texts (Borkenau 1981).

Modern Japanese literature provides additional insight into the contextual, multiplicity of selves. In the modern Japanese novel the narrator is frequently a participant in the story and does not stand apart as an omniscient observer. This is consistent with the sheer immanence of Japanese culture and the absolute continuity of its phenomenological field. The location of the narrator becomes especially prominent and ambiguous in the so-called 'I-novel' (*Shishōsetsu*). The 'I-novel' initially gained popularity as openly imitative of European confessional literature and was read as barely disguised autobiographical accounts of the author's more or less scandalous private life. But its popular manifestation was misleading and hardly represents its importance as a literary form. The genealogy of the 'I-novel' emerged retrospectively during the nineteen twenties as one of the most distinctive Japanese inflections of modernism, identified with Tayama Katai's *Futon* as its substantial founder and Naoya Shiga's *A Dark Night's Passing* as the apotheosis of the form (Suzuki 1996; Fujii 1993; Washburn 1995, 2007). In its developed literary form the 'I-novel' was neither autobiographical nor even first person narrative; but a statement of the 'I'. Shiga, reacting in a subtle and complex way to reading Rousseau, created a literature that ultimately 'questions the belief in a fixed identity of a subject as the origin of its actions' (Suzuki 1996: 112).

As distinct from western literature in which the novel is sustained by a transcendental myth of authorship, the Japanese 'I-novel' is participatory in the world it describes. The author has to be given a place in the narrative from which to describe the action, a device occasionally exploited by

European writers, notably Dostoyevsky in *The Devils*. The Japanese text must accommodate the author as one of its participants; insists on continuity between fictional and actual worlds. The Japanese form is saturated with immediacy (Fowler 1988). The 'I-novel' is witness to the ambiguities and contradictions of experience without positing as its transcendental possibility the psychic unity of author, reader, or character. The modality of Japanese prose (fiction and non-fiction) is not emplotment in terms of a narrative unity that 'makes sense' to the self-composed reader, but immediacy that undermines continuity, structure and the coherence of what western modernity designates as 'experience'. The predominance of the 'I-form' in modern Japanese literature has to do paradoxically with the absence of the 'self' from Japanese experience; the absence of experience as such. In Japanese narrative there is no essential difference between objective reported experience and direct transcription (Fowler 1988: 36–37). The immediacy of Japanese narrative, however, is part of its objectivity, its emotional exteriority. The modern Japanese author is a 'recorder-witness' rather than an omniscient and detached observer.

Modern Japanese literature, more generally and not only the 'I-novel' display a remarkable narrative objectivity that finds its coherence in terms of mood rather than character or plot. Literature strove after pure forms, including pure forms of emotionality not as expressive of specific characters or for the purposes of plot but, rather, as an interesting and detachable phenomena, to be described, recorded, classified, and examined. The Japanese I-novel does not work by a psychology of identification at all, it is an objective statement, a laying out of a variety of life histories as 'there.' The influential short stories of Akutagawa, during the 1920s with their shifting points of reference and narrative perspective, (brilliantly filmed by Kurosawa) is exemplary in this regard. These general features are common in much modern Japanese literature whether western in orientation, such as the novels of Natsume Soseki, or otherwise self-consciously traditional and 'Japanese', such as the later work of Junichoro Tanizaki and Kawabata. Mori Ogai, one of the most lauded of all Japanese writers of the Meiji era, is an interesting example. His major literary works rest on European psychiatry and the setting of Japanese student culture. But they remain unresolved, are non-romantic, and relationships are not founded on mutuality of feeling but convenience, contingency, and, habit. Ogai in fact gave up the western style, as did Tanizaki, and wrote historical novels and finally an enormously long reconstruction of the life of an eighteenth-century doctor. This amounted to a literary consecration of daily life and the unremarkable, unnoticed and forgotten as the real content of life. Self found itself in this forgotten world, only there could be found sufficient breadth and content to accommodate its many, unrelated, disproportionate and discontinuous forms. The celebration of the everyday, a major theme in Japanese literature that became a guiding theme also in literary criticism and the construction of its classical cannon, finds its 'theoretical' extension in aesthetics rather than theology or philosophy. More recent 'identity fiction', of which the novels of Kobo Abe (2002, 2006) is preeminent, embraces the paradoxical world of selflessness rather than posits lost selfhood as a problem. For many Japanese writers self cannot be narrated; identities can only be presented, floating, beyond the touch of selfhood; circulating in the space of modernity.

Literary convention is an important aspect of a more general aesthetic culture the significance of which was fully recognized during the eighteenth century when a number of 'nativist' scholars characterized 'Japaneseness' in terms of its distinctive valuation of transitoriness. This idea was fundamental to aesthetic theory. Original Japanese spirit, in this view, is primarily an aesthetic sensitivity; that is, it lives and responds immediately in terms of *feeling*. And feeling lies primarily in the character of things themselves; it is not a personal, subjective orientation towards, or reaction to, these things. Japanese spirit is, from a modern western viewpoint, *exteriority* and is peculiarly heightened and clarified just at the moment of things fading or changing form. The moment of transience is highly valued for the special intensity of its objective givenness, whereas the modern western fascination with the momentary lies precisely in its heightening of purely subjective impression. This characteristic sensitivity to the pathos of things (*mono no aware*), thus, does not depend upon a detached appreciation of the beautiful or intuition of the sublime, but arises directly in the immanence of a reality that included the subject as a fully involved participant. In this regard historical and linguistic shared common ground with the cosmopolitan modernist that frequented the pleasure zones. The 'floating world' of the urban pleasure zone was devoted to just such experiences of sensuous transience.

The sheer immanence of Japanese culture is also evident in its aesthetic, secular culture. Neither beauty nor significance depends on transcendental values. Japanese religious traditions, thus, are overwhelmingly practical and deal with everyday realities and everyday social relations (Reader and Tanabe 1998). *Shinto* the 'native' Japanese religious tradition is part animistic cult and part state ideology. It is non-theological and offers a magical technology to manage everyday changes in station (Kasulis 2004). Birth, marriage, the transformation associated with age-grades, education, employment, illnesses and much more involve visits and offerings, to Shinto shrines. *Kami*, (spirits) are felt to inhabit many special locations, including mountains, streams, particular trees, build-ings, gardens, and so on. *Kami* are not extramundane and dwell in the same places as people, animals and objects. They coexist effortlessly in the modern urban setting. Shrines are found in many streets, beside shops, pachinko parlours, offices and houses. Shinto also serves as a system of registration for local government and is the most immediate level at which the state impinges on people's lives; significantly by recording names.

The juxtaposition of seeming opposites, or incommensurable ele-ments, which is a common feature of acosmic spatial relationships, also finds institutional expression in the popularity of Buddhism. An over-whelming majority of people claim some sort of attachment to Buddhist as well as Shinto organizations and practices. Again there are no theolog-ical demands made in most versions of Japanese Buddhism. Indeed, it is institutionally, practically and liturgically highly differentiated and diverse.

The immanence of the real means also that symbolic relationships in Japanese culture have an immediate and practical aspect. They are neither metaphorical, nor part-whole relationships. Symbols, rather, are contex-tually rich points of interaction for many different contexts of interactive performance. Cherry blossom and rice, for example, like the multiple selves of ordinary people, appear in several different contexts in every-day life serve to distinguish characteristically 'Japanese' relationships (Ohnuki-Tierney 1993, 2002).

In the emergence of modern Japan the traditional warrior group, the samurai, were effectively disarmed and socially transformed. The new regime suppressed all *private* conflict resolution through arms and forbade the samurai to draw their swords in public. These traditional weapons became badges of office as the samurai took on new governmental func-tions, which did not require qualities of personal honour, but for which they received a stipend; 'The Tokugawa samurai were thought of as persons who combined the roles of the aristocracy, the military and the bureaucracy, three functions that were increasingly divided among distinctively different social groups in early modern Europe' (Ikegami 1995, 184). The samurai became urbanized and pacified; any were impoverished and many who were not became patrons and customers of new urban arts. The performance of civility became the key integrative feature of Tokugawa regime (Ikegami 2007). As this became well established its aesthetic values and forms in turn were elevated into the sources and substance of Japanese national culture.

Aesthetic networks, looking back to aristocratic ideals long since destroyed by factionalism and warfare, emerged in the interstitial regions of the new regime. This culture included tea ceremonies, games, and theatrical performances of all sorts. In larger cities specialized pleasure zones became the focus of an aesthetic life that valued the sensuous, transient experiences of the 'floating world'. The strong military dominance of Tokugawa was in practice allied to a shrewd and flexible policy of ceding near autonomy not only to regions and their *Daimyo* but also to occupational and status groupings and to voluntary associations of various sorts. These latter became the sites of cultural innovation and a new economy of pleasure. This was the first popular culture to be wholly commercialized; a world celebrated in immensely popular literary and theatrical works including many works of great distinction such as the novels of Ihara Saikaku and the plays of Monzaemon Chikamatsu for the *bunraku* theatre (Matsunosuke 1997).

What had characterized Japanese culture throughout its modern development, however, was the elaboration of performance codes of all sorts. The elaboration of appropriate standards of performance in all aspects of everyday life, as well as in the staging of theatrical events, was central to the development of Japanese culture from the beginning of the Tokugawa regime and remained fundamental throughout its modern development. Regulating the performance of everyday life was the key mechanism of state formation. Sumptuary regulations were introduced and regulated dress, food, housing and demeanor in public. Theatrical entertainments, which were exemplary performances and had an important educative effect in establishing conventions and, more importantly, on the capacity to learn and assimilate such conventions to the rituals of everyday life, were especially bound by official codes:

> ... regulations prescribed sites of theatre construction, the materials permissible for constructing the roofs of theatre buildings, the areas in which actors were allowed to live and move freely, access by the actors to the theatre's boxes and the kinds of clothes the actors were allowed to wear and the precise type of hat they were asked to wear whenever outside their territory,

permission regarding the performance of certain types of dances within *kabuki* presentations, permission for theatres to operate following major scandals, including minutiae which may appear embarrassing to a modern reader, such as prohibiting female impersonators from using public facilities reserved for ladies.

(Ortolani 1995: 163)

The distinctive historical-cultural context of developing Japanese modernity, thus, involved a quite different form of experience and awareness to the self-identical subject that characterizes modern western society. It is important also to grasp the institutional aspect of this difference, which involved not only a distinctive pattern of everyday life but a different relationship between everyday life and the state. For the modern west, the state represents itself as a transcendental body; it is above civil society, domestic and household economy, the differentiated spheres of experience and everyday life. But in Japan, a culture of sheer immanence, there is no such possibility so the state seeks to enhance and consolidate its power through direct participatory control of everyday life. It cannot stand above society as its uniting and integrating idea and, as a result, cannot establish itself as an ultimate authority. The Japanese state, therefore, does not operate by institutionalizing self-regulation (law, market, reason, pleasure), but seeks direct and continuous control of society through local community organization and local political bodies (Garon 1997), the household and domestic life (Sand 2003) and the ritualization of the life-cycle afforded in particular by its sponsored development of Shinto (Nelson 2000; Kasulis 2004; Hardacre 1989).

SELF-IDENTITY: MODERN WESTERN SOCIETY

Classic modernity in the west conceived of its world as autonomous self-creation in which, ideally, identity and self were in mutually supporting interrelation; the crucial problem of identity was focused on the issue of self-identity. The self, to be self, had to be constituted as an identity. This implied the separation of self from its world around and the subject's withdrawal into the security of an inner-space.

The problem of identity becomes acute just because it is held to be expressive, or indicative, of self; and self, for modern society which founds itself in a radical break from the past and rejection of subordination to God or Nature, is ideally free. Self-identity, then, becomes a matter of choosing, producing, expressing, and forming identities adequate to reflect the self that chooses and forms them. Unlike premodern western society identity is not given in the structure of society and its organized forms of interaction and, in comparison with modern Japanese society, the multiplicity of social roles, partial, segmented, and anonymous relationships, identity is a requirement of self-experience. For the modern west, that is to say, the fluidity and multiplicity of social roles each with their attendant self is ideally integrated into a singular identity. But this identity, in principle, cannot be constituted either in any one, or in the combination of several or all, of its instances. Yet the demand for valid and authentic selfhood persists. Self is an achieved experience; it is not inscribed in social relations. And self is required to identify itself and to express itself.

The immediate social transformation that both required and actualized self-identity as a new and distinctive experience of the world has been described and analyzed in a number of ways, most notably by the major founding figures of sociological thought. The transition from feudalism to capitalism, the rationalization of modern life, the differentiation of society into interdependent parts and aspects, the development of a money economy, the production of commodities, the centralization of the state with its complex impersonal institutions of law and government, the splitting apart of family life and the household economy, the spread of bureaucratic organizations – all these and other related changes that are highlighted in the classical literature as characteristic of and go some way towards explaining, the distinctive character of social life in modern western society, also constitute the meaningful context in which self-identity arose. There is a danger, however, in enlisting this powerful literature as a background to more recent sociological discussions that have focused on parallel transformations in, for example, image making, sensory awareness, intimacy and private life, bodily practices and techniques and the experience of illness and disease. It is easy to give the impression that such studies are simple additions of detail to older perspectives that had focused on the central and most significant features of the social transformation; that the latter are to be explained and understood in terms of the former and that the issues and phenomena with which they deal are secondary and derivative in some way. In the case of self-identity it might appear that contemporary scholarship is adding a more or less interesting psychological gloss to well known and still contentious, debates about the 'real' issues of modernity.

But this is far from the case. The emergence of self-identity is the central phenomenon of modern everyday life and should not be viewed simply in relation to, or as explained by, the transformation as understood in the classics; it has to be seen *as* that transformation. It is not just that self-identity seems to be important to us, or that we value our own experience over everything else. Nor is it the case that 'psychological' reality is inherently more important than anything else; far from it. Self-identity is not another and previously overlooked, aspect of the emergence of modernity; it is precisely what is meant by modernity itself. Self-identity is a new experience of reality; it is reality transformed *into* experience. It is important, therefore, not to isolate certain aspects of experience and treat them as somehow more 'real', or more fundamental than others. Thus, while it is clearly the case that the development of a money economy and the concentration of large numbers of people in urban areas had, as one of its consequences, the growing dominance of social relationships that were fragmented and anonymous compared to the more holistic and personal relationships that were thought to be more characteristic of premodern society, it is even more significant from the present point of view that *both* types of relation, neither of which were, in fact, exclusive to premodern or modern society, became distinctive self-identities rather than simply different kinds of social relation. The transfiguration of life, any aspect of life, into the *experience* of life is not just a descriptive generalization about the emergence of modern society, it brings into focus the sense in which modern society is a *radical* change. Modernity is a large scale, comprehensive transformation in the conditions of people's lives; it is, equally, a transformation in their world view, recreations and personal relations. It also transforms everything in the past that seems, in some form, to have persisted into the present. Everything that appears still to be premodern, including older religious perspectives, small communities and traditionalism of many sorts, is irresistibly and fundamentally altered in becoming part of modern society. They appear as other possible experiences of life, rather than, simply, particular ways of life. Modernity, in other words, is cunningly inclusive and does not readily allow people to 'opt out' of its radical break with the past. Every apparent survival of the premodern, along with every newly created alternative mode of life, is assimilated to another version of its own essential form and becomes just another possible experience.

Self-identity is not an afterthought. We do not 'have' experience and then interpret it in the light of a particular self-image; experience comes to us already formed and shaped (Ireland 2004; Jay 2005). And it comes to us as a self-experience and not just as an awareness of something external.

In experiencing the world we experience ourselves as the active subject of that experience.

In a strict sense the modern problem of identity stems from the rejection of substantial forms. That is, identity is not inherent in any particular appearance. One person can appear here as one self and somewhere else as another. This is the case not only for persons, but for collective identities, for all objects and things, events, places and periods of time. Modernity begins with a radical break between appearance and reality. And now, it seems, reality has become just another appearance. Nothing is fixed in the nature of things; identity is a problem just because it seems to have been abolished. All identities are simply conventional ways of seeing things, of describing and arranging things and of behaving in relation to them. All identities are, ultimately, arbitrary and reside wholly in the attitude of a community for whom such an identity is taken to be 'real'. The importance of, actual rather than theoretical, self-identity is that, in modern society, it is constituted as the inescapable and essential form of experience. Self-identity, in other words, unlike any other identity, successfully resists critical scrutiny; it is the non-arbitrary and essential distinction in which modernity takes root. Self-identity is not rooted in a natural category or in Divine Ordinance; it is because it inheres in the transformation of *every* aspect of modern life into a possible experience, that self-identity posits itself as the essential identity of modern society. In this sense self-identity is the essence of modernity; and is completely without content.

The separation of humanity from God and nature was given immediate force in a further and equivocal separation of self from its social relations. While the transcendental in its premodern form was firmly rejected and self formation was conceived and practised in a new, secular environment, self-identity as interiorized authenticity served as the transcendental point of integration of what otherwise would be the mere juxtaposition of meaningless difference. The Reformation provides a key example of this transition from medieval to modern forms of self-identity. Broadly speaking and by resorting to extreme simplification, the Reformation can be described as a movement from religious observance of an obligatory sort to a freely chosen religion of belief and conviction. That is to say, a specifically religious experience of the world is transformed into an inner experience of faith. The interiorization of religious practice as faith amounted to a relocation of the transcendental point of reference which had organized the premodern world. Absolute Identity (God) was rejected for a society and an age that demanded nothing less than human autonomy, only to take up residence in the remote inwardness of the Self. Self-identity, then, became the transcendental point of reference for all meaningfulness, significance, value, action and so on. The entire human world was ordered in relation to a self-identity that was removed to an infinitely remote point of interior subjectivity; as inaccessible and incomprehensible as the medieval cosmic God (Goldmann 1964).

But this was far from obvious; it is still far from obvious. Modern self-identity involved a continuous process of expressing inner selfhood and, whatever philosophical difficulties this might ultimately encounter, this seemed most of the time to be both possible and preferable to the obligatory tradition, confinement, and sheer physical struggle that was life for most people, most of the time and in most places. The single, overriding obligation in modern society was simply to 'be yourself'. Modern self-identity was the practice of self-actualization which had as its goal the complete articulation of authentic inwardness; evidently and openly to be just the self one was. This idea was rooted in the experience of modern everyday life in which social relationships were to an increasing degree anonymous, mobile and segmented. Only small parts of people, so to speak, met and interacted. People played a variety of different roles, requiring different skills, resources, attitudes and so on. In each of these roles they might appear as a particular kind of person. It seemed there must be, behind all these particular roles and orchestrating all these appearances, an authentic 'inner' self that monitored, controlled and acted out the innumerable parts in which any person found themselves. In the middle of the eighteenth century, thus, Jean-Jacques Rousseau already found much of concern in this situation. Everyone played a part to such an extent that they lost sight of the authentic self to which they should be committed and which, ultimately, required expression. In ordinary everyday life, Rousseau complained, people were called upon only to play a part and too easily came under the influence of other people's expectations. Vanity was the problem of the age; the corrupting sentiment in which self-identity dissolved.

Romantic writers, inspired by Rousseau's writings, championed the cause of authenticity and paraded before an enthusiastic reading public a succession of heroic individuals bent upon self-realization. The results, fictional and otherwise, were frequently catastrophic and commonly suicidal. Why, even imaginatively, was it so difficult to realize modern self-identity? The problem arose in part, but only in part, from a view of self that remained stubbornly individualistic. This was connected with powerful institutional forms, especially the market and the centralization of the state which maintained its authority over each citizen-individual, rather than over a subject mass or populace, through techniques of individuation (Foucault 1977). The result, as Rousseau had anticipated, was that the well-formed inner-self, wholly conscious of itself and its intentions, yet failed to express itself adequately because, in entering into communicative interrelationship with others, expressive self-transparency was obscured by external forms of life (Starobinski 1988). The problem was intractable. Authenticity, to be real, had to be expressed, but any form of self-expression distorted the purity of an inward vision and, thus, ended inauthentically.

The failure of Romantic selfhood points to a fatal disjunction between self and identity. Self-identity cannot be accomplished because the inwardness of self cannot wholly be expressed and, inasmuch as self puts itself into exterior forms of identity it does so, as it were, in disguise and fails to be itself. Alternatively, any effort to preserve selfhood in the purity of its interiority simply fails to appear. The root of the difficulty here is the non-social conception of self-identity that has been adopted. The Romantic position supposes self as an already formed, given, individual and interior self-image. But how, it might well be asked, could such a self take form?

The alternative was to begin with an interactive, social, conception of self whose interiority was just one aspect of its identity. This transposes the problem to one of social relations; authentic selfhood depends on establishing the right kind of social relations. It is an issue about how people should live. In this perspective, however, things fared hardly better. An historical-social view of self-identity is the critical insight contained in Hegel's (1977) *Phenomenology of Spirit* and prompted a reorientation in European philosophical reflection on experience. Hegel proposed a new view of self-identity as the movement from consciousness to self-consciousness, which he understood to be nothing other than the advent of modernity. Hegel's magnificent book, thus, belongs centrally to any historical sociology of the modern age. That it should appear in the form of a philosophical reflection should not mislead contemporary readers for whom philosophy has become, for better or worse, a technical subject. For Hegel, as had been the case for Descartes and his significant successors in the elaboration of modern European philosophy, his subject matter was nothing other than everyday experience. Hegel's historical understanding of spirit, in fact, represents the fullest development of Descartes' inauguration of a new philosophical method. By orienting his reflection to doubt, rather than wisdom or faith, Descartes effectively opened the modern world to philosophy. Doubt was both a new orientation to the world and a methodical starting point for thought. Doubt is the most general expression for the *separation* of human being from the world in which it lives. This is a new human situation; a decisive and irreversible movement from a God-centred objective cosmological order to human-centred subjectivity and, thus, withdrawal from direct participatory consciousness in any non-human reality. The object world is transformed into a wholly external region to which, no longer living immediately through its forms, human beings are related primarily in terms of uncertain knowledge. Human beings must make do with representations of external reality, but *self*-identity is exempt from doubt. Every uncertain representation simultaneously confirms the self-presence of the human subject. The existence of self is not doubtful in the sense that it is presupposed in *any* experience. There is no self-certainty in terms of psychic contents; we often lack clarity over our own motives, intentions, feelings and thoughts. The point Descartes is making is that neither doubt nor certainty are relevant to existence and this is simply because existence is immediate; there is no 'distance' between self-experience and the experiencing self, no *need* to represent the representing subject.

Where Descartes analyzes this situation in terms of a philosophical problem connected with the individual consciousness, Hegel provides a socio-historical vision of the origins of that problem. For Hegel the epistemological problem (how can our knowledge of the world be justified philosophically?), becomes the historical question (what is the origin of self-identity?). And the solution to that problem, he claims, rests in the social transformation of modernity. The conceptual-philosophical issue of consciousness dissolves in a proper historical understanding of changing social relations.

Hegel's initial step (and it was only the initial step) brings into focus the developmental character of self-identity. His approach built on and ultimately criticised, the idealist philosophy of J. G. Fichte (2008), whose influential *Science of Knowledge* went through several versions during the 1790s. Fichte argued that the sense of self present in immediate experience, what he called the 'I', was a uniquely human mode of being which *posited* both itself and its world. The 'I', thus, included the 'not-I'. The notion of positing marked a decisive shift in the philosophical development of modernity, away from a predominantly cognitive towards a more existential view of humanity. This made feeling, passion and commitment as fundamental as reason in the formation of modernity as self-identity. Hegel, in turn, provided a general history of that formation. What, for him, distinguished ordinary human consciousness from any other is its own sense of inadequacy; human consciousness is, above all, the consciousness of something lacking. In Hegel's terms human consciousness is characterized by *desire*. This is not to be confused with organic needs rooted in natural being; it is, rather, a sense of wanting and longing directed uniquely towards other human beings. Self is never self-sufficient and feels itself incomplete; desire is self-positing in relation to *another self*. This relation, according to Hegel, is inherently one of conflict and struggle. Striving for self-identity requires what Hegel called *recognition*. It is not sufficient that others are subordinated under the will or intention of a dominant and assertive self; self-identity is only achieved in a mutual act of recognition, that is, through a social relation between beings for whom the other is also recognized as being fully human.

Hegel's idea of the struggle for recognition underlying the historical process of self-formation has stimulated a good deal of contemporary discussion and is now central to debates over 'identity politics' (Taylor 2004; Honneth 1996; Fraser *et al*. 2003). Contemporary political issues, however, are concerned primarily with recognition in the somewhat different sense of, on the one hand, legal-institutional rights of specific groups identified in terms of some key characteristic such as gender, colour, or impairment and, on the other, everyday interaction in terms of a normative standard of respect and dignity. Hegel's conception, however, does not necessarily involve either; self-identity does imply recognition of others as essentially related to self and recognition that the other is also a centre of self-conscious experience, but this has no necessary consequence for behaviour. What is often described as inhuman behaviour *also* requires mutual recognition of self-identity; it would be naïve to suppose, for example, that atrocities are committed *only* where perpetrators regard their victims as less than human, rather than humans of the wrong sort. The key issues in identity politics, that is to say, are concerned with the identity of selves, rather than self-identity; not with the human status of contending groups, but with the claimed or attributed characteristics of groups of human beings. The issue is what makes a group a group, not what makes a human being human.

Self-identity as a form is obligatory; experience is given as self-identical. At the same time self-identity is distanced from its own experiences and the relations through which it is constituted. The issue is not just an epistemological puzzle, it becomes an existential problem.

Self-identity is a project, but one that cannot be accomplished. How can self express itself adequately in identities and through identities that are arbitrary and conventional arrangements with no more substance than an image? All sense of substantive selfhood requires that it withdraws and keeps its distance from the transience of everyday interaction; but, in haughty indifference to its own world, selfhood withers.

The most common 'solution' to the problem is to deny the problem in the first place. In terms of everyday life it is simply assumed that, after all, identity is somehow 'real' and adequately reflects the self.

The solution within the liberal-empiricist tradition was not much better. It is to search for the remaining 'real' bit of the self and make that the carrier of identity. This is equivalent of the search for the 'primary qualities' of matter instigated by Galileo and Locke. What is there, in the self, that is equivalent to mass, shape, motion? These qualities seemed to be resistant to subjective variation, to impose themselves upon all observers in an objective way and were thought, thus, to be 'real' in a way that, for example colour or smell was not. Similarly reason and passion, it was argued, or at least assumed, constituted the 'substance' of self. These were universal attributes without which self could not be said to exist. Identity could then be construed as a specific organization of inner parts, a specific affection of the passions and the interests ordered by reason and brought under the controlling agency of self. Self was a self-constituting complex organization that synthesized the dynamic substance of the person.

The weakness of the Romantic hope of self-realization was exposed by Hegel and, in different ways, during the 1840s by his brilliant critics, Karl Marx and Søren Kierkegaard. For both the issue of self-identity is viewed in terms of the existing *obstacles* to its free development. Both the liberal and Romantic visions of modernity, as reason and expressive authenticity, are flawed to the extent that they have wholly failed to reckon with powerful institutionalized resistance to the realization of their own projects. On the one hand, private ownership of capital and, on the other hand, the persistence of an authoritative and dogmatic church, both of which are supported by and are inseparably bound up with, the modern, centralized state, prevent the real implications of self-identity from breaking through into everyday life. For Marx, the alienation of labour, the need to sell labour power as a market commodity, means the mass of workers become detached from their own nature as human beings. Self-identity is not an inner psychic process; it is a practical realization of human potentiality in a free society. And for Kierkegaard, the stultifying respectability of bourgeois life, which is expressed most forcefully in an attitude of piety and, equally, the efflorescence of a trivial culture of pleasure that existed alongside it, plunged people into despair. Despair was simply not to be a self and modern everyday life was nothing other than despair,

Alienation and despair were the real conditions of everyday life, so Hegel's optimism was unjustified. In fact, from the perspective of the present, there is less difference between Hegel and his young critics than there appeared to be at the time. Hegel's later work became increasingly conservative and supportive of an authoritarian state as the adequate realization of 'absolute spirit'; and this was the main target of Marx's and Kierkegaard's withering assaults. The radicalism of the *Phenomenology* was something that re-emerged for later generations and it is now possible to see all three as part of a single, explosive movement in which modern social thought was profoundly reshaped (Nancy 2002).

The emergence of self into modernity means freeing it from hierarchy and dependence. Self becomes responsible for itself, responsible for finding and maintaining its own image. It does this through interaction with others, finding ways of socially supporting its identity through the acceptance by others of its image. This, roughly, is the position of social interactionism and might be seen as a positive variant of Rousseau's fierce attack on the society of players and role-takers.

In this context, the work of George Herbert Mead provides an important link between the European tradition of social thought outlined above and the subsequent development of American sociological perspectives on self-identity. Mead was a significant figure in the American philosophical formulation of modernity, which found its distinctive contribution in pragmatism (Joas 1993). A central theme in pragmatic thought, expressed forcefully, for example, by William James in his famous textbook on psychology, involved a post-Romantic criticism of the idea subjectivity as an interior self endowed with expressive and communicative intention. Self-identity, rather, should be grasped in its living, practical and ongoing activity. The self is a social relation and has no anterior psychic reality; 'the self, as that which can be an object to itself, is essentially a social structure and it arises in social experience' (Mead 1967: 97). The self is an interiorized representative of society, or a subdivision of society and Mead pertinently asks 'How can an individual get outside himself (experientially) in such a way as to become an object to himself? (Mead 1967: 138); how, in other words can the self be constituted as both interior subject and exterior object. The interactive, social character of all self experience, for Mead, rests on an incipient language of gesture and in the developing capacity of every self to take on the role of another self. Initially through play and participation in games, children develop this capacity and take the role not only of particular others but of a 'generalized other' which represents the participatory group as a unity. Mead insists that the mutual adjustment of gesture is a general feature of animal behaviour and is continuous with more developed forms of human communication. Both gesture and speech arises in interactive contexts for which they serve as a monitoring and controlling mechanism. And all this is largely unconscious;

> We are more or less unconsciously seeing ourselves as others see us. We are unconsciously addressing ourselves as others address us ... . We are, especially through the use of vocal gestures, continually arousing in ourselves those responses which we call out in other persons into our own conduct.
>
> (Mead 1967: 68–9)

In spite of Mead's robust pragmatism and commitment to what he terms social behaviourism, it is difficult not to see in the internal and self-referential conversation of gesture and in taking the role of the other, just the kind of internal rehearsal and dialogue of the Romantic inner-self that he opposed.

Symbolic interactionism became closely related to the development of American functionalism, but has had a more widespread and lasting influence in terms of its notion of self-identity sustained by mutual 'definition of the situation'. The importance of the key insight of Mead and his followers lies in its focus on the role of interaction in sustaining the reality of social situations. It does not make sense, in this view, to look for the 'real' foundation of self-identity. The point, rather, is to grasp that self-identity, as is the case for any other social reality, has no foundation other than the compliance of interactive participants who, for the purposes of that situation, treat it as 'real'. A recent film *Lars and the Real Girl* (Craig Gillespie/Nancy Oliver, 2008), nicely illustrates the point. A painfully shy and socially awkward man introduces a life-size inflatable doll to his brother and his wife as his girlfriend. Advised by a psychiatrist to 'play along' with the fantasy they, and their friends and neighbours, treat her as a real girl. Soon they begin to identify with her situation as well as his, demand the boyfriend treat her more considerately and feel anger, compassion, and pleasure on her behalf.

The uniquely rich work of Goffman is distinctive here in developing a dramaturgical view of society, with a more individualistic approach that is clearly related to the Romantic tradition of selfhood. Goffman stresses the ability individuals have of holding back from the 'discourse' in which they are implicated. This standing back, or 'role distance', is an important element in everyday interaction and recalls Georg Simmel's conception of sociability as stepping into and out of society. The presentation of self is by no means the same as taking a role and following a script and Goffman is concerned with 'impression management' rather than role play. It is the performance aspect of interaction that is of primary interest here. The organisation of society and the web of sociability is a formal interactive structure and process, more or less loose in different circumstances, into which human content flows and then again withdraws.

In Goffman the key relation is between role and self; not between self and other. He focuses on the ritual manoeuvring that stabilises and maintains interaction. The ritual of presentation and self-deception, polite fiction and half truth. The interacting individual has a ritual status as sacred. Participants enjoin each other to sustain the fiction that is operative at the time and sustain, thus, a certain self-presentation. '… the person insulates himself by blindness, half-truths, illusions and rationalizations. He makes an "adjustment" by convincing himself with the tactful support of his intimate circle, that he is what he wants to be and that he would not do to gain his ends what others have done to gain theirs' (Goffman 1973: 43). Tact and dissimulation keeps things going and protects the self; 'Social life is an uncluttered, orderly thing because the person voluntarily stays away from the places and topics and times where he is not wanted and where he might be disparaged for going. He cooperates to save his face, finding that there is much to be gained from venturing nothing' (Goffman 1973: 43). For Goffman, a degree of calculation enters into every self-presentation.

These developments are noted here to indicate the change in the *context* of modern self-identity. It is not as contributions to further conceptual clarification and theoretical elaboration that the above literature is noted here; it is as descriptive of actual change in the contextual field of self-identity that they gain their significance. Modern western society, which emerged in Europe around 1600, like self-identity which is its central form, is a continuing project rather than a completed form. Many of the historical and philosophical disputes over the character and idea of self-identity are, in fact, descriptions of different and varied practices which have developed within that society. concepts and their varied contexts, however, is the conviction that self-identity is inherent in modern society and that, however it is constituted, it is experienced as a unity. The question immediately arises: what is the character of this unity?

INTERRUPTION 3: HISTORY

Besides, it is not difficult to see that ours is a birth-time and a period of transition to a new era. Spirit has broken with the world it has hitherto inhabited and imagined, and is of a mind to submerge it in the past, and in the labour of its own transformation. Spirit is indeed never at rest but always engaged in moving forward. But just as the first breath drawn by a child after its long, quiet nourishment breaks the gradualness of merely quantitative growth – there is a qualitative leap, and the child is born – so likewise the Spirit in its formation matures slowly and quietly into its new shape, dissolving bit by bit the structure of its previous world, whose tottering state is only hinted at by isolated symptoms. The frivolity and boredom which unsettles the established order, the vague foreboding of something unknown, these are the heralds of approaching change. The gradual crumbling that left unaltered the face of the whole is cut short by a sunburst which, in one flash, illuminates the features of the new world.

(G. W. F. Hegel, *Phenomenology of Spirit*)

The recent and the more or less distant past (thus) combine in the amalgam of the present. Recent history races towards us at high speed: earlier history accompanies us at a slower, stealthier pace. . . . One must consult many different snapshots of the past, each with its own exposure time, then fuse times and images together, rather as the colours of the solar spectrum, focused together, combine at last into pure white light.

(Fernand Braudel, *A History of Civilizations*)

The history of all hitherto existing society is the history of the class struggle.

(Karl Marx and Friedrich Engels, *Manifesto of the Communist Party*)

All history is contemporary history.

(R. G. Collingwood, *The Idea of History*)

History is double-sided. It is the past and the study of the past; the past and our knowledge of the past; the past and the present as its culminating moment. History is stretched uncomfortably between story and theory. A dual perspective, characteristic of many aspects of contemporary culture, is constitutive of the historical consciousness of the present. History is at once universal and particular. On the one hand, history is the level of generality within which contexts are placed and ordered and, on the other, it is the specific social-cultural identity that stands out from that very background. History is background and foreground, the universal context within which civilizations, empires, societies, nations, peoples, classes, families, and so on, emerge and are interrelated, and the particular reality of any one of those socio-cultural unities. At one extreme history dissolves into pure temporality; at the other extreme it loses itself in the eternity of particulars.

History, thus, like science and modernity in its broadest sense, emerges and becomes meaningful as a way of grasping reality in a specific context, but makes universal claims. The peculiarity of history is that its claims to universality co-exist with an equal insistence on the particular character of its subject matter. There is a logically curious relation between History and history; between the universal framework of the human past and the distinctive process of unfolding manifest in any of its aspects or parts.

History, like theory, claims universal validity for its most general framework of understanding, and, like story, characterizes unities within this framework as self-identical unities. And history, unlike either story or theory, is the universal consciousness of the present, which it makes meaningful as the culmination of the past. All of which is to say that history is a *modern* conceit. History only becomes possible, and necessary, because modern society is conceived in, and as, a decisive break in the continuity of time. Modern society, at least in its self-understanding as modernity, is a revolutionary break with the past; it is radically new and supersedes everything prior to its birth and casts the past into oblivion (Blumenberg 1983; Koselleck 1985; Ankersmit 2005). Everything anterior to the moment of self-emergence is lost in the abyss of prehistory.

And, having thus formed a self-image of the modern subject, history turned towards the newly created prehistoric past and began the endless task of filling it with fresh content.

History emerges with modernity, and first of all in the recovery of the past as the emblem and ideal of the present. Ancient Civilization is, thus, selectively defined in relation to the relatively short period of cultural growth, and imperial greatness of Periclean Athens. The Renaissance grasps itself as the historical recreation of this greatness. This view is transformed in the development of modernity into a self-understanding of the present as possessed of its own dynamism, liberated from all past models and their prejudices. Like science and art, modernity is a breakthrough rather than another, ultimately arbitrary change; it arises spontaneously as the self articulation of humanity, for the first time free to generate itself and its own world.

The distinctive character of modern history as nothing other than the history of modernity was clearly established by Giambatista Vico (1984), whose largely overlooked masterpiece *The New Science*, published in 1725 but barely read for a hundred years, placed modernity firmly in a secular framework. Vico presented history, which included a compendium of what were to become modern social sciences including ethnography, mythology, and the study of language as a new science superior in its ambition and promise to the hugely successful and prestigious science of nature. As human history is self-created, the possibility of reaching an inner understanding of its course and development was, in principle, possible. Where the natural sciences were confined to abstract theory and meaningless empiricism, history could provide an account of events as an inner narrative. In this respect Vico pioneered a view of historical knowledge that finally came to fruition towards the end of the nineteenth century and the early decades of the twentieth century, preeminently in the impressive scholarly works of Wilhelm Dilthey and Max Weber.

History condescends to the non-historical world, embraces its illusions, and assimilates them to its own universal vision. This widespread current criticism of much historical discourse as 'Eurocentric' points to a more pertinent truth than most of the critics intend or would accept (Lambropoulos 1993). Universalistic claims arising in the context of classical modern European culture discount the separate history of other societies and peoples. However, accepting alternative histories, in fact, *insisting* upon them, and the rights of other societies and subordinate groups to a history of their own, is *also* part of the modern European historical consciousness. It is not just a question of imposing upon non-western societies an historical view of their world as conceived from the perspective of modern Europe (which is evidently prejudicial), but of incorporating what has first been discounted as non-historical societies into a common framework of world history. The multiplicity of alternative, subaltern histories, rescuing the oppressed from oblivion, succeed only in turning them into meaningful narratives constructed on the model of modern consciousness. Further, where other societies and communities already possess documented historical accounts of their own world, those accounts are discounted, or subordinated to a modern universal and inclusive history. The modern history of Ancient Society, or China, or medieval monasticism, for example, is quite distinct from *their* versions of their own, or other, histories.

History supposes universal continuity and presupposes discontinuity. The principle of continuous interconnectedness arises in a society that founded itself on discontinuity and its decisive break with the past. Confined to the present history could do nothing other than create images of the past that were meaningful in modern terms. The problem, however, is not that history invents, and thus distorts, the past, but that it invents the present. A methodological obstacle still blocks the path. A secret complicity links concepts to contexts in a mutually supportive relation. Concepts become fully intelligible only in relation to particular socio-cultural contexts; and contexts are established and described only in relation to discourses that presuppose those very concepts. Whatever the starting point, what emerges is an implicit or explicit affirmation of western modernity. Yet, to see this means that a point of view has arisen that lies outside the mutually reinforcing circuit of modern critical discourse. To locate this viewpoint requires yet another beginning.

3

UNITIES

Self-identity is the essential form of modernity; it is the constitution of reality as experience. But this experience is not itself given, it is, rather, just what self-identity creates. Self-identity is the subject of its own experience. Critical philosophical literature, and sociological responses to it, highlights the formal freedom of self-identity from any natural or divine constraint. Self-identity is an existential project of becoming. Even admitting that this is the case in a theoretical or ideal sense, and ignoring for the moment new kinds of constraint and suppression that emerge also with modernity, the issue arises, how can self-identity be constituted as a unity? What gives experience its peculiar coherence as a unified field of consciousness? And what, if anything, underlies its unity? Rather than pursue these questions immediately through further theoretical-historical analysis it is worth returning to everyday life.

Unity cannot reside either in the sense objects of experience, or in the intentional structure of the self. Both these are the result that needs to be explained. It is worth reviewing two possibilities; two forms of unity that seem to be given in a peculiar and privileged way and might serve, at least as models, upon which self-identity can be constructed. These are *names*, and *bodies*.

NAMES

The special status of names is indicated by their grammatical peculiarity. Names are singular, written with a capital letter, and, bereft of definite or indefinite article, they simply appear, as if from nowhere, and stand 'for themselves' unsupported by grammatical crutches, circumstantial description, or accompanying explanation.

This is the case for personal names and what are generally called proper nouns that denote particular places and things. Identity inheres in names, or adheres to names, in an immediately evident and compelling manner.

Being named

The simplest way to think about self-identity in an everyday sense is to consider names. Proper names, and pre-eminently personal names, are the ubiquitous and elemental instance of self-identity. We have a name but, in a highly significant and evident way, we *are* our name. In English, introductions are effected as a direct revelation of being; 'I am …' 'This is …' The name does not merely stand for or represent the person; the name *is* the person; the whole person 'in themselves'. And where an indirect form of address is used, 'My name is …' (as commonly, for example, in French or Italian) this is a formality of speech and not an evasion of self-identity. A name is neither a label nor a description; it belongs to the person in a peculiarly intimate and complete way. This relation is quite unlike, for example, the manner in which a valued possession that might, nonetheless, be sold or lost, is owned; or the way in which a particular part or aspect of the person, such as a physical feature or a personality trait, is identified *with* the person but is not identical *to* the person. For both latter cases it is possible to imagine the person without the particular possession or the specific feature. And while it is clear that the person *might* have had a different name; *that* particular name, nonetheless, becomes *essentially* who they are. The name, in other words, is self-identical and not just a means of identification.

Wittgenstein remarks that one cannot forget one's name. Of course, we are aware of many cases of amnesia in which forgetting 'who you are' is precisely the leading symptom; a pathological type that became common and was much commented upon in Wittgenstein's Vienna, and of which he was well aware (Hacking 1998). Wittgenstein is making a more subtle point that might be expressed as; 'if you forget your name, then you are no longer yourself'. And forgetting your name is, indeed, widely regarded as symptomatic of a serious neurological or psychological problem. He is also making an interesting comment in relation to Descartes's philosophy that might be expressed as; 'You cannot doubt your name'. Descartes, famously, had made doubt (rather than love of wisdom, or faith, or curiosity) the beginning of philosophy. But the *cogito* cannot question its own existence. And Wittgenstein's observation reminds us that the *cogito* comes with a name; it is not the anonymous subject of modern philosophical reflection, but a living person. This, indeed, is just Descartes' point. It is the *named* self that cannot doubt his or her own existence. Yet the name, obviously enough, might have been different; it is a contingent fact of experience that the author is named Harvie and not Thomas, or Stephen, or Bruno, or Michel. So, it seems, Descartes, in this respect, apparently contradicts his own argument. This would be the case, however, only if the name were a detachable property of the person. In the end Wittgenstein is supporting his predecessor. The name *is* the person, and it is just because of this that 'I' cannot doubt my name; I cannot forget who I am without forgetting myself, without becoming another person.

This strong identification is evident in the sensitivity with which we regard our name. We are readily insulted by our name being mispronounced or misspelled, yet are rarely even aware of the particulars of officially significant forms of identity. Few people know their National Insurance number, or passport number, and are apt to forget their Personal Identification Number required for credit card transactions. Interestingly, ex-service personnel usually recall their service number without effort, as do long-term prisoners, and survivors of camps; people, that is, whose names have been deliberately erased as part of an intensive programme of resocialization. But who could recognize their fingerprint, iris print, or DNA profile (all, in principle, unique) as indicative of, far less as part of, or as one with, himself or herself? And old photographs bear a resemblance that becomes distant with time and offers a substitute for, rather than an aid to, recollecting self-identity. Even newly taken digital images are often dismissed as 'a poor likeness;' not 'really' us. But we find it difficult *not* to respond to our own name. Whispered it will waken us from a deep sleep. Written on a printed page it leaps at once to the eye. The United Nations under its Charter recognizes the right to a name as universal. To be deprived of a name, or have your name forcibly changed, is to be violated (Kim 1998). Oddly, we advise children to pay no attention to being 'called names', or to being made fun of on account of their name, yet we know differently and recall, vividly enough, the humiliation of these games.

If our name belongs to us in a peculiar fashion, it is, equally, the case that we belong to our name. We are called and summonsed 'by name'. At school we answer the register with a cry of 'present;' and it is in school that we learn that the enunciation of our name *requires* our presence. We are frequently enjoined to 'live up' to our name, or discover that we have much to 'live down' because of it. Our reputation and standing in the community is a matter of gaining and preserving a 'good name'.

And we belong, in a similar way, to those larger and more inclusive self-identities that are signified by name. Family names, names of towns and communities, regions, countries, languages, and religions, however they are dissected and analyzed by sociologists, appear in everyday life first and foremost as names. Names indicate without describing; they refer unambiguously because they share directly the self-identity whose presence they announce. The 'I am', that introduces a personal self-identity, may continue 'I am Scottish', 'I am Japanese', 'I am Buddhist', 'I am Pagan', and so on. Interestingly, in English, we use this form almost exclusively for personal names, nationalities, and religions. Otherwise we use an 'improper' noun and an article, or a circumlocution of some sort; 'I am from …' 'I am a member of … '. In many other European languages the article is not used to indicate profession, and many other identifying characteristics. The elementary, psychologically most compelling, form of self-identity in all cases, however, remains the personal name. It is this relation, at once intimate and complete (we are and remain our name 'through and through') upon which all other relations of self-identity rest.

All the difficulties of self-identity that were raised and remain unresolved at the level of conceptualization and contextualization suddenly fall away; names return us at once, and effortlessly, to the everyday world for which such problems do not exist.

Or so it seems. We easily imagine that the link we have with our own name is 'given' in a primordial way. We experience our name as continually present to us, coterminous with us in time and space, and, so to speak, spontaneously 'in' us rather than merely a constant companion 'to' us. Our name inhabits our dreams, memories, and imagination as well as our ongoing experiences. And our name remains real to us even if we adopt an alias. Yet this easy assumption is suspect. On reflection, names and naming throw up issues of their own, which philosophers have worried over a good deal (Kripke 1980). And, as commonly with what seem to be abstruse philosophical problems, these issues usefully throw up real questions. They do so, in fact, because names occupy a position between the conceptual and the contextual and hence offer a way towards a fuller understanding of self-identity. Not only do naming practices vary enormously across different societies, the experience of having, being, and bearing a name also varies.

In a broader historical and comparative framework, the consubstantiality of name and self-identity is evidently far from being a universal or necessary relation. Curiously, in spite of being the dominant experience of self-identity in modern society, the immediate unity of name and self-identity is thoroughly unmodern in its assumptions, and, consequently, raise interesting and quite unexpected sociological questions.

The antiquity of naming

Modern assumptions about personal names resonate with ancient religious and philosophical worldviews strangely at odds with those comprehensive and radical transformations of social life and culture that otherwise closed off the past. In spite of its major spasms of creativity and rejection, the Renaissance, Reformation, Capitalism, Scientific Revolution, Enlightenment, industrialization, urbanization, and so on, for modernity the Judaeo-Christian tradition apparently survived in naming. For that tradition God confers reality, and identity, in a single act of naming.

Genesis describes Creation as a process of enunciation, of 'bringing forth' by naming: God created through the Word (as the later Gospel writer recognized 'In the Beginning was the Word'). He spoke, 'let there be light'; light was *named* as that which was to come into existence. Its name was given with its creation; it was its name. Subsequently, the separation of Light from Dark is also effected by naming; Day and Night. Similarly, on the Second Day a firmament comes into existence directly through the commanding voice, and is differentiated prior to the assigning of more specific names to heaven and earth. Creation is a two part linked process of naming. The essential name is given with creation; immediately followed by a process of differentiation and division that required the addition of more specific qualifying name. Both essential names and the bestowal of names on differentiated parts and aspects of Creation are non-arbitrary identities. There is no difference in Creation between the bestowal of a name and the conferring of identity; name and referent are brought into existence together as identical.

The Word (Creation) offers itself, reciprocally, as a 'way' to God. The self-identical being (humanity), aware of its name and the names of things from God, seeks God directly by finding His name. *Theology* is, first of all, the (ultimately defiant) act of 'naming' God. A strong and frequently renewed mysticism in the western tradition has sought God directly in the revelation of his Name. In principle, of course, God cannot be named, any more than He reveals himself in Creation. But the attraction of negative theology of Divine Names, notably in the writings attributed to one of the shadowy figure in early Christianity, Dionysius the Pseudo-Areopagite, has proved irresistible. Naming the unnameable (even as the Unnameable) in some sense raises human self-identity to a Divine level and frees the creature from its Creator (Pseudo-Dionysius 1940).

Surprisingly, the absolute, singular identity, God, has many names. Any divine 'attribute' could, arbitrarily, be chosen as the starting point for the contemplation of His essential being as the 'perfection' of that name. Yet God remains singular identity. He is One. God, who is the source of all His own attributes and transcends each, can be known through the absolute perfecting of *any* attribute. Power, presence, knowledge, love, freedom, and so on are divine attributes and apply to His ultimate self-subsisting identity only in their transcendental form as Omnipotence, Omnipresence, and so on.

Of course, the issue here has nothing to do with theology or even with the religious tradition more generally. The point, rather, is to emphasize the importance that is attached, in modern society, to naming. In bestowing names, and in relation to our own name, we retain something of the primordial notion of self-identity; a notion made absolute in the religious myth of the west.

We bring children into the world in a double sense; in creating them and in naming them. Naming bestows identity and establishes the self-identity of the new person. Re-enacting the story of Creation, identity is made co-substantial with coming into existence. Children are named at birth, as if they are born already with a name, and may be greeted by name. In many other societies there is a clear separation between birth and the subsequent bestowal of social identity through a naming ritual involving wider community participation. In this regard we act as we imagine God acted, and treat personal names as authentic attributes in which the ultimate reality of the person is, as it were, secreted. At the same time usurping the power of naming, human beings assert their autonomy and freedom from God. What seems at first to affirm the continuity of an ancient tradition, on closer inspection, reveals a wholly modern face. Naming is seized as a distinctively human power. Naming simultaneously affirms the self-identity of the parent and posits personal identity in the child. And while naming is a direct and institutionally recognized expression of parental power, the legal obligation officially to register a name accompanying every birth is a reminder of the role of the modern state as custodian of, and ultimate authority over, each individual. The census, unknown in premodern society, identifies every citizen by name, and the power of the state, elegantly illustrated in Saramago's contemporary fable, is vested, first of all, in an archive of 'all the names' (Saramago 1999; Groebner 2007).

The exception

Having begun by characterizing personal names as the exemplary form of self-identity, it is now clear that, this relation is, nonetheless, exceptional. The name 'sticks' to the person it identifies in a peculiar fashion. The ideal fusion of self and identity is a form realized uniquely in naming and, even then, only in historically localized naming cultures. The exemplary character of naming in modern society, after all, has little to do with its original context. It is not the religious or philosophical origin that is being invoked here, nor is the name being treated as the exception that, in fact, it is. Rather, the self-identical name serves as the deceptive prototype for all those less secure and equivocal identities that now bear the weight of social and political aspirations.

It is the ambition of many special interest groups, as well as their political opponents or competitor groups, for example, to have a distinguishing characteristic or attribute treated as a name rather than a category. There is an important difference, thus, between asserting 'I *am* black (disabled, gay, old, Glaswegian, and so on); and saying 'I am a person *of* colour, (disability, age, Glasgow, and so on). Treating a category as a name invokes the pure 'isness' of the name, and asserts self-identity in an uncompromising way. The power of naming, in other words, spreads well beyond the sphere of bestowing personal names.

Yet, the substantial unity assumed for the name is not just exceptional, it is highly equivocal. The modern western assumption, one name one self, is justified only by, viewing the name as a substantive form immanent in the self, which makes sense only in a premodern context. This is all the more remarkable in the context of naming commodities, brands, products, and companies. The most contemporary aspects of modern society, its fashionable emblems of newness, which might be expected to be free of all premodern prejudice, yet cling to the magic of names. The most effective selling technique is to have a product recognized as a brand, and both as a name. It is not that the name means something in particular, or that its lexical meaning is related to the product or services it identifies; the effective device is the name recognized as a name (Nike, Sony, Apple, Virgin, Orange, and so on). And the simplest way to do this is to use a 'real', single name, such as Chanel, or Armani.

Variation

If naming in modern western society shows some connection with an older religious worldview, however much transformed in the context of a secular society, is it the case that naming generally, and the notion of self-identical unity that it apparently assumes and inspires, is quite generally connected with religious traditions in other societies? If names are, in fact, primordial instances of self-identity, then much of the historical-sociological discussion in the previous two chapters is very wide of the mark. Might it be the case that self-identity is a name, and the ontological status of the name has nothing to do with modernity, or modern society?

The response to such a question has to be firmly in the negative. For us names, however ancient, have nothing to do with ancient society and appear in an entirely new light. Names are not lexical; that is to say, they do not have a unique meaning in the sense of a dictionary definition (Wilson 1998). Popular name books list *original* meanings for many names, but few are well known and hardly ever chosen for their meaning. And even where the meaning remains clear, or the name is identical to a word (Prudence, Constance, Frank), the name refers exclusively and without any associative significance to the person. At the same time, names are not without meaning. Names are defined within a *system* of possible names and it is through this system that they can be used to represent a variety of social differences. National, regional, gender, and class differences in naming are commonly recognized (Smith-Bannister 1997). Names, in this regard, are signs rather than symbols. The naming system, as Levi-Strauss demonstrated, includes other beings such as pets and racehorses as part of its overall structure (1966). The difference between, for example, William, Jack, and Brian to name boys, and Claire, Nancy, and Jane to name girls, is arbitrary. There is nothing in the names themselves that designate gender, but gender is effectively coded in the naming system as a matter of convention. The meaningfulness of personal names is, thus, of two quite distinct kinds. The name is the person and the name is an arbitrary sign in a system of classification.

This duality, and its relevance for the issue of self-identity, as well as the historical transformation of naming in western society, raises the issue of naming and self-identity in other societies. The comparative context outlined in the previous chapter can be used and extended to clarify the significance of naming for modern self-identity.

In some systems names are unambiguously tied to the system of identities as social relations. The name is predetermined by the position of the individual or collectivity within a system of social relations; names are, so to speak, held in readiness and allocated according to a strict rule. Other systems, allow a choice to be made from a more or less extensive group of possible names. Some systems require a unique name to be assigned, one not known to be shared by any other member of the society (vom Bruck and Bodenhorn 2006). Marcel Mauss points out that in many societies there are a multiplicity of names for the same individuals, varying by context, age; discussing the Kwakiutl Indians he remarks

> ... each moment of life is named, is personified, by a new name, a new title, of child, of adolescent, adult (masculine and feminine). Then the individual has a name as a warrior (excluding women, of course), as a prince and a princess, as chief and chieftainess, a name for the feast they give (men and women), and for the particular ceremonial which belongs to them, for their age of retirement, their name in the society of seals... Finally names are also given to *their* "secret society", the one in which they are protagonists ... *Names* are also given to the chief's house (with its roofs, posts, doors, decorations, roof-beams, openings, double-headed and double-faced serpent), the ceremonial canoe ...
>
> (Mauss 1979: 70)

This profusion of naming does not imply a casual use of terms, or confusion of identities, it indicates, rather, the extent to which their lives are marked by real metamorphoses. They are not so much different names for the same individual, as transformations of personhood.

In modern Japan the name culture is strikingly similar to Mauss's description of the Kwakiutl. Names in modern Japan are individuated and refer to identifiable selves. But, because self is a multiplicity of distinct context-bound performances, the same person may be the bearer of a number of different names. The self is not nebulous or indistinct, in any context it is clearly identifiable and names, but each context requires fresh identification and, in principle, its own name. Furthermore, as self is ubiquitous spirit, names include many non-personal, and non-human beings:

> names in Japan are metonymic, symbolically linking human institutions, often at a level of essences. For example, a name, beyond being attached to a person may be tied to a piece of land, to a government office or position, to a family or group and its political and territorial rights, to a house or a shop, or vice versa, that is, to any extrapersonal institution from which the persona draws his livelihood and his identity. A name may indicate political affiliation, rank, eligibility for office, family or group belonging, economic revenue, and cultural as well as religious identity.
>
> (Plutschow 1995: 2)

Thus, for example, *Ujina* are clannames which serve as 'important means of identification and claims to power and office' (Plutschow 1995: 5); *Myōji* or *azana* are private names of families that have become semi-autonomous in relation to clans. They are literally name fields, and distinguish those who live off the same fields. And *azana* are place names, from the smallest administrative unit. *Tsūshō* common appellative names or 'middle names', infiltrated into family names to indicate clan membership, or to indicate birth sequence. Personal names were given at initiation (*genpuku*). Boys at age 15, and girls at age 13, had new names bestowed on them by a 'name father' (*nazuke-oya*) in an effort to forge lasting bonds with officialdom. It is hardly surprising then, that the celebrated writer Takizawa Bakin (1767–1848) changed his name 35 times and Bashō, 17 times.

Significantly, as part of the general policy of aggressive westernization that followed on the Meiji Restoration, many of the complexities of the Japanese naming system were officially abandoned in 1874.

In premodern western society and among the aristocracy in the modern west 'personal names' classify and are modes of collective identification. Names here are kinship terms and place the individual appropriately in a lineage. Names, in such cases, are impersonal and 'belong' to particular families and descent groups rather than individuals. The self-identity substantially united with the name and expressed in it is collective. Elite names in medieval society may also indicate place and community, locating and fixing people in the social cosmology; as, for example, Anselm of Canterbury, Aelred of Rievaulx, Duns Scotus and so on. Most family names, in fact, are place names before they are occupational or functional identities. In premodern society, for the vast majority of people living in stable, small, and relatively enclosed communities, a single name was sufficient for purposes of personal and social identification (Beech *et al.* 2002).

Imposing names

Names connect self and identity. On the one hand the name objectifies self and converts the living moment of self-presence into a communicable identity; and, on the other hand, the name absorbs and draws into the self all those identifying relational features of social life through which particular individuals, places, and traditions are constituted. For modern western society self-identity is articulated, first of all, by naming.

This, certainly, is the conventional view and one sanctified by everyday practice. It is appropriate at this point, however, to ask to what extent this adequately describes *contemporary* social life. The idea of the postmodern is now widespread and, indeed, in many formulations has already become banal. But the degree to which contemporary life is no longer lived out through classically modern social forms is obviously central to the issue of self-identity. If self-identity is simply the experience of modernity, and reality given as experience, then the postmodern must be a break with this form of self-identity and all that it implies. Where, for modernity, self-identity is the uniquely essential identity, indeed, the *only* identity, the postmodern finds itself in the embrace of the non-identical. An indication of both the plausibility and difficulty of such an idea is evident in the more recent discussion of names and naming.

Jacques Derrida, thus, the leading exponent of the art of postmodern deconstruction, insists, against everyday assumptions and previous reflective discourse, that *we are not* ever our names. Far from articulating the hidden but vital link between self and identity, the name is and remains exterior to all subjectivity. Not only are we not our name, we encounter our name as the primordial other, as pure, imposed exteriority. Derrida preserves the elusiveness of the name under the Greek term *Khōra*; a ghostly presence which, neither the sensible nor the intelligible, yet encompasses both, and oscillates between story and theory; '*Khōra* reaches us, and as the name. And when a name comes, it immediately says more than the name: the other of the name and quite simply the other, whose irruption the name announces' (Derrida 1995: 89). Naming is an 'irruption of the other' or 'originary violence', which imposes identity upon us and suppresses the immanent freedom (non-identity) of self.

Naming is a powerful device of containment; it is the prison of the self. Derrida was influenced in this view by the daring and highly original speculations of Jacques Lacan, a maverick psychoanalyst whose increasingly influential ideas emerged in the immediate postwar period in close interrelation with French surrealism and aesthetics as well as Freud's clinical (1990) and theoretical (1991) writings. Lacan argued that the subject, far from being an inner, psychic unity, is constituted in and through language. The psychic subject is the metaphysical myth of modernity, in fact an anachronistic illusion. However, rather than wither away, the psyche takes possession of subjectivity and gives it the (false) appearance of identity. Naming confers identity, and asserts itself as an alien encumbrance on the freedom of experience. In this view self, in principle, cannot find direct and authentic expression and, pushing Romantic imagery to new extremes, is in continuous conflict with its interiorized name as well as its exteriorized identity. Naming is a tyranny and it might be expected that, to an increasing degree, individuals and groups resist being named, and reject the names bestowed upon them.

The rejection of many national identities, certainly, involves resistance to naming; Catalan not Spanish, Scottish not British, Flemish not Belgian, and so on, but such examples oppose one named identity with another rather than renounce being named as such. Similarly women's rejection of their husband's family name as their 'married name' is an explicit appeal to the continuing significance and value of their original family name. And where names have been changed as a result of colonial status, such as Koreans by Japan during the Pacific War, bitter resistance to adopting Japanese names was at the same time an assertion of their continuing self-identity as Korean (Kim 1998).

Derrida's and Lacan's extreme formulations nonetheless convey an important insight. Self is just what cannot be named. 'Pure' subjectivity is the unnameable. In Romantic thought this is just because self is prior to any identity, and can appear only by, as it were, borrowing an identity from the range of existing possibilities. For Derrida, and in different ways also for Michel Foucault (2005), Judith Butler (1997), Slavoj Žižeck (2006), and other influential sociologists and cultural critics, it is unnameable because there is nothing to name. Self is a fiction that exists exclusively in the language and discursive practices that describe its activities. There is nothing behind, beyond, or beneath the name. The name posits a psychic unity that does not exist. There is agency but no agent. There are only identities, no self-identities. This idea is part of Derrida's lifetime assault on the modern western philosophical tradition, what he calls the onto-theology of the west (and all west actually means modern west because Ancient Greek and Medieval philosophy and literature, which he frequently discusses, is a contemporary interpretation of positions rather than a an appeal to their original insight). Derrida tirelessly exposes the illusory hypostasis of the subject throughout its unhappy philosophical history. It is ironic that this process of dislodgement should finally settle on the renunciation of the name; bringing his project into close interrelation with the western mystical tradition that refused the rationalizing theology of naming God; it is as if Derrida has ended by consecrating self as Divine, rather than deconstructing its metaphysical pretension. The shadowy interiority of the subject is driven from its hiding place, and stripped of its most successful disguise, its name. In this perspective, self has a performative rather than an intentional structure. It is nothing other than the performance from which we (wrongly) infer its existence. Self, in other words, is not an entity, does not posit its world, or act in it.

But the matter can be put somewhat differently; as Žižeck remarks, self is *only* a name. So, rather than renounce the name as the illusionary foundation of the entire edifice of ideological suppression and reclaim the absolute freedom of the unnamed subject, it may become all the more important to cling to a name; not as a presumed identity, but as the unique *habitus* of a self with whom we can live. Self may be displaced from its hidden interiority, as from the remembered warmth of its exterior traditions and community; but the name continues, for a moment at least and from sheer inertia, to offer its empty shell to a fugitive subjective presence.

The name offers itself as an alias and pseudonym as well as an ambivalent self-identity. Many nineteenth-century women writers adopted pennames to preserve their anonymity and public respectability, as do some popular or sensationalist contemporary writers. Many actors use stagenames and performance names, in part to free themselves from a sense of self-exposure. Interestingly, Søren Kierkegaard published many works devoted to issues of self-identity under fanciful pseudonyms, not to keep secret an authorship he welcomed as notorious, but to distance himself from the life-views they expressed. Surrendering authority over his own words he forced his readers to reach their own judgements and conclusions. His pseudonyms proliferated to such an extent that publications he signed S. Kierkegaard became equally suspect. His 'official' and publicly acknowledged name was transformed into another pseudonym. He concealed himself perfectly, and appeared in public disguised under his own name.

Names, far from being the primal unity in which self-identity arises, chart the construction and deconstruction of self and identity. And whether or not a postmodern view is adopted, the historical variability and cultural ambiguity of names and naming preclude their being understood as the original ground in which self-identity takes root.

BODIES

The human body, *our* body, is different; it is different to anything else. The human body appears to be the most natural of objects. We feel our body as a unique presence which constitutes a reality of its own; a reality which seems to us to stand outside of the conventionality and arbitrariness of daily life. Overwhelmingly we are aware of our corporeal nature as given; as that which we offer or withhold in every action, the modality of volition and pleasure, which remains the natural ground of every experience of unity. Unlike our name we cannot take a new body. Certainly, we can alter our bodily appearance, sometimes dramatically so, and bodies undergo significant change through aging, suffer accidental damage, and may undergo transforming surgery; yet, through all such change the body, as the secure, irreducibly natural carrier of self-identical unity, remains, and cannot be otherwise than, *my* body. The claim that the body is the natural unity in which self-identity inheres does not imply that the body is not subject to change and transformation but, rather, that its unity is unaffected by such change.

It seems obvious that what makes the body 'mine' is the overwhelming sense that conscious experience is strictly localized to its bounded space; that, on the one hand, sense and feeling continually wells up within it and, on the other hand, we have no immediate access to the continuous flow of experience that animates any other body. The body is the 'natural symbol' of all unities (Douglas 1978). The ceaseless flow of experience is uniquely open to me, and always in relation to my body. The body seems to be the natural unity that underpins every experience of identity and self-identity. The body, of course, can be taken apart, analytically and actually, into distinct functioning organs and subsystems, its internal structure and processes analyzed in terms of general chemical and physical laws, or aggregated into larger structures and groups. There are no special laws of nature applying uniquely within, and no social conventions that operate exclusively outwith, the body's apparently sharp and unambiguous boundary. But, at an experiential level, the body stands out, inescapably, as a primordial unity.

And it is not only in terms of its immediate physicality that the body obtrudes self-evidence. The body seems evidently to be the source of all 'clear and distinct ideas;' its structural integrity and organized form is the initial point of orientation of and within the world (Husserl 1990). The body seemingly possesses a compelling logic of its own; right and left, up and down, front and back, inside and outside; the body is a veritable architectonic plan, more than forests and the rich variations of other species the body is 'good to think', and might be thought of as an original table of categories. The thinking subject of Cartesian philosophy is not only a named person, but an embodied mind.

Yet the bounded and individuated character of the body is misleading. It is not that the body, in its nature, gives rise to the experience of unity upon which self-identity rests. It is, to the contrary, the historical emergence of a society constituted through and as self-identity that inscribes itself in the body and makes it unitary. For modern society, in other words, the body is not so different after all. It is not as a physical entity, or as a concept, that the body is significant in everyday life. The body appears simply in the continuous momentum of life. Life is always and wholly embodied, so that the body, as an experiential mode and living being, is fully assimilated to the historical process. The body-image, which we live through, cannot be grasped as a natural structure, or logical plan, but flows along with the social transformations that affect every aspect of life. This amounts simply to saying that the body is a social phenomenon and, therefore, must be grasped historically and contextually. For a society in which self-identity is of paramount importance and is constituted as the unity of experience and the singularity of the experiencing subject, the body-image is individuated, bounded, and uniformly structured. For societies such as those characteristic of the medieval west, however, in which reality is given as a hylomorphic cosmic order, the human body, rather than standing out with seemingly primordial distinctiveness, is lived through as a symbolic *microcosm* of that order. And for a society, as exemplified by modern Japan, in which no difference ultimately has categorical significance and everything is interconnected in the sheer immanence of being, the body is a participatory channel for communication and interrelation which is 'attuned' to reality in a distinctive way and is not a detached 'model' or metaphor for reality (Nagatomo 1992).

The modern body-politic

How does this come about? How can we grasp self-identity as a social relation that is inflected in the body as the experience of corporeal unity? This is a central issue for the understanding of western modernity, and one of the essential features of the emergence and development of its distinctive social form and culture. Two pioneering sociological works propose related perspectives which have been important in reaching new insight into this issue; the work of Norbert Elias and Michel Foucault.

At roughly the same time two books appeared in English translation, one an older German work and one a more contemporary French study, together made the social and historical character of modern embodiment central for contemporary reflection and practice. Norbert Elias's (2000/1939), *The Civilizing Process* (English translation 1978) and Michel Foucault's *Discipline and Punish* (English translation 1979) unlike and even antithetical in so many respects, shared a common *topos* in the human body both as an historical subject and as a key to a fuller understanding and deeper insight into the character of modern life and modern society.

Elias's work suggests a historical sociology of embodiment which grasps the specific character of modernity in the inculcation of new codes of bodily self-control and self-discipline. In his view the Northern European humanism, associated in particular with the writings of Erasmus, transposed the call to human self-dignity which lay at the root of the artistic and scientific ennoblement of humanity in the Italian Renaissance into a universal pedagogy of the body. The culture of modernity begins in the general demand for good manners; that is, with bodily self-control. Continuous and effortless self-control over bodily comportment, gesture, disposition, state of need and readiness for public activity should be exercised. In a word, decency was the first requirement of modern society; a requirement which in turn demanded constant vigilance. Where traditional local forms of political-legal control were no longer effective because of large scale movements of population due to disease and warfare, and feudal social relations had dissolved, social order seemingly depended on the capacity and willingness of individuals to control their own behaviour. New controlling mechanisms were 'interior' to the subject. Modern values were effectively embodied as reason, responsibility, and decency.

The locus of social control decisively shifted and effected 'a change in the relation between external social constraints and individual self-constraints'. Psychic mechanisms correspondingly became socially more significant, resulting in:

> ... firmer, more comprehensive and uniform restraint of the affects ... together with the increased internal compulsions that, more implacably than before, prevent all spontaneous impulses from manifesting themselves directly ... without the intervention of control mechanisms – these are what is experienced as the capsule, the invisible wall dividing the 'inner world' of the individual from the "external world" or, in different versions, the subject of cognition from its object, the "ego" from the "other", the "individual" from "society".
>
> (Elias 2000/1939: 211)

The 'threshold of shame' was lowered and made more specific; it became 'bad manners' to relieve oneself in public, spit in the street, and so on (though not all at once and not all the time). Conduct was continually regulated by the effort not to cause embarrassment or to be embarrassed by others by the untoward negligence over appearance, behaviour or temporary loss of self-control. However, bodily self-control was at the same time a spiritual liberation and the realization of a particular kind of individuality. Control over the body was achieved by the agency of the body's own self-presence; manners provided, above all, a modality for the development and expression of a new form of embodiment. It is worth noting that Elias thus provides an insightful and important historical-cultural context to symbolic interactionism and, particularly, the work of Erving Goffman, for whom the avoidance of embarrassment provides an important focus for the regulation of everyday life.

The History of Manners (Elias 1982) addresses itself above all to the question of whether the supposition, based on scattered observations, 'that there are long-term changes in the affect and control structures of people in particular societies; changes which follow one and the same direction over a large number of generations can be confirmed by reliable evidence and proved to be factually correct'. Additionally, given that such a general tendency can be demonstrated, then 'the increased tightening and differentiation of controls' suggests a related question; 'Is it possible to relate this long-term change in personality structures with long-term structural changes in society as a whole, which likewise tend in a particular direction, toward a higher level of social differentiation and integration?' This latter question becomes the general theme of *State-Formation and Civilization,* the second volume of *The Civilizing Process* (2000/1939). Elias links these two levels of analysis through the notion of *figurational change*. Manners and state-formation are continually interrelated aspects of figurational changes which involve, at every level, processes of differentiation and integration.

If the term 'personality structure' is replaced by 'body-image' a genuinely inter-relational historical sociology of embodiment becomes possible. A sociological perspective is established, that is, in which 'society' and 'body' do not appear as hypostatised entities which are subsequently 'related' on the model of mechanical interaction but, rather, as a complex relational process in which, progressively, body and society become identified as specific domains of experience and reality; in short a 'sociogenesis' of the body and self-identity.

Substantively Elias brings to light the crucial historical significance of the social processes through which an unambiguous boundary between one body and another was established. It was a boundary which was, in fact, a kind of reflexive formation of new social interests and social requirements. The social character of the body and the social relations that were inherent in all bodily experience (and all experience is bodily experience) were manifest first and foremost in its isolation. The apparent independence and self-subsistence of the human body was, in fact, the consequence of new forms of social regulation. Self-control was a principle of social control; close attention to conduct, appearance and the etiquette of everyday interaction created a new individuated body-image and a new society; the history of manners, that is to say, was at the same time the history of state-formation.

Similarly Elias's discussion of the modern 'individual' and the self-perception of the modern subject as *homo clausus* – 'a little world in himself who ultimately exists quite independently of the great world outside' – not only 'determines the image of man in general' but applies, above all, to the classical modern body-image as a closed structure. What might be termed an isolated 'body in space' can be understood in this perspective not only as the social foundation of modern individualism but' simultaneously' as the socially meaningful starting point for Newtonian science and modern philosophy in which the world is conceptually reconstructed from an initial process of imagining a singular body in space.

Typically modern society is composed of 'People to whom it seems self-evident that their own self (or their ego, or whatever else it may be called) exists, as it were, "inside" them, isolated from all the other people and things "outside", have difficulty assigning significance to all those facts which indicate that individuals live from the first in interdependence with others'. That this sense of individuality is itself a social relation was already stated by Durkheim, but is usually taken to refer to a nebulous sense of self as a personal identity and self-presence, rather than to the more concrete and everyday sense of 'body'.

The social division between the individual and others is replicated internally as an immediately felt relation between an 'interior', non-material individuality and *its* body. The human being is locked-up within a protective corporeal shell. Thus, Elias remarks, 'his true self appears likewise as something divided within him by an invisible wall from everything outside'. But what is the nature of this wall 'Is the body the vessel which holds the true self locked within it? Is the skin the frontier between "inside" and "outside"? What in man is the capsule, and what the encapsulated? The experience of "inside' and "outside" seems so self-evident that such questions are scarcely ever posed' (Elias 2000/1939: 204). Elias argues the sense of inside and outside is itself a product of the civilizing process, and the self-restraint or 'repression' of emotional and aggressive expressions which are still felt as 'inclinations' that are controlled.

Both Elias and Foucault describe the modern body as the outcome of a process of ideological and practical activity in which bourgeois values and a bourgeois way of life became idealised and dominant. For Elias, 'the voices expressing the social beliefs, ideals, hopes, and long-term goals of the rising industrial classes gradually gained the advantage over those seeking to preserve the existing social order in the interests of the established courtly-dynastic, aristocratic, or patrician power elites'. For Foucault, however, this 'early-modern' period, what he terms the classical age or baroque period from the late sixteenth to the late seventeenth centuries, though still dominated by dynastic courts and hereditary aristocracies, was revolutionary in its own way and had decisively broken with the past and its feudal ideal.

Foucault epitomises the radical character of this period in corporeal terms; 'The classical age discovered the body as object and target of power'. The absolute power of the early modern state was made visible, above all, in the spectacle of public torture and execution. Premodern forms of community and an earlier corporate and functional organisation of social life had been swept aside. There emerged, amidst uncertainty and the continuous threat of disorder, a new individualistic world. But the individual was created, first of all, as the absolutely powerless subject of the state; a being whose body was wholly at the command and under the will of the monarch. Modern society in a more developed sense – indeed, modernity in the most general sense of the term – consisted primarily in making this power invisible through new constitutional arrangements and, more significantly, in inculcating a particular form of 'reason' in the soul that now lay within the subjugated body.

The modern period, that is to say, extended new techniques of governance to the body – but did so as the intermediary between the state and the soul of the citizen. The disciplinary regimes of monastery, barracks, factory, prison, school, were developed and generalised into a universal technique of governance; a 'political anatomy' aimed at the production of 'docile bodies'. Foucault is interested less in the disciplining of the workforce, where individual reason develops as an interior and continuous monitor of right conduct (all individuals can be trusted to recognise the need to work in a society which systematically destroys all non-market means of subsistence), but those whose lives were led outside the immediate constraints of employment; principally children, lunatics, the ill, and women. The political motive at the heart of all modern institutions of confinement is revealed, for example, in the economically groundless imposition of labour in prison, where there is no guiding no profit motive 'nor even the formation of a useful skill; but the constitution of a power relation, an empty economic form, a schema of individual submission and of adjustment to a production apparatus'. These groups must be disciplined directly by the state rather than through the coercive self-regulation of market rationality. La Salle's pedagogics, in this perspective, becomes a general model of modern disciplinary regimes. There La Mettrie's *L'Homme Machine* becomes 'both a materialist reduction of the soul and a general theory of *dressage*'. The disciplinary mechanics was one of individuation, separation, monitoring, measurement, the imposition of time-table, the precise control of gesture, handwriting, endless drill, intense and continuous supervision and the ubiquitous 'normalizing judgements' of formal examination.

It was through techniques such as these that a responsible and responsive psyche was created; 'The soul is the effect and instrument of a political anatomy; the soul is the prison of the body' (Foucault 1977: 30). Recalling Marcel Mauss's account of 'body techniques', Foucault regards the modern body-politic as 'a set of material elements and techniques that serve as weapons, relays, communication routes and supports for the power and knowledge relations that invest human bodies and subjugate them by turning them into objects of knowledge (Foucault 1977: 28).

It is again worth noting the relevance of Foucault's work in providing a rich historical context for the reading of Goffman's well known interactional account of 'total institutions'.

Transformations of the modern body-image

Both Elias and Foucault were preoccupied with investigating the origin, rather than the contemporary reality, of modern embodiment. In particular both stressed the profound shift in culture and forms of government between the early modern period, which reached its apogee during the first half of the seventeenth century, which still depended upon a forceful imposition of externally imposed norm, and the period of classical modernity, which developed continuously from the mid-seventeenth to the mid-nineteenth century and was ideally self-regulating through effortless conformity to interiorised standards of reason and conduct. Consequently, neither Elias nor Foucault proves to be altogether reliable guides to the later development of modernity and contemporary postmodern culture. Each is concerned with the development of the classical bourgeois age and provide, in different ways and from related but distinctive perspectives, compelling accounts of the establishment of the self-subsistent and 'closed' body-image; a body-image overwhelmingly male, bourgeois, healthy and respectable; the controlling monad of high capitalism. Twentieth-century embodiment, however, reveals an affinity with the early modern period from which this classical picture departed and favours body-images suggestively 'open', female, dangerous and unhealthy.

Elias, certainly, concedes that a degree of 'informalization' characterizes bodily comportment and inter-personal relations during the twentieth century. But, he insists, this does not indicate a reversal in the general direction towards more completely internalised forms of social control. Thus, for example, codes of behaviour regulating the relationship among young people is certainly less formalized and more 'open' than they were in the nineteenth century, but this is only because the entire process of selecting a suitable partner has become exclusively their own responsibility; so that 'dating and pair-formation are individualised to a greater extent'. The 'emancipation from the external constraint of a preordained social ritual, makes higher demands on the self-constraint apparatus of each individual participant. It requires the partners to test themselves and each other in their dealings with each other, and in so doing they can rely on nothing and nobody except themselves, their own judgement and their own feelings'. At the same time, however, Elias admits that the large-scale social developments which constitute the foundation (the sociogenesis) of civilization also generate specific conditions in which 'manners' in the most general sense of cultivated behaviour are liable to break down completely. Barbarism, as well as civilization, characterise the century. Episodes occur in which there is a genuine 'lowering' of the threshold of shame and disgust. Similarly, contemporary society and culture seems to be more adequately described by, so to speak, running Foucault in reverse. The present seems, in many ways, an inversion of the 'panopticon'; surveillance once again gives way to spectacle.

Thus, rather than view contemporary society as the 'fallen' state of classical modernity, it is illuminating to view the peculiarities of the twentieth century as a rebirth of early modern culture and, correspondingly, to reinterpret the Baroque Age as anticipating many aspects of postmodernity.

Considering the body-image only in relation to self-experience and the issue of self-identity, a variety of highly original studies provide striking accounts of a general process of *disembodiment* that now seems to characterize contemporary experience. It might be argued, indeed, that just as sociologists had come to realize the importance of embodiment as one of the most significant ways in which both the institutional order and practices of everyday life in modern society were established, those very processes had already been put into reverse. Contemporary society, that is to say, rather than being embodied in the effortless self-identical unity of immediate experience, is found only in remote, abstracted, and inconsistent images. Far from founding itself in the primal unity of the body, the fragmentary character of modern experience indicates the *incoherence* of contemporary body images. This incoherence is evident in a confusion of language, disciplinary perspective, and political orientation present in many contemporary studies that take 'body' as their theme; studies that display, in fact, a multiplicity of divergent themes united under has become an almost meaningless label. *The* body has given way to the bewildering variety of *which* body? And *who's* body? The real difficulty is that the plurality of bodies does not map directly on to the plurality of individuals or persons; there are not just distinctly different but self-identical bodies, self-identity is no longer located in any body.

Corporeal flux

The extent to which contemporary body-images are in continual flux is an underlying theme of many literary, as well as philosophical and scientific works of the twentieth century. These works are descriptive of important changes in bodily experience, and are treated with exemplary eclectic sympathy in the still unsurpassed descriptive psychology of Paul Schilder, whose *Appearance and Image of the Human Body* (1935) might be read as a rejoinder to Norbert Elias's *The Civilizing Process* (2000/1939), conceived in the same period and cultural setting to which it responded in quite a different way.

Schilder treated the body-image as the focus of intersubjective communicative and emotional processes which is continually undergoing change. But it is in terms of the 'postural model' that he makes the most original and striking observations:

> The image of the human body means the picture of our own body which we form in our mind, that is to say the way in which the body appears to ourselves ... We see parts of the body-surface. We have tactile, thermal, pain impressions ... and sensations coming from the viscera. Beyond that there is the immediate experience that there is a unity of the body. This unity is perceived, yet it is more than a perception. We call it a schema of our body or bodily schema ... a self-appearance of the body.
>
> (Schilder 1935: 11)

Schilder is at pains to stress the complex process of construction that goes into the experience of the body-image as a unity. In fact, it soon emerges that process of destruction and fragmentation are also at work giving rise to transitory and partial body-images; 'living in its continued differentiation and integration' (Schilder 1935: 15–16). We do not have direct access to all parts of our body, there are parts we do not see or touch, we are completely ignorant of the organic interior which makes itself felt as a 'heavy mass;' a dark viscous fluid that moves and settles according to its own, slow rhythm.

Schilder was able to draw on a wealth of medical research conducted on war injuries to illustrate the creative and shifting character of the body-image; 'One of the clearest expressions of the existence of the postural model of the body is the so-called phantom of persons who have undergone amputation ... chiefly represented by tactile and kinaesthetic sensations ... It is as if the phantom were trying to preserve the last moments in which the limb was still present' (Schilder 1935: 63–64). But the phantom is only the most dramatic example of a general process that characterizes all body-images; '... we continually change our images; we multiply them and make them appear differently ... We have, therefore, an almost unlimited number of body-images ... emotional processes are the force and source of energy of these constructive processes' (Schilder 1935: 67). Where Elias, and later Douglas, stress the integrity of the body-image in terms particularly of its continuous, sensitive, and ritually protected boundary Schilder draws attention to the precarious and incomplete experience of bodily boundaries. According to Schilder we have no complete experiences of ourselves as bounded space:

> A more careful analysis about what is felt on the skin immediately reveals astonishing results. There are vague feelings of temperature. It is more or less a feeling of warmth. But the outline of the skin is not felt as a smooth and straight surface. This outline is blurred. There are no sharp borderlines between the outside world and the body ... The skin that is felt is distinctly below the surface of the optic perception of the body ... when we touch an object with our hands or with another surface of the body. At this very moment, the surface becomes smooth, clear, and distinct. The tactile and the optic outlines are now identical with each other ... They are not fused together. There is a distinct space between.
>
> (Schilder 1935: 85–86)

The body-image is not shrink-wrapped to the physical body surface. It expands and contracts, withdraws into the interior, detaches parts, and makes daring leaps into empty space, 'the most important parts of the body are the openings' (Schilder 1935: 88). The body-image twists, breaks apart and reassembles; it is the instrument and medium for 'the playful multiplication of psychic experiences' (Schilder 1935: 68).

Sensuous histories

Freud's pioneering psychology broke with the modern Cartesian subject between extended substance (body) and thinking substance (mind). He also rejected, what ultimately was related to this duality, the antithesis between biological determinism and Romantic expressionism. The body, for Freud, was the meeting ground and merging of physicality and meaningfulness. Freud's work took the form of a baroque merging of subject and object, in which all sensuous categories were spiritualised, and spiritual categories were sensualized. His understanding of the psychical mechanism, allowed him to see the formation of consciousness not only organically and functionally, in terms of the discharge of excitation and the emergence of a reality-testing mechanism, but schematically, in terms of the organizing principles given in a number of different body-images. In the present perspective what is striking in Freud's work is not only the variety of these of body-images, or schemata, but their distinctive historical references points. Hysteria is not only a vivid example of somatic incoherence and splitting of the body-image, it reproduces body-images that were active in childhood and, indeed, historically in archaic, ancient, and premodern times.

Thus, in the ancient world, a disunited assembly of organs, which bears some resemblance to the earliest erotogenic zones Freud (1991) outlined in his *Three Essays in Sexuality*, is evident. Neither the Homeric body, nor the body in the Ancient Judaic tradition, acts and thinks as a unity; its various organs are subject to specific passions of which it is the passive victim. Both Christianity and Neoplatonism imposed upon this 'primary process' a spatial differentiation of inside and outside with a consequential unification in terms of spiritual values over organic processes. The 'orality' of the ancient world was gradually 'oedipalised'; that is its openness to the abundance of spiritual value which flowed ceaselessly from its gods, became closed-off and made conditional on acts of obedience and, ultimately, upon the spontaneous conformity of an inner-will. Subsequently, in the context of the development particularly of feudal society, this unification was reconceptualized as a microcosmic order, which operated both as a mirror and as a replica of the macrocosmic structure of the world. These developing body-images, related to the Freudian discussion of anal eroticism, might be elaborated in terms both of the symbolic order of everyday life and of the organisation of nature. Renaissance body-images established the separateness of the human realm and understood the cosmological structure in terms of its mirroring in the mind, rather than in terms of direct participation in the substantial unity of creation. Withdrawn, and therefore privileged, the human body took on the character of a world apart. The reflective body-image, redefined within the bourgeois epoch as the infinite inwardness of the human subject, became self-sufficient and cut-off from the cosmos of which it could only dream. Then as advanced societies broke down the absolute distinctions introduced into the post-feudal epoch as characterising human dignity, the body once again opened itself towards, and fused with, the world; giving rise to a surface across which energetic and playful forces shocked first one, then another, element of consciousness into life (Ferguson 1997).

Alienation and exhaustion

The 'stream of consciousness' was also, and principally, a 'stream of physicality'. Freud was not alone in merging the languages of body and mind. In the latter part of the nineteenth century 'sensitivity' and 'nervousness' became commonplace symptoms of turbulence of everyday life in the modern metropolis (Beard 1881). At the same time a new freedom of movement and sensuousness was encouraged as both healthy and enjoyable. Sport, recreational exercise, including cycling, walking, climbing, swimming, dancing, and gymnastic training, all appeared and became popular aspects of the 'physical culture' of the most advanced societies . Typically these forms displayed the body in a vigorously active mode, in a public or semi-public place. And though usually a collective experience many of the participants would be and would remain otherwise unknown to one another.

Marx, in a different context, had anticipated the emergence of the 'pure physicality' of the contemporary age; anonymous labour power, which was no more than the bare possibility of energetic movement, characterized the worker reduced to the commodity form. The worker becomes indifferent, one from another; equivalent, interchangeable, and indistinguishable. Equally, the commodities the worker produces become indifferent; interchangeable, and equivalent; indistinguishably the same and, therefore, uninhibited in their circulation, defined by a single essential property of value expressed as money. This renewed physicality is quite distinct from the concentrated mass with its closed hard shell that characterized the classical modern period. This is physicality liberated from ponderous dead matter; *energetic* rather than statuesque. Energy, in fact, became the central *motif* of cultural innovation, the natural sciences, and popular culture (Clark and Henderson 2002). The body image of advanced society, like the transformed conception of space and matter in physics, was a local concentration of flowing energy rather than an isolated mass drifting in space. The body as an architectonic structure dissolved into various channels of conductivity and sensitivity. The human body, like any motor, was subject to entropy, and suffered exhaustion. Fatigue, as much as hysterical energy, became the characteristic disease of the most advanced societies; 'Exhaustion was not merely the consequence of physical overexertion, but the cause of a variety of physical and mental pathologies born of the languid and torpid state of men, women, and especially school-age children. Fatigue was also a metaphor for the

modern form of ontological suffering, for inertia, loss of will, and deple-
tion of energy' (Rabinbach 1990, 20). Fatigue is disembodied weightiness.
It is both the residue of physicality and the trace of spirit; the contemporary condition of the *flesh* (Chrétien 1996).

Phenomenal volatility

The philosophical movement of phenomenology, and particularly the
variant proposed by Maurice Merleau-Ponty (1962), also articulate the
transformation of late modernity in terms of new styles of embodiment.

Merleau-Ponty begins by discounting the idea of the psyche as the interior subject lodged in a body; 'there is no inner man, man is in the world,
and only in the world does he know himself' (Merleau-Ponty 1962: xi). It
is as being-in-the-world that human beings exist, and body, like mind, and
name, is not coterminous with that being. Merleau-Ponty, thus, emphasizes the importance of the difference between the immediacy of embodied experience and the 'anonymity of the body' (Merleau-Ponty 1962: 84).
The pure exteriority of the body, like the otherness of the name, is highly
significant for contemporary society and culture. It is in an *encounter* with
our own body that we grasp the sheer transcendental objectivity of experience. As Paul Ricoeur (1996) also points out, we do not choose our
body, and the existential focus on the ultimate freedom of self-identity is
one-sided in its failure to acknowledge the ultimacy with which we are
bound to our bodies. For Merleau-Ponty the relationship between the
objective body, the phenomenal body-image, and the body experienced
as something objective, is in continual flux.

Not only is the body present, therefore, in a number of different ways
perceptually, it also appears in ontologically distinctive modes of willing
and feeling. The active, wilful body is not an 'object' in the world that has
to be moved and directed as if it were an instrument; it lives through a particular intention and trajectory. Thus, while, 'we must provide the subject
of perception with the unity of the bodily schema', that schema, even at
the perceptual level 'is open and limitless' (Merleau-Ponty 1962: 233). So
the unity of the body, and that which it posits, is always provisional, fragile, and limited to the project for which that unity is adequate. The body
'as such' has no existence and no real meaning, it is subsumed in all its
experiences and 'we grasp the unity of our body only in that of the
thing ... the body by itself, the body at rest, is only an obscure mass'
(Merleau-Ponty 1962: 322).

The surface of life

Deleuze and Guattari (1983), like Freud recalling ancient body-images, refer to the 'body without organs', which is also to say 'organs in search of a body'; a body for which everything takes place on the surface. Contemporary life is embodied as skin. Anzieu (1989), for example, describes in psychoanalytic language, the 'skin-ego' and the whole development of ego-psychology from the wreckage of 'depth psychology' as part of the process of opening the body and bringing to its surface everything that had been separated from it as external and internal realities; as matter and mind, object and subject. The contemporary body is nothing other than a sensitive surface for recording changes in appearance. The body is without a form of its own; it is *indeterminate* and, subject to the ceaseless volatility of everyday life, radiates the energy of all those collective sentiments with which it is overwhelmed.

Name and Body are not so perfectly our own. The body slips and leaks, withdraws and expands, it is also over against me, heavy, fatigued. The name is obscure, tyrannical, and demanding. The body is multiple and volatile (Grosz 1994). Not only like itself (modern, individuated, closed), but like its others; at times carnivalesque and transgressive (Bakhtin 1968), at times, like modern Japanese embodiment, 'attuned' to cosmic spirit (Nagatomo 1992). Neither name nor body are the privileged source for the experience of unity, or furnish the prototype for self-identity. This is not because self-identity is not implicated in names and bodies. In so far as self-identity can be experienced as unity it experiences name and body as unity. The point, rather, is that self-identity, like name and body, can *also* be experienced in multiplicity, fluidity, and volatility. Name and body, conformed to social reality, indicate a significant transformation of experience in falling apart from self-identity. The alienation of name and body reveals something important about the fate of experience in contemporary society. Name and body are social relations; that they are no longer simple unities is simply an aspect of a social transformation towards an indeterminate condition. This also indicates that self-identity is *also* a social relation and subject, therefore, to the same transformation.

The large-scale social structure of self-identity must now be taken up directly.

INTERRUPTION 4: MEMORY

And suddenly the memory returns. The taste was that of a little crumb of madeleine which on Sunday mornings at Combray (because on those mornings I did not go out before church-time), when I went to say good day to her in her bedroom, my aunt Léonie used to give to me, dipping it first in her own cup of lime-flower tea. The sight of the little madeleine had recalled nothing to my mind before I tasted it; perhaps because I had so often seen such things in the interval, without tasting them, on the trays in pastry-cooks' windows, that their image had dissociated itself from those of Combray days to take its place among others more recent ... But when from a long distant past nothing subsists, after the people are dead, after the things are broken and scattered, still, alone, more fragile, but with more vitality, more unsubstantial, more persistent, more faithful, the smell and taste of things remain poised for a long time, like souls, ready to remind us, waiting and hoping for their moment, amid the ruins of all the rest; and bear unfaltering, in the tiny and almost impalpable drop of their essence, the vast structure of recollection ... And just as the Japanese amuse themselves by filling a porcelain bowl with water and steeping in it little crumbs of paper which until then are without character or form, but, the moment they become wet, stretch themselves and bend, take on colour and distinctive shape, become flowers or houses or people, permanent and recognisable, so in that moment all the flowers in our garden and in M. Swann's park, and the water-lilies on the Vivonne and the good folk of the village and their little dwellings and the parish church and the whole of Combray and of its

surroundings, taking their proper shapes and growing solid, sprang into
being, town and gardens alike, from my cup of tea.

(Marcel Proust, *Swann's Way*)

... it was so long ago that I cannot remember anything about myself then.
(Michel de Montaigne, *Essays*)

There is no experience of the past. Memory is always a present experience; it is here and now. Just as all history is contemporary history; all
memory is present memory. It is surprising, given the unique authority of
experience for modern society, that memory should be regarded as the
guarantor of self-identity. All that memory can confirm is the presentness
of the present. *That* we are remembering, rather than perceiving, reflecting, or dreaming, and so on, and *what* we are remembering in terms of its
specific present content is given with the incontestable self-evidence of
immediate experience; but whether the recollection corresponds to an
actual event in the past is as doubtful as any perception. Memory is not
only fallible, it is deceptive.

And because memory is always present experience it is absolutely
bound to the flow of time. A memory I am going to have tomorrow will
not arrive until that moment, a memory I had yesterday is already in the
past and, while I might recollect having had it, cannot be revisited. But,
whenever it comes, and in a remarkable way, memory is completely free
from the temporal constraint of immediate experience. We play over the
entire range of possible past experiences in recollecting events and
incidents; free from the ordering of time's original flow. And, in fact, we
can exercise some limited control and direction over memory, and use it
deliberatively

Memory also comes unbidden; an involuntary flood of recollection
fills every present experience with haphazard references to events and situations that we assume 'belong' to the past. But spontaneous recollection,
which, just because of its involuntary character is often charged with a
sense of 'reliving' rather than simply recalling the past, also exists exclusively in the transience of now. Proust, in the famous passage above,
rightly consecrates such images, vivid with self-presence, not to the
illusion of memory, but to the eternal moment of recollection.

Memory, like history is always contemporary. And like history, it
assumes continuity and creates discontinuity. That is to say, memory
arises because we have rejected the past. In this sense memory is also like
science. We *need* memory, as we do knowledge, because the past as well as

nature, stands over against us with impenetrable objectivity. Knowledge becomes our key interrelation with nature, and our means, to some extent, of controlling our world. And memory is our privileged means of grasping the past. We need to do this to assure ourselves of the continuity and authenticity of the self-identical subject of experience. It is not Romantic striving and self-realization that actualizes the self; rather it is recollection of a past for which the present is the culmination. The self's medium is time, so memory is a necessary tool for the creation of psychic life. Interiority, a spatial category, implies duration and an existence in time.

For modern society, then, because self-identity is the only non arbitrary identity, and reality is given as the experience of reality, memory becomes significant in a new way as the continuous unity of the psyche. John Locke had argued, in modern fashion, that self consisted simply in the continuity of consciousness revealed by memory. Self-recollections seem inexhaustible and apparently reveal our continuous existence throughout a particular period of time. But this is an illusion, which David Hume effectively exposed. The self cannot extend itself in time. Just as the succession of events does not demonstrate the operation of causality in nature, but only suggests it to our mind; so memory of apparently successive events fails to demonstrate the real continuity of self and, thus, fails to demonstrate the reality of self-identity at all. Self is not even the memory of self.

The now common insistence on distinguishing memory from history, thus, obscures significant characteristics of both. Nevertheless Pierre Nora is justified in distinguishing memory from history in a somewhat different way. For Nora memory, what he calls collective memory (although ultimately all memory is collective memory just because consciousness is a social relation), is living tradition and habit, embedded in the practices of everyday life. History is compiled from official archival deposits, and the anonymous, written records that inscribe the institutional rationality of advanced societies; 'Memory and history, thus, far from being synonymous, are in many respects opposed. Memory is life, always embodied in living societies and as such in permanent evolution, subject to the dialectic of remembering and forgetting, unconscious of the distortions to which it is subject, vulnerable in various ways to appropriation and manipulation, and capable of lying dormant for long periods only to be suddenly reawakened. History, on the other hand, is the reconstruction, always problematic and incomplete, of what is no longer. Memory is always a phenomenon of the present, a bond tying us to the eternal present; history is a representation of the past' (Nora 1996: 1–3).

Memory is founded in 'emotion and magic' and, consequently, is vague, selective, and impressionistic, whereas, because history is 'intellectual and nonreligious', it analyzes and locates events. The adequacy of memory is not what it reveals of the past, but how it creates the present; 'Memory wells up from groups that it welds together'.

But, in a larger context, what Nora says of memory applies with equal force to history. History is also consciousness of the present as secular, modern, and universal. The difference lies, primarily, in the locus of unity. History is directed outwards towards the establishment of a universal framework of otherness; memory is directed inwards towards the articulation of the continuity of self as community and person. In this sense the history of memory, its transformation in the emergence and development of modernity, offers a striking illustration of the emergence, development, and ultimate failure of memory as a 'technology of the psyche'.

Memory as the inner unity of self-identity is almost unknown in the ancient and medieval west. Habit, embedded in everyday practices, does not require conscious recollection any more than it demands objective and systematic knowledge of the external world. It is simply what is done. In the premodern west there is a real sense in which memory is superfluous; things continue as they are. There is no need to know 'who you are'; the question does not arise because you are co-substantial with your place. There is no need for inner self-knowledge and, therefore, interior memory, because self is objectified through fixed social relations. Highly sophisticated techniques for training and practising conscious recollection did develop, but in the limited and highly specialized context of 'artificial memory'. These techniques were derived from texts, going back to late antiquity, used for training in oratory (Yates 1966).

This already reveals a process of rationalization and distancing. The Homeric songs were masterpieces of an oral culture, a performing art in which rhyme and rhythm assisted the memorizing and repetition of enormously long passages; stories that took on a life of their own in the exteriority of speech. But the oratorical demands of the Roman polity required protracted public speaking, not as ritual performance, but as statements. The art of rhetoric required first of all that rules of composition be strictly observed and that the content was organized in terms of images that could be readily recalled. The artificiality of the procedure is instructive. Memory worked best when material was subject to a wholly arbitrary mechanism. The poet Simonides of Cos was said to have discovered the art of memory; 'He inferred that persons desiring to train this faculty (of memory) must select places and form mental images of the things they wish to remember and store these images in the places, so that the order of the places will preserve the order of the things, and the images of the things will denote the things themselves, and we shall employ the places and the images respectively as a wax writing-tablet and the letters written on it' (Yates 1966: 17).

Memory, unlike theory, operated through personal and unconnected associations. The art of memory, neglected in the medieval west, became an esoteric art that was revived in the anticipatory, early Renaissance writings associated with the Platonic revival spearheaded by Marsilio Ficino. At the heart of this revival was a new and powerful assertion of the human against and over both nature and God. The aim of various forms of hermeticism was to unlock the secrets of nature and appropriate powers that had hitherto been regarded as divine. The art of memory played an important part in this ambitious project. And central to the revival of that art was the replacement of the artificial context of memory with a natural theatre of place; the *loci* of an immanent system of logic through which nature remembered to do everything that, predictably and in orderly fashion, it performed.

Memory was a kind of logic, a natural logic that aided recall by its replication in consciousness of a system 'hard wired' in nature. For the modern period this system underwent an important transformation. The conscious system became self-conscious; that is, became the consciousness of self, recollecting itself through remembering past events. The interiorization of memory was important for a society in which individuation was fundamental, and everyday life was thought to depend on the personal commitment of its members. Modern individuals had to 'put themselves' into society if society was to operate effectively. The individual, furthermore, had to enter society through the free operation of specific inner-qualities. It was important that everyone 'knew themselves' in the sense that they identified fully with a controlling self-image felt as uniquely their own.

Continuity could only be the inner continuity of the self-identical subject of experience. Thus, whether or not the Romantic gesture towards authenticity was justified, everyday life was supported by the assumption that experience, however disjointed and chaotic it might appear in a modern world for which relationships were partial, transitory, and often anonymous, the synthesis of self carried along, as a running commentary on the events of the world, an observing, reflective, and active subject. Memory was the medium of interiority and the carrier of selfhood.

Modern self-identity came to suicidal maturity in autobiography, pre-eminently in Rousseau's *Confessions*.

Self-identity was reconfigured as *narrative*. This brings the idea of self-identity into close relationship to the literary history of modern society. Around the turn of the nineteenth to twentieth centuries, Wilhelm Dilthey leant his extraordinary weight of scholarship to this task (1988), and more recently Paul Ricoeur has devoted a notable series of studies to its elucidation (1990, 1994, 2004).

Ricoeur argues self is best understood in terms of narrative; that is, through memory of its role as the active agent of 'emplotment'. Self-identity has to be reckoned in terms of the inner connectedness 'of an entire life' (Ricoeur 1990: 115). This is not a reworking of the Romantic theory of selfhood; emplotment is not the continuous striving of an interior subject towards self-expression. It is, rather, the continuous self-recollection of developing character. Ricoeur is borrowing and adapting a literary-critical idea of narrative here. Literature is not a direct model, but 'a vast laboratory in which we experiment with estimations, evaluations, and judgements of approval and condemnation through which narrative serves as propaedeutic to ethics' (Ricoeur 1990: 115). Narrative takes precedence over character as interior unity, 'It is the identity of the story that makes the identity of the character' (Ricoeur 1990: 147–148).

Self-identity is not simple experience, or even the memory of continuous experience, so much as the 'capacity to model experience' (Ricoeur 1990: 76). Narrativity is a form of unity that accepts its own contingency and finitude. Yet the assumption of unity and sense is counterbalanced in Ricoeur by a realistic recognition of the confusion and indistinctness of the present: The told story 'is in "continuity" with the passive entanglement of subjects in stories that disappear into a foggy horizon' (Ricoeur 1990: 75).

Yet, memory works against itself; against the self. Self and identity dissolved into pure sensuous awareness, made eternal, rather than actual, in recollection. The Proustian moment is torn from the past, but does not fall into a rational sequence of events, and knows nothing of succession or duration; it has nothing to do with temporality. It is a version of selfless non-identity that stands positively at the outset of the contemporary postmodern.

The difficulty of contemporary life does not stem from our inability to recall the past, but from our failure to forget the present. Memory begins on this side of the break; memory requires trauma; modernity requires rejection of the past.

4

TOTALITIES

'We are fascinated by the unit; only a unity seems rational to us', remarks Michel Serres, voicing a persistent modern orthodoxy. However, the search for an underlying, indivisible, identity in any aspect of experience has been disappointed; 'The bottom always falls out of the quest for the elementary. The irreducibly individual recedes like the horizon, as our analysis advances' (Serres 2004: 2–3). Can the experience of unity be found, rather, in the construction of totalities? Or, to be more precise, it is not unity as an experience of separateness and indivisibility that is significant here but, rather, that of completeness and wholeness.

Analytic, individualistic ways of thinking have been institutionalized in modern society and a powerful orthodoxy reduces the phenomenal world to an appearance that requires explanation in terms of underlying unities. This approach includes all psychic and social, as well as natural phenomena. Unity is grasped as the individual, identical, and equivalent carrier of the requisite primary qualities from which totality emerges through interaction. In terms of the totality of modern society, the individual human being is defined as a social being in terms of the possession of reason, passion, and will. In pursuit of pleasure, and the satisfaction of wants, what generally are termed interests, individuals enter into relations of mutual benefit, which results, ideally, in an ordered society (Unger 1975). Looking at it the other way around, however, is illuminating. Beginning with the totality of society, an interrelational order is established in such a way that the experience of individual unities emerges as one of its conditions. Unity is a consequence of, rather than a foundation for, a particular kind of totality. The individual is constituted in terms of specific qualities just because those are the required characteristics of the totality. This is approximately the view of Émile Durkheim (1984, 1995, 2002), whose incisive criticism of the utilitarian position remains formative for the development of sociological thought.

Collective identity, then, might be considered the source of self; and individuation the result of a process of differentiation within totalities rather than totality being the consequence of aggregating individuals. Interestingly, at just the time Durkheim was developing his pioneering sociological method, Edmund Husserl adopted this approach in his *Philosophy of Arithmetic*, which was devoted, above all, to the experience of unity. 'One' could only become a numeral, he argued, when it was the terminus of a process of division within a group or set. The idea of oneness arose through subdivision of a set; and individuality might be thought of as a set or group with one member. What was important for the idea of unity *and* totality was how classificatory groups were formed; a process that drew Husserl into the radical reconstruction of modern philosophy (Husserl 2003/1891; Ferguson 2006).

The issue of social totality, in one sense, is just the same as that of unity. Is there a non-arbitrary foundation for the experience of totality? Is there a natural or spiritual community that is realized in the experience of living together in a particular way? Many of the problems of unity including the ambiguity of boundaries, unstable and uncertain forms, and the ultimately elusive character of the experience itself, recur and result similarly in inconclusive and vague characterization of phenomena. Additionally, however, the internal constitution of totality must also be considered. Totality, in its simplest sense, is an aggregation of like units. This is just the model of the social totality endorsed in the utilitarian perspective. But, as the sum of individuals this amounts at best to a collection rather than a totality; 'A cartload of bricks is not a house', remarks Michel Serres, 'we want a principle, a system, an integration' (Serres 2004: 2). In relation to social totalities, then, that might qualify as houses rather than cartloads of bricks, two rather different approaches to understanding integration are common. First, totality is viewed as an emergent property of interaction at various levels. Totality describes a distinctive and relatively autonomous field of interrelational activity giving rise to phenomena that belong properly to a collective level and taken together describe a totality that cannot be predicated on the characteristics of the relational elements themselves, whether these elements are individuals or groups. Society, Durkheim insisted in opposition to all forms of reductionist thinking, is a reality *sui generis*. Totality here has no definite implication for the kind of relations involved, which may be relations of domination, conflict, mutual interest, exploitation, and so on. Second, totality may be grasped as a pre-existing collective phenomenon, the character of which determines interrelational structures and typical forms of consciousness subsumed within it. The first view is summed up in the notion that 'the whole is greater than the sum of the parts', and the second approach might be characterized as 'the whole is prior to any of its parts'. There is a difference, roughly, between viewing totality as coming before or after the differentiation of social relations and, more significantly between an interactive and a collective subject.

Formal and historical issues are interconnected in assertions and denials of self-identical totality. The notion of 'modern society', for example, not only asserts a particular socio-historical coherence that claims distinction from (its conception of) premodern or Ancient society, it does so in terms of a distinctive mode of integration institutionalized as the nation-state. And other evident totalities, including world, nature, spirit, and humanity – totalities that have played a significant role in the developing of modernity not only as concepts but in the ordering of experience – are distinguished in terms of the specific region of reality integrated under them, and are constituted in distinctive ways. And, like other totalities and unities, on closer inspection, are less distinct and coherent than they at first appear.

World, for example, is distinct from environment, or globality, but the distinctions are shifting and insecure (Oelschlaeger 1993; Nancy 2007). Nature, even more obviously, dissolves into a number of different kinds of totality with diffused and overlapping boundaries; as environment, wilderness, landscape, ecosystem, park, garden, and so on. This is not just a series in which nature is progressively affected by human activity and human presence, but refers to nature differently constituted as a totality; that is, to different natures (Latour 2004). It is not one but several totalities. Similarly large totalities such as spirit, humanity, history, and so on are unstable and unsystematic. No totality is perfectly systematic, coherent, and ordered by a consistent and lucid principle. And every totality is both incomplete and contains extraneous elements.

Modern society constitutes a totality as a narrative of self-identity. At the same time other societies are constituted as historical totalities of different kinds. A number of ancient societies are grasped as proto-self-identical, that is as civilizations. Some large-scale societies are taken to be totalities of the non-self-identical, notably Oriental, or Asiatic society. And in relation to modern society, totality is also constituted in terms self-identical attributes or qualities, notably in terms of gender, or race.

It is important to bear in mind that in arguing that any or all totalities are arbitrarily constituted and have no necessary existence is not to say that they are insignificant or simply mistaken ideas. There are experiential unities and totalities that, however ill-conceived and unfounded, constitute important points of reference for any sociology of everyday life. If self-identity is a relational historical phenomenon manifest in, and as, lived totalities, then what kinds of totalities are there? And how are they constituted?

THE AXIAL AGE

Taking a long view, the entire question of self and identity arises, historically, in the context of the social transformation of ancient civilizations during the period often now referred to as the 'axial age' (Eisenstadt 1986; Arnason *et al.* 2005). Generalizing, refining, and giving empirical historical content to the term introduced by Karl Jaspers to describe the more-or-less simultaneous appearance of the great world religions and major philosophical schools, contemporary scholars have enlarged our understanding of the social origins of self and the characteristic experience of the world it entails.

Around the fifth century BCE (stretching from mid-sixth to mid-fourth) in Mesopotamia, North India, China, and the Mediterranean Ancient Empires underwent a series of linked changes as fundamental and far-reaching in their consequences as had been the Neolithic transformation to settled agriculture and the domestication of animals (Childe 1964/1951). Axial age societies developed in scale, internal complexity, external relatedness, centralization of power, and, most noticeably, cultural sophistication. The most significant features, in the present perspective, was the emergence of cities and the establishing of social elites detached from 'everyday' tasks related to agriculture. The power of centralized rulers, to become effective, was expressed in mythic forms that, simultaneously, described and interpreted the world. Within this development there arose a specific sense of 'inwardness' as an ethical demand, a spiritual force that required commitment to a specific way of life and a new and organized perspective on the world. This transformation, the first form of conversion (Nock 1933) to an inner conscience and moral imperative, manifested itself in religious-spiritual revolutions of the most varied kinds.

The rise of world religions all took place in this context, as did the emergence of disciplined philosophy, science, and literature. The philosophical 'schools' that emerged were, thus, very similar to religious movements in setting up communities, ordering the everyday lives of its members, and demanding a particular kind of spiritual practice (Hadot 1995).

The axial age civilizations, in other words, developed the social complexity and inner differentiation of structure, that was a prerequisite for the emergence of self; the internal differentiation and interrelation of experiential forms under a principle or value, hypostatized as a superior and demanding being. The inner demand of this relation was experienced as something distinctly personal, as an encounter; but, for the first time perhaps, the demand was not fully externalized or projected on to a mythical figure. This was, in other words, the beginning of the long process of secularization; the first secularization of a primordial, sacred cosmos (Voegelin 2000). The social processes, that is to say, broke free of its mythological context and the beginning of the process of human self-making began.

Self emerges here as a self-moving synthesis, as an awareness of human difference from the world, its special status marked by at least the possibility of bringing its nature and future under its own control.

The breakthrough of the axial age, a shift at the level of consciousness from *mythos* to *logos* and, simultaneously, from *mythos* to *theos* is not yet the formation of what is here termed self-identity (Buxton 1999). But it is the beginning of a process that develops in a distinctive way as a *history* of selfhood and, indeed, many contemporary scholars, as well as famous philosophers including Hegel and Nietzsche have sought, in different ways, to understand contemporary self-identity as continuous with this ancient beginning (Sorabji 2000).

CIVILIZATION

The coherence of civilization as a particular kind of human totality is equivocal. The term is new, and used as a substantive only after the mid-eighteenth century, and considerably later than the terms civilize and civility (Febvre 1973). Braudel points out that in 1732 the term civilization (as later feudalism) was used exclusively in a technical legal sense as a judgment that turned a criminal trial into a civil proceeding (Braudel 1995: 3). Later the notion of civilization came to include a number of societies dispersed over a considerable area. Civilization constituted both a totality (viewed internally) and a unit (viewed in relation to other civilizations) in a developmental-evolutionary sequence. Civilizations can include a number of distinct societies, regions, and persists over long periods and through more or less rapid institutional changes.

The crucial idea of civilization is bound up with the emergence and organization of higher-order forms of consciousness, and its use to gain political control over non-immediate and distant members of the society. Civilization brings together two forms of totality; power and culture. The unitary, archaic sacred world is split apart and assigned to distinct zones of activity and institutionalization. They remain closely interrelated, but the separation is ultimately decisive. It is not that one takes priority over the other; it is rather that the formation of large-scale totalities requires the continuous application of power and culture; totality has a cultural and a military aspect (Eisenstadt 1986).

Civilization was a modern creation; but lay decisively in the past. Civilization was ancient and belonged to antiquity. It was the creation of free and well educated elites in whom were combined military-political and cultural virtues. Modernity was the rebirth of civilization and a work still in progress. And the idea of civilization was closely tied to the strictly modern conception of progress which took shape in the eighteenth century and which stimulated and, in turn, was supported by, new scientific notions of evolution (Burrow 1966; Detienne 2007).

Two more particular developments were significant in the formulation of the modern, distinctively aesthetic idea of ancient civilization. The first was the rediscovery and reassessment of ancient art and architecture pioneered by Johann Winckelmann, whose impressive art history (2006/1776) of ancient Greece and Rome based on extensive, but little seen and never studied collections in Rome, particularly in the Vatican. Europe was the storehouse of ancient civilizations that, receding into the past, lay half concealed. Winckelmann's writings were enormously influential and provided a common point of departure for both classical and Romantic aesthetic idea of civilization in the work of, among others Goethe, Lessing, and Herder. The second, which brought to light in a yet more vivid and literal sense the historical layering of civilizations stretching from antiquity to the present, was the emergence of a systematic science of archaeology stimulated by the Napoleonic Wars which took French scholars, as well as soldiers, into North Africa and what later became loosely termed the Middle East.

The discovery of many impressive ruins spoke eloquently of the scale, complexity, and sophistication of forgotten societies and cultures. Excavation brought much to light. Ancient civilizations constituted complex totalities; the first surviving traces of a self-identical historical subject. Ancient civilization was not *other* to ourselves. There was something familiar and comprehensible in their ruins, however incomplete and puzzling they might be. It was a recognizable human world that underlay our own. Classical studies became popular, and competence in Greek language, history, and art became the common currency of European elite education. The recovery of such a distant pass did not seriously threaten the conviction that modern society was new in a radical way. Long intervening centuries following the collapse of ancient empires had obscured its real significance, which could only be recovered, in fact, by a decisive rejection of the immediate past.

The rediscovery of civilization was a psychological as well as a historical insight. The process of brushing away accumulated sand and debris, then interpreting and translating exposed material ('reading the stones'), portrayed as the investigative technique of the archaeologist, was later adopted by Freud as a model for psychological investigations. Freud claimed to have read more archaeology than psychology, and accumulated a large and varied collection of antiquities. Like Hegel, he held that all culture and civilization was created through a process of repression. In undeveloped societies immediate, organically based wants took precedence over any 'higher' values; but in more advanced society, and as a condition for its appearance, these needs had to be suppressed in the interests of developing purely human creative activities, directed towards the satisfaction of other wants, including aesthetic satisfaction, curiosity, and ethical consciousness. Civilization was costly and painful; it meant the renunciation of more immediate gratification and the relative devaluation of everything connected with immediate necessities of animal existence. Classical civilization was the beginning of the process of repression in which the self-identical subject, individually and collectively, was born.

Alternative views were rarely expressed. The striking exception was Friedrich Nietzsche's (1999) brilliant, and almost universally rejected, interpretation advanced in *The Birth of Tragedy*, originally published in

1872. Nietzsche characterized the orthodox modern view of classical civilization formed by Winckelmann and his followers as Appolonian. Civilization arose with an elite that was powerful, detached, and serenely confident in its own superiority. He contrasted this with a dark and turbulent Dionysian spirit that, he claimed, equally made its presence felt throughout classical culture. Excess, violence, and self-abandonment oscillated with calm self-control. Nietzsche views were rejected, ostensibly on technical philological grounds, and the idea that ancient civilization might be more than simply an early version of our conscious and rational identity, but the primal source of another, transgressive, unruly, creative and destructive self that modernity failed either properly to acknowledge or wholly to repress, lay dormant until the ferocity of twentieth century history invested his conjecture with frightening plausibility.

Throughout the latter part of the nineteenth century the exploration of ancient civilizations suggested a number of precursors and rivals to Greece and Rome. Extending the field of operations throughout Turkey, and east through the ancient Persian Empire and into North India enormously complicated the picture. Philological studies provided many clues that were hastily interpreted and encouraged quite grandiose conjectural histories of what was by then called Europe. Max Müller, for example, pushed the linguistic and spiritual history of Europe back beyond Egypt to what he believed was the primal source of all civilization centred on North India.

The diversity and richness of the material raised a new problem of classification. How many civilizations had there been? How might they be distinguished and characterized, not simply in terms of their localized historical and geographic range, but in terms of their inner coherence and achieved totality? And if all civilizations had in fact perished, would this not also be the fate of modern western civilization? So much, at least, was suggested by Oswald Spengler's popular dramatization of world history, *The Decline of the West*. The modern was already decadent and decaying; a view encouraged to some extent by the development of the idea of *entropy* in physics. Nature was running down, so was human society; the human motor was exhausted and could no longer build and rebuild the great structures of civilization (Rabinbach 1990).

The zenith of infatuation with civilizations as a socio-cultural totality was reached in the prolific and very different writings of Arnold Toynbee and Eric Voegelin. Toynbee's multi-volume work is curiously titled *A Study of History*, in which twenty three civilizations are characterized, and their rise and fall outlined. History, it seemed, had shifted from the universal narrative of the past leading to the present, to a typological game with an uncertain number of corpses, of which the present might become another. Voegelin, in a sociologically more sophisticated and equally monumental study, takes civilization as his basic unit of analysis and provides a comprehensive account focused on the emergence, development, and decline of religious world views as their central *motif*. Under the general heading of *Order in History* he analyzes civilizations in terms of their constructive, world-building processes. Linked to the work of Max Weber, and Wilhelm Dilthey the study of civilization is transmuted into an analysis of world-views.

The structural and typological notion of civilization is further dissolved in Norbert Elias's influential work *The Civilizing Process*. Elias takes a rather different meaning civilization as his central theme; the inculcation of manners. In an important respect this acknowledges the impact of modern democracy on the idea of civilization. No longer referring to an exclusive 'high' culture associated with the exercise of political and military power, civilization became an aspect of everyday behaviour. In a fully developed modern society civilization, in the sense of the continuous exercise of bodily self-control and the regulation of everyday social interaction through peaceful conventions, is accessible to all. The totality of civilization was dissolved in its transformation into civilized behaviour.

Civilization was always an uncertain totality. The boundaries of any designated civilization proved to be porous, the principles and world views that made them intelligible historical objects on closer inspection turned out to be composed of complex, unresolved and contending discourses.

PRIMITIVE AND ARCHAIC SOCIETY

Ancient civilizations were initial steps out of the mythic-sacred world, the unprecedented appearance in an undeveloped state of a self-identical subject; the maker of history. Modern historians, looking back, thought they caught a glimpse of themselves, as if in a clouded mirror. It was not always an encouraging image. The instability and ultimate incoherence of civilizations, their inhumanity, and ultimate failure raised worrying questions. Older than the oldest civilization, however, and still surviving in their original, or near original, form, many small-scale, isolated, and undeveloped societies provided a quite different and possibly more compelling model of social totality.

What anthropologists studied as primitive or archaic society were apparently isolated, small-scale, and untouched by modern or any other civilized society. In fact these groups were the dispersed remnant of once much larger and complex structures destroyed by colonization and, as in central Asia, not always western colonization. The primitive was constructed by systematic inversion of the idea of the modern; it was irrational, characterized by collective participatory consciousness, fetishisms, immediate contact with nature, superstition, magic, and minimally organized in terms of kinship. Anthropologists extended backwards a model of premodern community 'but in practice primitive society proved to be their own society (as they understood it) seen in a distorting mirror. For them modern society was defined above all by the territorial state, the monogamous family and private property. Primitive society therefore must have been nomadic, ordered by blood ties, sexually promiscuous and communist. There had also been a progression in mentality. Primitive man was illogical and given to magic. In time he had developed sophisticated religious ideas. Modern man, however, had invented science' (Kuper 1988: 5). In spite of being radically other than modern, the primitive was not alien and offered in its purest form a an important model of self-identical totality as the commonality of cosmos and human life, and the wholeness of the sacred world.

Émile Durkheim posed an interesting question in relation to this idea of the primitive. How could such a simple society be constituted as a totality? The very lack of internal differentiation and complexity made it difficult to understand how, to use an image from early modern theory of matter, it could be self-adhering. His solution was to suppose a social totality was formed through a *conscience collective*; that is, a common or collective consciousness. In the simplest societies people's lives were uniform and similar to one another; everyone had the same experiences of the world. They shared the same world in all its aspects, and could not imagine any other. For Durkheim an original 'social protoplasm' was formed into a totality through the moral force of 'solidarity'. Totality is not simply the operational integrity of a society, its viability as a functioning whole; this functionality, in fact, depends on the development of bonds of solidarity, which is simply the social relations of belonging. Solidarity is 'belonging' to society, and primitive society is constituted through 'mechanical solidarity'; that is, through relations of similitude in which people experience their belonging together. Solidarity is a primordial 'social fact'; it is something exterior to and constraining the individual. In fact, in primitive society there is nothing other than solidarity bonds; all relations partake in a striking manner, in the collective, and there is no separate, withdrawn existence of individuals. Most primitive societies are somewhat more complex, extended, and internally differentiated than the social protoplasm that Durkheim had in mind as his logical starting point. In fact the critical problem for primitive society is how to bring people together in order to generate and sustain solidarity. Particularly for hunter–gatherer societies people were dispersed over large distances for significant periods of time. Durkheim argued that the key role of religion, in such societies, is to bring people together in the celebration of specific, cyclically repeated rituals. The observance of rites held to be sacred (set apart and above everyday life) served to generate relations that might otherwise not exist, increased the 'dynamic density' of society and ended in the creation of solidarity bonds and a vivid *conscience collective*.

Durkheim's work has often been used somewhat against his own argument to suggest that modern society is less 'solidarity' than primitive society; that modern society lacks the moral cohesion that constitutes society as a totality. In fact Durkheim argues that modern society is constituted differently. The modern totality exists, first of all, in the purely rational and factual division of labour; in the necessary social relations subsumed in everyday life. Solidarity also develops, but of a distinctive 'organic' type. There is however, an undeniable sense of loss involved in the development out of primitive society. And this loss is expressed more clearly in an influential essay on the social character of the gift and gift relationships by Durkheim's student and nephew, Marcel Mauss.

This involves and important revaluation of the idea of the primitive as an original totality; not the undeveloped and simple so much as the primordially human and sociable. Still measured by the standard of the modern, the primitive exemplified what we had lost, rather than what had been gained, in the transformation of modernity. The original organic wholeness of society was the first totality; a form displayed in all its parts, processes, and aspects. Primitive society was founded on the 'total social phenomenon' rather than differentiated and structured through relationships of different sorts, economic, political, religious, and so on. A certain awkwardness in Durkheim's analysis was evident. Primitive society was 'all of a piece', yet required specific forms of social representation, religion and its sacred rites, to generate and maintain the totality. Totality seemed to refer to both the whole and an aspect of the whole that had the specific function of representing totality. Marcel Mauss, in analysing the gift as a 'total social' phenomenon avoided the problem of having to represent totality separately from its active performance in social life. In primitive societies, he argues, 'social phenomena are not discrete; each phenomenon contains all the threads of which the social fabric is composed. In these *total* social phenomena ... all kinds of social institutions find simultaneous expression: religious, legal, moral, and economic. In addition, the phenomena have their aesthetic aspect and they reveal morphological types (Mauss 1952, 1). The exchange of gifts is not, as it largely is in modern society, to a specific class of objects deemed appropriate to particular occasions, but involves all kinds of objects and, indeed, every aspect of social interaction; 'What they exchange is not exclusively goods and wealth, real and personal property, and things of economic value. They exchange rather courtesies, entertainments, rituals, military assistance, women, children, dances, and feasts; and fairs at which the market is but one element and the circulation of wealth but one part of a wide and enduring contract' (Mauss 1952).

Through the mutual obligations of gift relations solidarity is generated, expressed, and reinforced in an immediate way. It is not that gifts 'represent' the totality of society as a network of moral obligations and, at the same time, establish 'real' economic and political relations. In primitive society these are one in the same relation. The totality of society is preserved in all its parts and aspects without the need of a special integrative, symbolic medium, as it were, gluing things together. The collective reality, the totality of society, is continually and immediately present in all the activities of daily life.

The importance of the model of primitive society, then, was twofold. On the one hand, it confirmed the superiority of modern society in terms of its scale, complexity, mastery of nature, and rational understanding of the world. On the other hand it presented in its purest form the image of one kind, and perhaps the most successful and complete kind, of totality. The irony was that the primitive was ignorant of their own advantage. They lived immediately in their social totality and were unable to reflect on it. So the totality of the primitive could never be a model of self-identity. The consciousness of the primitive lacked self-understanding and self-consciousness, and it is here that Durkheim is more insightful than his talented student. As individual consciousness, in modern society, is itself a social form, and must in some sense rest on and represent society, self-identity had to be guaranteed by something other than mechanical solidarity and its glowing *conscience collective*. In modern society the totality of society had to be characterized by just those features of self-identity that were experienced individually. Reflexivity, that is to say, had to be built in to the social totality and otherwise would never have emerged in the consciousness of individuals. For this to occur, a specific 'function' of reflexivity had to appear in modern society. And it could only emerge in a specific modern form if it already existed in a potential form, in primitive society. Religion, for the primitive, thus, had to be a special symbolic relation, and a special representational field. Then modern self-identity and reflexivity could be understood through a long process of social change in which this original religious function was transformed and re-emerged as the psychic life of individuals. This is indicated, in fact, according to Durkheim, in the peculiar value that we place on the individual in modern society; the 'sacred' of modernity is the social totality represented in the experience of individual life.

The primitive and archaic were conflated in the context of late nineteenth-century evolutionary thought. The primitive was thought to be isolated and literally unchanging so that, never coming into contact with more progressive and developing society, preserved a living museum of human and cultural types.

WEST AND EAST

Ancient civilization and primitive society offered two contrasting images of self-identical totality; the former similar to, and the latter different from, us. Neither was sufficiently stable and transparent, however, to found modern self-identity. A vaguer designation, yet one destined to play a much greater role than either civilization or primitive society, is the notion of the west.

Clearly, the west cannot constitute an historical-geographical totality. 'West' is an arbitrary relational term; everywhere has its own west. West and east have no fixed point of reference. Contemporary 'western' societies include North America, Australia, and possibly Japan. Somewhat more definite, but not identical, is the related distinction of Europe and Asia. In any event all these terms are vague, change over time, and are difficult to divide one from another. Where is the boundary between Asia and its peninsula, as Braudel nicely calls Europe? Continents are also unstable and internally heterogeneous totalities (Richards 2003; Lewis and Wigen 1997).

The significance of the west as an idea of totality is that it seeks to characterize the origin of *modern* society in features of socio-cultural traditions that go back to ancient civilizations and establish that origin as a unique world event. The comparative historical sociology of Max Weber is pre-eminent in this context. Where Durkheim began with the present for which he constructed a conjectural starting point founded on its own principle of mechanical solidarity, Weber, also starting from the present, projected its immanent principle of rationalization into the past so that the entire historical narrative of western society fell under its aegis. The unparalleled richness of Weber's work is allied to extraordinary conceptual skill in presenting a sociological narrative that seemingly achieves the impossible. Modern society is grasped in its radical difference from the past while, at the same time, connecting it with a lengthy all-encompassing prehistory. For Weber rationalization is the central phenomenon of western society since its inception; but in its most recent, modern form it has as a consequence the separation of the present from its own past.

Weber's argument is often misrepresented. The process of rationalization is not uniquely western; it is a general developmental process at work in every large-scale social formation. What is peculiar to western society is the depth, generality, and ubiquity of the process. More significantly, Weber views radical rationalization as a *consequence* of the fundamental religious position of western society. It is the developing religious world view of western society that makes coherent and meaningful the complex, differentiated structure of its political, economic, and social life, and distinguishes it from other major world civilizations with their own distinctive religious presuppositions. Weber's original sociological insight in fact leads him away from the central modern narrative that founds western civilization in the rational spirit of Greek Antiquity. He traces western civilization, rather, to origins in Ancient Judaism and its religious orientation. What emerges in Ancient Judaism, and remains central to the entire subsequent development of the west, is an uncompromising monotheistic, transcendental, and personal religious world view that is made essential to the conduct of everyday life. God, as distinct from pagan gods, does not share the life of human beings but remains absolutely apart from His creation. God imposes upon humanity commandments to be observed in everyday life but, as a consequence of His incomprehensible mystery, humanity is driven to make sense in its own terms of his world and its relation to God. It is the gulf, and tension, between the everyday world and the religious promise that stimulates the expansion of rational thought and rational action beyond its fugitive presence in archaic society.

Polytheistic religions posited a world that was an 'unordered miscellany of accidental entities' (Weber 1965: 2), whereas monotheism required the world be made coherent as a meaningful whole. And, as distinct from varied cultic and magical practices, monotheistic religion required a continuous regulated relationship with the world and with God. A permanent priesthood emerged, armed with doctrine 'marked by the development a rational system of religious concepts... and a systematic and distinctive religious ethic' (Weber 1965: 29). The absolutely unfounded, non-rational religious assertion, that is, resulted in a powerful tension with the world that was the condition for rationalization; 'The conflict between empirical reality and this conception of the world as a meaningful totality, which is based on a religious postulate, produces the strongest tensions in man's inner life as well as his external relationship to the world' (Weber 1965: 59).

The tension between the human world and religious assumptions leads not only to the rationalization of the world but to a rational understanding of those assumptions; 'The more the development tends toward the conception of a transcendental unitary god who is universal, the more there arises the problem of how the extraordinary power of a god may be reconciled with the imperfection of the world that he has created and rules over' (Weber 1965: 138–139).

The discrepancy between transcendental norms and everyday life cannot ultimately be resolved. In the west institutional compromises develop that provide specialized intermediaries between the human and divine, and routinized means of acquiring salvation. Tradition, however, and not only in a specifically religious context, is always threatened by the renewal of founding assumptions of transcendentalism. The process of rationalization, thus, while in tension with everyday life serves primarily in the premodern period to clarify, and order a theological discourse. And, in fact, according to Weber, the Reformation is primarily a consequence of this continuing process. What Luther and Calvin asserted was, in effect, the ultimate, logically coherent, and internally consistent version of western religious assumptions. At the same time it involved a complete overthrowing of prior religious practices. If the idea of an absolutely transcendental, omnipotent creator God upon whom every person depended for their ultimate salvation, was grasped as a reality, then the religious individual was left in an utterly helpless position; 'the Calvinist god's absolute inexplicability, utter remoteness from every human criterion, and unsearchableness as to his motives' destroyed the efficacy of every tradition bound mechanism of salvation.

For Weber, the long-term consequences of the Reformation lay partly in its fostering a specific worldly ethic as part of the emerging psychic economy of modern society. The Protestant Ethic formed as the afterglow of the Reformation, and was its first compromise with the realities of everyday life. The extreme anxiety of the believer in Calvin's god was relieved by continual hard work treated as a vocation. This did not itself guarantee salvation, but it made bearable life in the face of ultimate uncertainty. This ethical life-view was the immediate antecedent to the spirit of capitalism that stimulated and made meaningful the institutional and everyday practices of modern rational capitalism. But what was even more significant, for Weber, was the implication of the Reformation for the meaning of religious faith and *ipso facto* all other ultimate values. For modern society all ultimate values became matters of conscience, and everyday life is organized exclusively in relation to secular goals. In modern society rationalization takes the form of the continuous adaptation of technical means for the achievement of specified, empirically verifiable, goals; whereas for it long prehistory rationalization was a process of continuous clarification, and interrelation, of religiously inspired values. Rationalization underwent a profound, religiously motivated transformation that had the effect of establishing a completely new context for its meaning and operation.

Weber's complex narrative cannot be reduced to any simple idea that the west is inherently more 'rational' than any other major historical tradition, or that any other tradition is, as a result, inferior or less valuable. Weber makes clear that ultimate values, the character of which he uses as a means of identifying major world traditions, are incommensurable. It is not possible to make relative judgements of value; this is just what is meant by 'ultimacy'. The decision among conflicting values is always an existential decision, rather than an intellectual or aesthetic judgement. There is, nonetheless, an obvious sense in which Weber's account is focused on the emergence and transformation of western values that leant themselves to the continuing development of rationalization in all its forms. And while, in Weber's view, the contemporary consequences of rationalization are far from benign, he clearly argues that its unprecedented grip on the institutional structure and organization of everyday life is at the root of modern western economic, military, and political ascendancy.

The detail of Weber's historical sociology is not here the central issue. What counts is the extent to which he succeeds in framing an idea of the west as a coherent socio-historical totality. And in this context, his own writings suggest caution. Weber was reluctant to commit his work to a concept of society as an essential point of reference. He prefers to think in terms of social groups of different sorts, pursuing a variety of interests, including intellectual and aesthetic interests, contending for power and, where possible, establishing their rule. Emerging religious and other world views do not characterize societies as such, but the specific social groups that, for varying periods of time and with varying success, are able to dominate others. The finality of an ultimate value, even where it is successfully promoted by its carrier and becomes the dynamic historical vision of a powerful society, is never identified with a social totality. Society is always differentiated, unequal, and unjust. It constitutes a totality only to the extent that one or other group is able to enforce its rule and, thus, can claim, against all alternatives and challengers, that its world view is ultimately valid (Bendix 1960). In spite of the clear thematic focus on rationalization, it remains the case that, whether in relation to ultimate value, world view, and social structure, Weber reveals multiplicity, differentiation, conflict, and transformation rather than unity and totality.

Weber takes seriously the idea of the west, but, in the end, cannot present a coherent and convincing narrative of its totality. More recent studies have tended, rather, to treat the west as an important political-ideological notion that lacks real substance. The west is now likely to be treated academically as a significant, and misconstrued, totality intimately related to the development of modern self-identity as 'rational'. The modern west conceived of itself as uniquely advanced technologically, scientifically, and morally. Other significant world cultures, or civilizations, were, by contrast, viewed as undeveloped, unscientific, and sensual. Edward Said's (1978) influential and timely book, *Orientalism*, has already become orthodox. It is something of a commonplace to charge modern European bourgeois culture with denigrating of the other. And, of course, this is all too evidently justified. Oriental was sensual, lazy, slovenly, and uncivilized in the contemporary meaning of manners and behaviour. They were unreliable, and untruthful, they resembled children. Actually all the leading characteristics of the other, officially renounced, as it were, by respectable western middle-class men, were also admirable in their own way and the subject, as Said points out, of secret longing. Sexual freedom, spiritual creativity, social sensitivity; all existed elsewhere and had been sacrificed to reason and the demands of the market place. It was a cost worth paying, but a cost nonetheless.

Said makes his point boldly but, as a result falls into an 'occidentalism' of his own in which the west is implicitly characterized as arrogant, over bearing, complacent, domineering, insensitive, and so on. Prior to Said's refreshing text, however, John M. Steadman's *The Myth of Asia* (1970) provided a nuanced and comprehensive view of Orientalism, that paid more attention to the diversity of the Orient, and was more alert to oriental misconceptions of the west and of their own societies.

Steadman points out that the contrast between calculative and commercial west and spiritual-sensuous orient does not bear scrutiny at any level, a view amply supported by much contemporary scholarship. The scientific and technological precocity of China, for example, has been highlighted in Joseph Needham's exceptionally impressive works. Immediately prior to the emergence of modern society in Europe it was far from obvious that the west constituted a significant world region at all, far less the nascent totality of a world dominating economic and political system (Abu-Lughod 1989; Levathes 1994; Pomeranz 2000). In many ways the 'east' was always in and part of the 'west' and vice versa (Goody 1996; Montgomery 2000).

In recent, challenging, and insightful works by scholars familiar with Greek and Chinese sources, however, the distinctiveness of east and west as cultural totalities has been reassessed and reasserted (Jullien 1999, 2004, 2007; Lloyd 1996, 2002, 2005; Faure 2003; Hall and Ames 1995, 1998; Schwartz 1985; Shankman and Durrant 2002). François Jullien, for example, in a fascinating work argues that 'When compared with the elaboration of Western thought, the originality of the Chinese lies in their indifference to any notion of *telos*, a final end for things, for they sought to interpret reality solely on the basis of itself, from the perspective of a single logic inherent in the actual processes in motion' (Jullien 1999: 17). This is a view that Weber would have endorsed. It is the transcendence, as against the immanence, of all social values that distinguishes the west from the east. Even accepting this, however, it has to be treated cautiously as a comparison between the world views and cultures of two dominant social groups, rather than self-identical totalities in which are subsumed all internal social differences.

THE MODERN STATE

Hegel viewed the modern state as the institutional realization of absolute reason. He argued that modern society in the usual sense given to it since the early seventeenth century meant civil society, rigorously conceptualized by Thomas Hobbes, as a collectivity of private individuals whose wants were insatiable and whose interests were insatiable. The resulting 'war of all against all' could be overcome only by a centralized authority, in Hobbes's view, a particular person, a monarch or emperor. Hegel argues that the modern state emerged from this period of absolutist rule, replacing personal command with institutional and impersonal rule in which were embedded universal criteria of justice. The distinction between civil society and the state, in his view, was akin to the difference between consciousness and self-consciousness. The state was the higher development of humanity, its universal ethical conscience; an ideal humanity. The state, thus, rightly regulated and controlled the life of civil society in the interests of humanity's own best interests. The state in fact protected people from their own less developed nature. The state is the self-identity of the modern human as universal being. Kant's ethical injunction to self-restraint, in the end, was insufficient; compulsion was required to ensure that people acted in their ultimate best interest. The passions are overcome first by those willing to suppress (sublate) their lower nature in a form of life that gained universal value as reason.

This description was applied to post-revolutionary reactionary states throughout Europe. Hegel's own reaction to revolution had moved on from the excited moment of the *Phenomenology of Spirit* (1977/1807) to the authoritarian rule of the 1830s. Younger, radical intellectuals sought to still follow the earlier work and Marx, impressively, mounted a critique of his doctrine of the state, a critical analysis that turned eventually into his full-scale critical analysis of modern capitalist society. Marx argued that, in fact, the classical account of civil society was misleading. Modern society is not an atomised maelstrom of private individuals driven by inner, unexaminable passions. Rather, it is already a well defined social field of contending organized interests; social classes. The state, far from transcending private conflicts and expressing universal human values, represents the interests of a particular social class; the capitalist or bourgeois class who own the modern means of production in the form of private property and exercise rights over it. The working class, who are forced to live by selling their labour power as a commodity, are subordinated to the state as citizens bound by its laws and jurisdiction; laws framed and executed in the interests of the property owning class. The state disguises its partiality; expressing the particular interests of the capitalists as the general interest, imposing its laws as universal principles, claiming for itself the privilege of universal reason.

Both Hegel and Marx treat the state as a particular kind of experiential totality; the disagreement is over its scope. For Marx it is an adequate expression and practical political defence of the interests of the bourgeois class, including their cultural interests which did aspire to universal validity. The totality in question is not society, far less humanity, but a social class; the class who made the modern world in its image.

For Hegel and Marx the state is a political totality, it represents, organizes, and controls the life of society in the interests of some part of it. It is a totality that is not coterminous with society. In Max Weber's monumental historical sociology the modern state emerges in a new way, as a centralized 'imperatively co-ordinating body', ultimately with interests of its own. The totality that is the state is organized around the exercise of domination; it is in the business of power. Weber insists that the state does not exist to serve the interests of one section of society over another; albeit it in practice it often does precisely that. Rather it has an interest of its own, which is in the continued concentration of its own power and its continuous exercise to guarantee an orderly society. Weber insists that the modern state rests ultimately on the use of force and violence; 'A compulsory political organization with continuous operations will be called a "state" insofar as its administrative staff successfully upholds the claim to the *monopoly* of the *legitimate* use of physical force in the enforcement of its order' (Weber 1979, 1:54).

However, the effectiveness of the state depends upon its capacity to mobilise *authority*, or *legitimate domination*. Legitimation depends in modern society on observing correct procedural rules, enacting laws through constitutional government, and organizing the rule of the state in terms of impersonal criteria. This is the basis of the *claims* ruling groups make in justifying their rule; Weber points out the ultimate success and sustainability of this rule depends still on force; legitimation is a form of self-justification, not primarily a mechanism of imposing rule by an ideological means.

Weber's stress on the role of force and violence in the formation of the modern state, as much as in the founding of ancient empires and premodern and non western societies, is fully justified. More recent research has highlighted the significance of warfare and military revolution for the emergence of the modern state. During the second half of the sixteenth century royal households and courts began to use mercenaries to augment or replace the uncertain military resources of the nobility. Using the surplus rural population as fighting men under the direct control of 'professional' soldiers proved to be highly effective and led to the formation of small regular armies. These forces were held in a continuous state of readiness and constituted 'expendable' troops. Commanders, depending on the patronage of the monarch, had a strong interest in short and decisive campaigns. They sought decisive engagements with consequentially high losses. The strategic balance swung heavily in favour of massed infantry over less controllable cavalry. Provisioning troops usually meant the destruction of local communities, and the seizure of 'booty' was a major motive and form of payment throughout the military hierarchy. The new social-technology of war required new military virtues. Effective forces were now composed of a mass of soldiers immediately responsive to officers' commands. The commander's skill consisted primarily in a clear tactical plan and clear battle instructions. Warfare no longer depended on the valour and traditional fighting skill of individuals. Throughout the latter part of the seventeenth and eighteenth centuries military training techniques were developed. Military personnel were separated from the working population and their communities, housed in barracks, and subjected to rigorous training. Habits of obedience and the development of *esprit de corps* became increasingly intensive and sophisticated. Military training became one of the key models for the development of modern 'disciplinary regimes'. Schools, in particular, specialized in 'moral training' that inculcated habits of obedience. Michel Foucault's *Discipline and Punish* draws attention to the significance of this process. The 'self-regulating' character of modern society, he argues, depends not only on the free exercise of reason (the Enlightenment conception of modern society), but also on *moral* regulation. In the early modern period regulation took the form of spectacular public displays of the overwhelming power of the state. This involved impressive architectural construction, public festivals and parades, as well as executions. 'Training' was (more or less) effective in 'internalizing' the power of the state as the self-regulation of 'respectable' citizens.

Armies and their training were expensive. From the late sixteenth century, states had supported military activities in part from taxation. A strong positive relation developed between the growth and centralization of state powers and increasing levels, uniformity, and generality of taxation. The major effect of the military revolution was to increase the size and power of the state (Glete 2002). Warfare rapidly developed as a technique of state-formation. European states fought each other to establish territorial boundaries *and* top establish firm control over their own population. Warfare, through taxation and the direction of economic resources, extended the power of the state over society as a whole. The growth of state power, rooted in the exercise of military force, increasingly became autonomous from other sources of social power. In particular the state established its interests as distinct from those of its original sponsors; either an aristocratic court (Spain) or a rising merchant-bourgeois class (England).

The issue here is not to establish the validity of a particular view of the modern state but simply to point to the variety of plausible interpretations of the state as a particular kind of totality. What these views have in common, however, is an identification of the state as a concentration of power that exercises control and direction; that is as a part rather than a whole, an effective mechanism rather than a totality.

NATION

The idea of the nation was also born in the modern period and is closely related to the emergence of the modern state. The territoriality of the state defined a heterogeneous population bound by its laws and subject to its authority. In principle the nation includes all those within its boundary, but the totality of the nation is defined as a people rather than a state or a society. The people, as distinct from subjects or citizens, are defined by a common culture and heritage, a shared language and customs. At its simplest it is the idea of a life in common. This may or may not include an ethnic identity, that is to say a common ancestry, passed down through intermarriage.

The nation defined the people in a distinctive way; ideally the boundary of the state and the nation were the same. Throughout Europe in the late sixteenth century societies differentiated into functional and qualitatively distinct groupings of estates, orders, and communities, and were dominated by nobilities dissolved and began to reform as nations. The term (new born) referred in principle to all the members of a single territorially based society, rather than corporate elites within it (Greenfeld 1993: 6). This, of course, was an unrealized conception. Although the nation emerged at approximately the same time as the state and is clearly related to it, there is no simple connection here, and the connection became more evident only in retrospect. In the early modern period the emerging state was in many ways in competition with the ideal of the nation for the allegiance of the population. Once again the critical role of the Reformation is significant in the emergence of modernity. One of the most significant consequences of the Reformation was the translation of the Bible into vernacular languages, a process pioneered brilliantly by Martin Luther himself. If nothing was to stand between the individual believer and God it was important that the mass of people could read scripture for themselves, which meant in their own language rather than the Latin of an historic, and more or less pagan, empire. This challenged the authority of the Catholic Church, and also of the emerging state, both of which were threatened by the zealous independence of a large number of 'its' people.

The development of a vernacular language coincided with the spread of printed books and not only made more available devotional as well as unorthodox works, it made possible for the first time the sense of a common culture shared by many people outside the immediate community and available outside the authoritative institutions of ecclesiastical schools (Anderson 1991; Eisenstein 1983). Though the impact of printing has been somewhat exaggerated (Johns 1998), the general adoption of national languages for official purposes is the first great victory of the nation over the state.

In many cases the development of nationhood lagged behind and was a sort of after image of the dynamic development of the state. Warfare between states and the mobilization of increasingly large numbers to fight them was instrumental here. Nationhood, rather than the interest of the state, became the primary declared justification for warfare.

Internal struggles also adopted the language and imagery of the nation. Revolutionary change in the aftermath of the French Revolution was driven by class interests and the development of a modern state, but was made through the rhetoric of the people and the national idea.

The crucial difference between the, equally imaginary, totality of state and nation, is evident in an interesting debate between Immanuel Kant and his one time student and collaborator Johann Gottfried Herder (Zammito 2002). Kant expressed most fully the idea of modernity as enlightenment; the claims of universal reason. His *Critique of Pure Reason* set out the formal conditions for any possible experience. This was hugely influential for many reason; but one of the earliest critical responses and the most interesting came from Herder. He argued that the idea of pure reason was illusory; simply, there was no such thing nor could there be. Reason was always local; there was only reason embedded in the actual social life and practices of specific groups of people in particular places and times. Reason was embedded in language and every language uniquely created a world of experience that remained distinctive and characteristic of those who lived through it. Herder's idea of language as expressive of the spirit of its community of users became the starting point for the development of the Romantic idea of nationhood as the soul or spirit of the people. The actually modern totality of the people was transformed into a premodern myth of ethnic community. von Herder claims, for example, that 'each language has its distinctive national character' (Herder 1992: 30); our experience is formed through the sensibility embedded in a particular language, not the universality of reason applied to experience.

After the 1848 revolutions throughout Europe the idea of the nation was increasingly invoked in a quite self-conscious way as a response to sharpening class conflict. As international economic competition temporarily replaced armed conflict, class conflict intensified. Industrialization and urbanization brought widespread and drastic impoverishment, disease, insecurity, and hardship to the mass of working people. The emerging totality of class was softened through appeals to a purportedly national interest. New emblems of the nation were invented, ceremonies hastily rediscovered, pastimes apparently hallowed by tradition introduced as collective celebrations of being a collective, a constituting a totality of people in spite of discrepant life experiences and grossly unequal life chances (Hobsbawm 1992; Hobsbawm and Ranger 1992).

Nationhood, and especially ethnic nationality, has become prominent in recent years and demonstrate the effectiveness, in particular circumstances, of self-identical totalities modelled on myths of the past. Patrick Geary despairingly, seeks to put the record straight:

> Any historian who has spent much of his career studying this earlier period of ethnic formation and migration can only look upon the development of politically conscious nationalism and racism with apprehension and disdain, particularly when these ideologies appropriate and pervert history as their justification. This pseudo-history assumes, first, that the peoples of Europe are distinct, stable and objectively identifiable social and cultural

units, and that they are distinguished by language, religion, custom, and national character, which are unambiguous and immutable. These peoples were supposedly formed either in some impossibly remote moment of pre-history, or else the process of ethnogenesis took place at some moment during the Middle Ages, but then ended for all time ... Actually, there is noth-ing particularly ancient about either the peoples of Europe or their sup-posed rights to political autonomy. The claims to sovereignty that Europe is seeing in Eastern and Central Europe today are a creation of the nineteenth century, an age that combined the romantic political philosophies of Rousseau and Hegel with "scientific" history and Indo-European philology to produce ethnic nationalism.

(Geary, 2003: 11–13)

MODERN JAPAN

Interrelations between west and east, state and nation, society and indi-vidual make clear the extent to which all such totalities and unities are constructed from continuous, complex processes of translation, inter-pretation, and interaction. It is helpful to focus the discussion at this point on a particular, significant example; the emergence and development of modern Japanese society.

Modernity emerged in Europe and Japan at around the same time, fol-lowed distinctive trajectories, and came to maturity as specific experien-tial unities identified with the collective life of the people. Societies were established as 'imagined communities' formed through shared history and experience and identified by unique proper names. These societies were, in fact, temporary worlds crystallized from the deconstructive flux of cultural translation that continued, almost invisibly, to form global net-works into which they would, or will, ultimately dissolve. The processes through which modernity emerged from pre-existing territorial, linguis-tic, and cultural traditions were not everywhere the same. Indeed, modern societies are characterized by imprecise 'family resemblances', rather than the possession of a limited number of essential features (Goody 2004). Thus, while it no longer makes sense to regard Japanese development as an exception to a normative standard set by Europe, it remains important to acknowledge the distinctive trajectories of *both* Europe and Japan as self-defining cultural fields.

The complex interrelation of state and nation west and east modern and traditional is brought into focus by returning to one of the contextual fields already used, Japanese society is a significant example that forces important changes of perspective. It is not a question of balancing a western, eurocentric view of the world with a different, eastern perspective. Rather, what is at issue is decomposing *both* ends of such a relation to reveal the global interaction involved in the constitution, simultaneously, of both terms and the relation between them.

Eisenstadt, in a substantial study that exaggerates the separateness of Japanese historical development, nonetheless provides a penetrating insight into the sources of the difference between European and Japanese civilization. Locating the emergence of major cultural fields in the ancient world, he claims that, 'the most important feature of the Japanese historical experience is that it is the only non-Axial civilization to have had a continuous, autonomous – and very turbulent – history up to and including modern times' (1996, 13). The Axial age model posits the fundamental tension between immanent and transcendental values and knowledge that emerged around the sixth to fourth centuries BCE in a number of ancient empires stretching from the eastern Mediterranean to north Indian. In Japan from its earliest history, the resistance of forms of life and reflection to transcendental systematization and the seizure of ultimate values in terms of meaningful interiority established a pattern that remained significant throughout its modern development:

> Unlike modern Western – and after also Asian – national or nationalist ideologies, the ideology of the Meiji regime did not formulate the distinctiveness of the Japanese collectivity in relation to some universal religion or civilization of which it was a part ... Building on the basic conception of the *kokutai* as developed by the nativist schools of the Tokugawa period ... it defined the Japanese nation as a unique type of collectivity, defined in primordial social-natural terms.
>
> (Eisenstadt 1996: 32)

In the specific context of emerging modernity this difference takes on a strikingly distinctive institutional pattern. While modern European societies created themselves through the mutually reinforcing processes of state formation, administrative centralization, and warfare (Poggi 1978, 1990; Glete 2002), Japan emerged as a distinctive political and cultural unity from a 'medieval' period of endemic warfare. The Japanese polity founded by the Tokugawa in 1603 succeeded in maintaining its rule for more than 250 years, in disarming the samurai, and in pacifying regional and lineage based conflicts, but without establishing a strong, centralized, and authoritative state.

The unique system of rule created by the Shogunate was, first of all, the product of military supremacy. During the second half of the sixteenth century the Tokugawa were able to subjugate all their rivals; and while it has been claimed that Japan never underwent the military revolution that characterized early modern state formation in Europe, it is certainly the case that their ultimate victory depended on the use of western firearms introduced by Portuguese traders in Nagasaki and, even more significantly, on the ruthless destruction of the enemy through sheer force of numbers (Totman 2000: 199–221). The growing dominance of massed foot soldiers over smaller numbers of highly trained mounted warriors transformed armed combat. It placed a premium on defensive positions, logistical effectiveness, and tactical manipulation of organized and highly disciplined fighting groups. The steeply rising costs of such warfare gave the Tokugawa an advantage they were able to exploit, further driving up the economic and organizational costs of taking to the field. The ruthless pursuit of ultimate victory by the Tokugawa in fact signaled the end of traditional warfare and, in part, they were successful just because, in advance and more completely than their rivals, they were willing to abandon old conventions.

But whereas the European military revolution, which comprised similar technological and social transformations, was related directly to *political* centralization and an emerging administrative apparatus that continued to rest ultimately on the threat of violence, the Tokugawa regime, having won the day, relied on their economic power and ingenious new mechanisms of social control to sustain its rule. Regional control was ceded to local rulers (*Daimyo*) who were allocated revenues in proportion to the rice production of their region and, in return, rather than furnish military services were made responsible for 'public works' of all sorts. Crucially, this involved establishing an effective road network; making hitherto isolated regions more accessible and controllable. In the new capital, Edo (present day Tokyo), the Shogun established a political-administrative centre separate from the historic aristocratic-political centre of Kyoto. However, he made his presence felt in Kyoto through the construction of a magnificent residence in a modern style that rivaled the imperial palace. In addition to having a permanent presence through close family members and officials in Kyoto, he imposed strict residence requirements on all *Daimyo* and their households. They were required to establish a residence in Edo in which they to be personally present every alternate year, and some members of their household were required to be present at all times.

The system had important implications for the future development of Japan. The system required the first full scale land survey, which was carried out in a highly detailed fashion, and included the production of the first usable maps of the country which could now be visualized as a whole (Berry 2006). Additionally, the need to transport rice for tax payments, then have it distributed as food, had far reaching implications for the centralization of internal trading in Osaka and the development in connection with it of varied and sophisticated financial institutions, including the first effective futures market. One of the most striking features of the entire Tokugawa period is the dramatic growth in urbanization. Edo, Kyoto, and Osaka, were only the most spectacular examples of a general process that made Japan by the mid-eighteenth century the most highly urbanized population in the world (McClain *et al.* 1994). Yet Japan remained a pre-industrial society; the movement from rural to urban was not associated with the transition from an agricultural to an industrial economy.

In the emergence of modern Japan the traditional warrior group, the samurai, were effectively disarmed and socially transformed. The new regime suppressed all *private* conflict resolution through arms and forbade the samurai to draw their swords in public. These traditional weapons became badges of office as the samurai took on new governmental functions, which did not require qualities of personal honour, but for which they received a stipend; 'The Tokugawa samurai were thought of as persons who combined the roles of the aristocracy, the military, and the bureaucracy, three functions that were increasingly divided among distinctively different social groups in early modern Europe' (Ikegami 1995: 184). The samurai became urbanized and pacified; many were impoverished, and many who were not became patrons and customers of new urban arts. The performance of civility became the key integrative feature of Tokugawa regime (Ikegami 2007). As this became well established its aesthetic values and forms in turn were elevated into the sources and substance of Japanese national culture.

The idea that a distinctive spirit underlay Japan's modern development was made more plausible by the relative isolation in which its cultural unification had been formed. Culturally shaped in the nativist school of thought which, in fact, assimilated many aspects of western as well as

Chinese culture. Christians had been expelled in the 1630s and travel to and from Japan severely restricted thereafter. However, a significant relation with both China and the west was sustained throughout the period, particularly in the southwest of the country where Nagasaki remained open to trade and intellectual contact. 'Western learning' took root there and, through translation of Portuguese and Dutch as well as Chinese translations of western works, resulted in the assimilation of various aspects of modern western medicine, botany, and other sciences (Blussé *et al.* 2000).

It was from this region of Japan that the Confucian ideal of self-cultivation and modern western notions of individualism, entrepreneurship, and social mobility were merged into a new progressive idea of Japanese modernism. Well before Perry arrived to force one-sided trade agreements on Japan, disaffected political elites in Satsuma and Choshu together with the regime's own 'service intelligentsia', had been calling for a general opening to the west as the prerequisite for all future development (Huber 1981). The final collapse of Shogunal power in 1868, though involving military action, was a less intense and protracted affair than its inauguration. And, following the pattern set by the Shogun, the new regime immediately declared itself to be a restoration rather than a revolution (Jensen 1995).

The Meiji Restoration, a three-decade long process of institution building and cultural consolidation, projected modern Japan as simultaneously rooted in the unique character of its people and wholly committed to progressive, western oriented change. The spirit of Japaneseness was given living form in the unbroken continuity of the restored imperial lineage and in public celebration of re-established, and in many cases newly invented, traditions (Gluck 1985; Fujita 1996). At the same time the Emperor himself wore western dress and embraced 'progress and enlightenment' as the urgent need of the time. For the Meiji reformers modernization meant westernization; indeed, the renewal of imperial ceremony and sacralization of tradition mirrored the latest trends in European nation building (Hobsbawm and Ranger 1992). Throughout Europe nation building during this period had been designed to promote social and cultural integration in response to class, regional, and gender conflicts engendered by over a century of industrialization, and to mobilize the population for the increasing intensity of economic and imperial political competition. In Japan, however, nation building was a mechanism through which the nascent state appealed to a culturally homogenized population as a means of increasing its political power and administrative effectiveness. In global terms the state lagged behind the nation, while in Europe the nation lagged behind the state. A modern society, it was claimed, required advanced education, a dynamic industrializing economy, and a strong centralized state.

GLOBALITY

The recent resurgence of global history has already gone some way towards undermining confidence in the coherence of large-scale totalities, as concepts and as socio-cultural entities, in which history is normally written. It is not just the casual assumption and massive orthodoxy of national histories that has come under scrutiny, but the meaningfulness and actuality of continents, countries, epochs, peoples, cultures, and so on (Duarra 1995; Crossley 2008; Hodgson 1974; Reiss 2002). This has to be distinguished from the post-colonial literature that champions a previously suppressed narrative and view of the world, and obscured the role of minority populations, marginalized groups and, above all, the major historical actors colonized in the hectic expansion of capitalist modernity.

Global, in this sense, is not a totality, but the largest arena of historical interaction; an unfolding region or field with an open and indeterminate horizon.

Duarra, for example, refocuses historical studies on global questions outside the narrow conception of the western model of state and nation, and questions more generally the privilege of modernity as the sole constructive force of large-scale political identity. The approach of global history challenges the assumption that a cohesive historical subject can exist at all, or that there are any fundamental differences between the modern historical subject, misconceived as the nation, and earlier forms of collective life.

The deconstructive tendencies of global historical perspectives provide fresh insight into the formation of the mythic totalities of the present. But this does not efface the significant difference between modernity and premodern society. The distinction is not between imagined and real totalities but, rather, the manner in which they are constituted. The imagined totality of modernity has as its essential characteristic the rejection of the past and its dependence on quasi-naturalistic and spiritual categories. In principle, modern totalities are formed transparently in relation to newly emerging collective and interactive subjectivity.

ATTRIBUTION

As distinct from structural and regional totalities; aspects and characteristics of individuals and groups constituted originally in different ways seem unlikely to found totalities. But in surprising ways the emergence in the recent past of identity politics of, primarily, race, gender, and disability provide impressive evidence for the formation of self-identical totalities founded on characteristics rather than whole social actors. In these instances characteristics become categories and then communities; the life of the person or group is shaped in every way by the possession of a specific characteristic.

Exploitation, suppression, and rejection are the common experiences that found such self-identities. The totality of race or gender, for example, is primarily a consequence of the development of social relations in which these aspects were used as classificatory principles for the unequal treatment of human beings. The universal identity (humanity) is differentiated (men and women) in such a way as systematically to disadvantage women, whatever the situation. Consequently the devalued attribute becomes the point around which a general identity forms; and serves to identify common interests and the possibility forming a community of interests, and possibly life styles and cultures more generally.

There are two puzzling aspects to such developments. First, why should people identify positively with a devalued self-image? And, second, why should such attributes be devalued in the first place? Nietzsche provides a clue to the first problem. In a famous essay on the origins and meaning of religious valuation of morality in western society he coined the term *ressentiment* to describe the process of repression and inversion which occurred in the religious consciousness of early Christians (Nietzsche 2008). Within the Greek and later Roman empires most Christians were part of occupied colonies in which any resistance to imperial rule was ruthlessly suppressed. Christianity, during its first three centuries suffered brutal attacks whenever and wherever its unorthodox religious ideas and practices could be interpreted politically as critical of established rule. Early Christian communities and scattered groups were in a powerless and insecure position. Nietzsche suggests that in this situation of suspended rebellion, forced to dissimulate and conceal their real beliefs, Christianity was profoundly changed. From the natural Greek mode of valuation, seizing the evidently good and avoiding the bad; the Christian vision of the world was organized in terms of good, which, as the preserve of colonial rulers, was unattainable, and evil, which described the fallen state of humanity. But redemption was assured through self-identification with the fallen state of sin. Human weakness, humility, vulnerability, and passivity were revalued as the 'highest' human attributes. The Christians identified with the colonial rulers' devalued image of a weak and pitiful captive population, but transferred to this image the higher value of religious suffering and future redemption. In a similar way, for some (and only some) who are treated as generally inferior by virtue of their gender, race, or impairment these attributes may be transformed into the focus and carrier of higher values. Femininity, for example, rather than being rejected as itself a prejudicial stereotype and ideology of suppression, may be embraced in a positive light as the exclusive self-identity of women. Similarly racial stereotypes can be made the focus of a new positive self-identity rather than simply rejected as a baseless but debasing characterization. An important feature of this situation is that both the original attribution and the transformation of *ressentiment* assume a natural connection between the categorical and the characterological aspects of identity. Women and a range of characteristics loosely grouped together as 'feminine' are viewed as 'going together' in a natural way; the issue is just how femininity (emotional sensitivity, capacity for nurturing, patience, and so on) should be evaluated as human traits. Self-identity which begins with an imposed and devalued image is transformed, according to Nietzsche, where the despised group are powerless in the face of a ruthless aggressor, and make a psychological adjustment of suppressing their original sense of identity and self worth. The position of women, racial minorities, and the disabled are not often as starkly subordinate as that of early Christians. But where the key attribute is viewed as 'natural' it is assumed that there is nothing that can be done to change the fundamental situation.

Contemporary identity politics makes claim and counter claim formed in just such a way. The entanglement of identity issues with naturalistic fallacies is difficult to understand. The essential feature of modern society is just that self-identity is its only essential identity and that identity is formed as a project just because it is without natural foundation or determination, on the one hand, or Divine guidance, on the other. Women and men can, and do, display all the characteristics usually assembled under the heading 'masculine' as well as 'feminine', and any assertion of exclusivity in relation to attributes is unconvincing. As, indeed, they are for national, ethnic, religious, or any other category treated as a 'real' totality.

And this raises the second question all the more acutely. It might be plausible to see subordinate groups responding to attribution with the identity politics of *ressentiment*; it is not, after all, a simple matter of rejecting a description but of living with, and overthrowing, a complex and continuously active network of institutional assumptions, regulations, and discriminatory practices seemingly based upon naturalistic fallacies. But it is implausible that these discriminatory practices should have arisen in the first place. For a modern society gender, race, religious conviction, sexuality are no different to nationhood, ethnicity, or world view. No totality is actually complete and systematic. The very idea of self-identity requires a radical rejection of all classificatory processes that make naturalistic claims. Modern society *should* be a society whose members, individual and group, parts, and aspects are freely constituted *social* relations. The real difficulty is to explain why the bourgeois class, the group most self-consciously identified with modernity, should itself have created a society in which organized social life is carried on in terms of premodern assumptions.

SOCIETY

Is society always experienced as a distinctive reality, with a specific structure, and characteristics of its own? We are used to thinking this way. Especially for contemporary sociologists this seems to be self-evidently the case. Wherever people regard reality differently this is simply a result of the kind of society in which, in fact, they live. Most societies conceal themselves and appear, fugitively, in minor roles and fragmentary parts. But, insists the sociologist, this is an illusion generated by the very relations that constitute society 'as a whole'.

But is this really the case? Is 'society' a *necessary* totality? How can sociologists escape the kind of deconstructive critique they obligingly provide in relation to all other constituted realities? If self, and identity, and body, in the end cannot sustain the myth of primordial unity, how can we claim for 'society' the privilege of 'necessary being?' After all, is there any important difference between tracing the apparent realities of immediate experience to a 'pre-given' psyche, or body, or self, or soul and then fabricating society from these elements? Sociology is too easily seduced into doing the reverse; and assuming what must be demonstrated in treating its object of knowledge, 'society', as a pre-given and essential unity-totality. Of course societies differ, but so does the content of the psyche or the form of the body. The priority of society that is assumed is not the dominance of this or that society, but of society 'as such'.

Durkheim made some powerful arguments against the modern tendency to reductionism and the utilitarian view of society as the result of interaction motivated and sustained by individuals in pursuit of their own interests. This view, he argues convincingly, presupposes a society as the source of background normative order that makes possible these very lines of action and interests. But this is not the issue here. The question is whether 'society' is experienced in an immediate way. Clearly we do not experience society in its totality, all at once, so to speak. But we do experience 'the social' in specific ways, some or all of which may be said to be 'society' in an immediate way.

Durkheim's work (1984, 1995, 2002) can be seen as a commentary on his own society. It is in modern society that 'society as such' appears, and appears pre-eminently in everyday life. Durkheim makes this appearance the starting point for his sociology, the foundation of any society is the original differentiation of reality into sacred and profane; and the sacred is society writ large, society in the very act of self-creation. The insight that allows us to 'see' society in the formation of arbitrary but compelling conventions is the work of late secularization. Durkheim supposes that, in previous societies, society has installed itself, so to speak, in everyday life and in cultural assumptions (*conscience collective*) that ascribe all such conventional order to a superior, non-human source; thus assuring or at least making more likely, that the norm 'sticks'. The real problem in Durkheim's sociology is how in modern society, now that we have seen through (and made into an elegant theory in Durkheim's own works) the social, and seen that there is nothing in it or beneath it that compels assent, how will it continue?

In Durkheim's own work two possible answers emerge and the ultimate priority of one over the other is never settled. To ensure that society continues it is essential still to generate those images and representations of society as a whole or as such, to which people will unthinkingly identify themselves, and thus be formed into a single community. And, alternatively, he argues that in modern complex societies there is no longer any requirement for such an overarching community of feeling, sentiment, or belief. What holds modern society together is simply the factual interconnectedness of its parts and elements. Modern society is so highly differentiated, and everyone is therefore dependent on many other people of whom they know nothing. In other words, just as society emerges and, so to speak, shows itself for the first time (hence the appearance, with it, of sociology), it vanishes. If Durkheim's (1995) second, more radical, answer is taken as a starting point we can see that 'society' is sustained even though we see its utter conventionality because of its sheer weight of exteriority. It is not 'common values', 'shared expectations', 'religious orientation' or its substitutes in secular ideologies, civic virtue, or national identification that 'holds society together'. What makes society a society, in this view, is the absolutely mundane character of everyday life, which implicates everyone in complex networks of social relations that have 'a life of their own'.

Durkheim's approach makes society, like language, a complex structure that exists only in the interaction of those who daily act according to its conventions, and, even when they see these conventions are arbitrary, nonetheless cannot significantly alter its common usage. Society predates and outlives any of its members.

Durkheim was not alone in this insight. In different ways all the classical writers in sociology reject nineteenth-century views on the nature of modern society and stress the way in which society carries with it an enormous inertial mass. In Marx, the everydayness of the commodity makes all organized opposition to capitalism more difficult and tends continually to undermine its political impact. For Simmel, the growth in objective culture in the modern metropolis is on a scale that overwhelms not only collective efforts to grasp and direct its flow, but generates a new psychic reality. And Weber, pessimistic and resigned, looks forward to a modernity continuing in the bleaker side of rationalization, in the perpetuation of a widespread cultural nihilism.

All these views make it clear that self-identity has irreparably parted company with the structure of modern society. To put the matter another way; now you can be anything you like because what you are and who you are has nothing to do with how society works. There is a particular kind of liberation consequent on surrendering to the forces of modernity. And it is this compensatory freedom that, for the postmodern era, is the precondition of new kinds of experience.

Self-identity is not founded on the experience either of unity or totality; it is not founded on anything and does not constitute a determinate structure, or a coherent process. Self-identity is both more and less than unity or totality; it is a fragment. And the fragment is not more than the sum of the parts it is only one of the parts.

INTERRUPTION 5: SYMPTOM

... a symptom signifies the representation – the realization – of a phantasy with a sexual content, that is to say, it signifies a sexual situation. It would be better to say that at least *one* of the meanings of a symptom is the representation of a sexual phantasy ... a single unconscious mental process or phantasy will scarcely ever suffice for the production of a symptom.

To be sure, she would not hear of going so far as this in recognizing her own thoughts; and indeed, if the occurrence of the symptoms was to be made possible at all, it was essential that she should not be completely clear on the subject. But the conclusion was inevitable that with her spasmodic cough, which, as is usual, was referred for its exciting stimulus to a tickling in her throat, she pictured to herself a scene of sexual gratification *per os* (by mouth) between the two people whose love affair occupied her mind so incessantly. A very short time after she had tacitly accepted this explanation her cough vanished.

... a single symptom corresponds to several meanings *simultaneously*. We may now add that it can express several meanings *in succession*. In the course of years a symptom can change its meaning or its chief meaning, or the leading role can pass from one meaning to another.

(Freud *Case Histories* Vol 1)

Trauma is a break, an interruption, to which the self-identical subject is oblivious. The trauma initiates a process of forgetting that enfolds and conceals the break in a new continuity. But the trauma is not annulled; it is hidden, and from this invisible core a fragmentary discourse of perplexing bodily malfunctions furnishes a silent commentary on the banal spectacle of everyday life. The resulting symptom, in its turn, is the starting point for a deranged path of interpretation and detection. It follows the associations of everyday life, and with unpredictable inventiveness links together discontinuous, disproportionate, and qualitatively distinct events in order to trace out the figure of an earlier experience. The symptom is hieroglyph; a somatic text message from the unconscious.

Symptom is the trace of the primary process and, at the same time, the embodiment of a discursive memory; a reminder that something is forgotten, and an encrypted message to the present of what lies obscurely and for ever in the past. Symptom is also an ontological variation; a transformation of conscious experience into bodily symbol.

Oblivion stands at the origins of self-identity, for the individual as for the collective, for history and for philosophy. Freud's psychoanalytic method uncovered the birth of self-identity in a moment of forgetfulness; that is, in the process of repression. Modern society and modernity begin, similarly, with the decisive annihilation of the past and the creation in its place of a prehistory of self-images. Autonomy is declared and grasped in the process of interruption. Self-identity, that is to say, is a story, it simply begins, but it cannot remain in this state of unselfconscious innocence. In grasping its own reality it generates itself as a continuous unfolding narrative, which rests upon, and arises from, the lost world prior to the break. Modern self-identity *requires* trauma (Ankersmit 2005).

The overwhelming character of events, not only emotionally and physically but cognitively, has the effect of preserving a detached fragment of psychic life that, unrecollected, unassimilated, and dissociated, intrudes an alien presence in conscious experience (Caruth 1995, 1996). Trauma is the actual deconstruction of experience; it may be repeatedly witnessed without ever entering experience. And symptoms then become indicators of real past events rather than pathological 'illusions' of some sort; relics of the non-identical.

Modernity institutionalized trauma; the shock of the modern was the shock of war, the destruction of tradition, the spread of disease, the forced movement of people into unfamiliar and insecure environments (Leys 2000). And it was shock repeated, over and over again, because the very condition of trauma was that it should be forgotten. The shiny newness of modernity had a sinister undertone; the self-identical subject, serene in its naked existence, was born from forgotten catastrophes, and set about preparing another.

The narrative of self-identity posits its own prehistory consciously to fill the blank of an annulled past; but the gradual adjustment to the post-traumatic is evident in the diminishing urgency and gradual extinction of the need for all such grand narratives of the personal and collective past. And after the break the narrative is not rejoined. Self is just what cannot be narrated, and even Braudel's ample and leisurely history breaks down into 'different snapshots' of civilizations. Self, if it is born from trauma, cannot risk losing itself in its own fabricated history. In any event, as Freud's case histories so wonderfully attest, there is too much, not just forgotten, but not, in the first instance, actually lived through. More recently Javier Marías, in a narrative that lacks nothing in the scrupulous attention to detail, reasserts Freud's insight; self eludes narration because there is

> too much vague material collected together and yet somehow dispersed as well, too much for one story, even for a story that is only ever thought. Not to mention the infinite number of things that fall within the eyes' blind spot, every life is full of episodes that are literally invisible, we don't know what happened because we didn't see it, couldn't see it, much of what affects and determines us is concealed or, how can I put it, not available for viewing, kept out of sight, out of shot. Life is not recountable and it seems extraordinary that men have spent all the centuries we know anything about devoted to doing just that, determined to tell what cannot be told, be it in the form of myth, epic poem, chronicle, annals, minutes, legend or *chanson de geste*, ballad or folk-song, gospel, hagiography, history, biography, novel or funeral oration, film, confession, memoir, article, it makes no difference.
>
> (Marías 2006: 97–98)

Judith Butler, similarly, warns against the comfort of narrative; 'Telling a story is not the same as giving an account of oneself' (Butler 2005: 12). And, although the latter presumes the former, it absolves the subject from the demands of inner-connectedness and ethical intentionality; 'Suspending the demand for self-identity or, more particularly, for complete coherence seems to me to counter a certain ethical violence, which demands that we manifest and maintain self-identity at all times and require that others do the same'(Butler 2005: 42). And, in fact, the more closely 'an account of oneself' approaches the truth of being the less it makes sense (Gilmore 2001).

The fragmentation of narrative marks the present, and creates, from nothing, a huge assembly of possible worlds in which to live. Contemporary life is the post-traumatic, the post-war, the postmodern; it is discontinuity, repetition, oblivion, the merging of incommensurable aspects of awareness, and the splitting apart of every substance and form. It is the fragment.

5

FRAGMENTS

The matter contained in the following pages will be of two kinds. In the first place I shall give some fragmentary extracts from the history of a case of obsessional neurosis ... In the second place, starting out from this case and also taking other cases into account which I have previously analysed, I shall make some disconnected statements of an aphoristic character upon the genesis and finer psychological mechanism of obsessional neuroses ... A programme of this kind seems to me to require some justification. For it might otherwise be thought that I regard this method of making a communication as perfectly correct and as one to be imitated; whereas in reality I am only accommodating myself to obstacles, some external and others inherent in the subject and I should gladly have communicated more if it had been right or possible for me to do so ... if I were to reproduce the analysis, it would be impossible for me to make the structure, such as by the help of analysis we know or suspect it to be, visible to others through the mass of therapeutic work superimposed upon it.

(Freud *Case Histories* Vol 2)

Freud's case histories are all fragments. He was not alone in resorting to fragmentary presentation; it had been pioneered as a literary form a century earlier by the Romantics, most notably Novalis (Friedrich von Hardenberg) (1997) and Friedrich von Schlegel (1971). And in a highly significant way Kierkegaard (1988) titled or subtitled many of his pseudonymous works of the 1840s 'Fragments', including his most famous work *Either/Or: A Fragment of Life* and a short, important work *Philosophical*

Fragment: or a Fragment of Philosophy in relation to which he subsequently published the much larger *Concluding Unscientific Postscript to the Philosophical Fragments*. These titles do not refer to unfinished or occasional pieces of writing, nor do they betray any lack of rigour or methodological sophistication on the part of their authors; to the contrary they are among the most comprehensive and insightful accounts of life in the society of their time. The fragment was the appropriate form in which to grasp and through which to convey, the real character of contemporary everyday life. The fragment is both a comment upon and an actual form of, contemporary experience. Of course Schlegel and Kierkegaard were well ahead of their contemporaries and it is only in retrospect that the device of fragmented and fragmentary writing appeared as anything more than a literary stunt.

The fragment is the epitome of contemporary life. Where classical modernity can accurately be described through the experience of self-identity, the premodern world as selfless-identity and modern Japanese culture as non-identical-selves, contemporary everyday life is best described as selfless-non-identity. The double negative of the present seems at first to leave the observer helpless. The radical deconstruction of experience, if taken seriously, leaves us in the sheer flux of awareness, which cannot be grasped, understood, explained, adequately described, or communicated. But this is not the case, or not necessarily the case. We are not left either with chaos, or with nothing, but find the fragment.

In this sense the fragment is not like a splinter of wood or a shard of glass; a piece broken off from an intact and uniform whole. The fragment is a detached portion that takes on a life of its own and may even gain the appearance of self-sufficiency as something *unlike* its parent body; 'A fragment, like a miniature work of art, has to be entirely isolated from the surrounding world and be complete in itself like a porcupine' (Schlegel 1971: 189). Commonly, the notion of the fragment is taken as synonymous with disintegration; a piece of coal turned to dust, for example. But what emerged in the works cited above, as in many others, is an appreciation of the constructive character of the fragment. The process of deconstruction is always, at the same time, a process of constructive fragmentation. It should be borne in mind, for example, that the modern individual, the self-identical subject, is *already* a fragment. In premodern society the human being is always absorbed in and dependent on, a community of some sort. The modern period is distinctive precisely in establishing and identifying the human being as an individual. And, as individuals, human beings become self-referential and experience the world firstly in the context of their own particular situation. The individual, a fragment of the community, has a new life in modernity, not as a dissociated part of a once larger whole, but as a new centre of life and activity. In a very similar manner and at the same time, Giordano Bruno remarked on the fragmentation of the heavens. Stars, rather than being points of light in a continuous luminous substance, became separate 'self-adhering bodies', each an inward focused mass; the cosmos, far from being the unity-totality of a singular identity was an infinite collection of fragments, a 'plurality of worlds'. Schlegel's observation that 'as yet no genre exists that is fragmentary both in form and content' (Schlegel 1971: 170), was effectively contradicted by the collection *Athenaeum Fragments* (1798) in which it was published. Following its appearance the fragment became the preferred literary-philosophical trope for the depiction and exploration of ordinary experience. But the literary philosopher was already behind the times; Bruno had grasped two centuries before him, as Freud was to do a century after him, that 'every whole can be a part and every part really a whole' (Schlegel 1971: 144). And in the early seventeenth century the fragment had already appeared in its definitive mode; the still-life painting (Bryson 1990). The fragment, that is to say, entered the modern world in intimate association with the depiction of everyday life and just because everyday life was in the process of being reconstructed as a vast collection of fragments.

It is appropriate to grasp contemporary life in a fragmentary way; as the repetition of trauma and its aftermath, rather than as a continuous developmental history of self-identity. It is a growing consciousness of the foundational significance of the break. The postmodern is simply the consciousness of the break, as distinct from the self-consciousness of an identity liberated into the empty space of the post-traumatic void; a transition from self-consciousness to consciousness of self-aware experience. Now everything is in fragments; everything has its own fragment (Baudrillard 2004), God is in fragments (Pohier 1985), the body is a fragments and a history of fragments (Feher 1989), history and the philosophy of history are fragmentary (Vinen 2002), the nation comes with its fragments (Chatterjee 1993) and the best social theories of modernity appear as fragments (Frisby 1989). The post-traumatic is a world without memory, or, rather, a world for which memory has to be invented; it is the sense that 'this is happening – here and now'.

FROM SOCIETY TO EVERYDAY LIFE

However appealing the 'method' of the fragment might appear, is there not still a level at which fragments are interrelated, conjoined, synthesized and made whole as 'society'? This remains an orthodox view in sociology. But if the notion of fragment is taken seriously it must refer to *dis*connection, *dis*continuity, and *un*related phenomena. The continuity that characterizes the present is the continuous processes of fragmentation, emerging in every aspect and dimension of social life. Thus, where modernity grasped reality in the unity of experience, contemporary life is a process of radical disaggregation and splitting. 'Contemporary life' is not used here as an implicit, unitary concept; as if, beyond the classical notion of experience, fragmentary consciousness is synthesized in a new way within a larger and ultimately coherent field of awareness.

Experience is not just taken apart and rearranged in some way; it is fragmented. This means that self-identity is not simply emptied and refilled with fresh content, while remaining the underlying bearer of unitary experience. Certainly, self, in-so-far as self sustains a fugitive presence in contemporary society, becomes plural. As a result either of involvement in distinct and differently constituted relational networks and contexts, or its detachment from any forms of commitment, self may, indeed, appear to be a continually transforming project of some kind. Both role-involvement and role-distance, in other words, can be adduced as the significant context for the multiplication of selfhood. There are different selves for different occasions and contexts and different selves, over and above these contexts that constitute part of the characterological and narrative discourse of a self-project. Fragmentation, however, goes much further than this and has to be considered primarily as a process affecting the unity of experience itself.

Collectively and individually, extensively and intensively, and in terms of place and time, what had been experienced as continuous dimensionality has broken up, re-arranged, turned inwards and parts made the focus and boundaries of separate and distinct levels of awareness and existence. What had been varied aspects of a singular experience became divergent and unrelated modes of awareness. Thus, for example, where sensing, reasoning, willing and feeling had constituted the varied functions of a singular self, they became, to an increasing degree, autonomous ontological regions of experience, each presenting a qualitatively distinct world of its own. And each region offered itself as the constituting medium of a fragmented self-awareness. Self might emerge momentarily as will and intention, then as feeling, or in particular sense impressions; turning one way then another, being pulled deeper into one region before switching abruptly to a different modality of appearance.

Bruno's insight remains relevant; the fragment is greater than the world of the whole or the totality; it is greater than the sum of parts. The fragmentary is *many* worlds. The post-traumatic fragmentary is suggested by the discontinuous and disproportionate; by multiplicity, diversity, and transition. At the same time, however, society 'as a whole;' a world of 'shared values', historical communities, centralized institutions, the concentration of power, the integration of markets, global economic interrelationship and a more highly differentiated division of labour *also* appears. *Society*, that is to say, has become a fragment that exists alongside and at the same level as any other fragment. But it is everyday life, rather than society, that is the theatre of fragmentation; the arena in which all fragments appear and in which none can establish priority. And everyday life is an indeterminate region; the unbound eternity of dissolving experience as distinct from the objective forms located in the empty extension of the spatio-temporal world.

Whether society is viewed in terms of solidarity, the *conscience collective* and a shared collective memory, or as a structure sustained by the concentration of power and unequal access to economic, political, and symbolic resources, contemporary sociology has continued to ground its explanatory and interpretative framework in the assumption that, conceptually and actually, all distinctions are ultimately interrelated in a systematic whole. And modern psychology and philosophy has been constructed, correspondingly, as a project to 'save the phenomenon'. Like the medieval astronomer forced to construct an imaginary geometry of epicycles to bring the observed, eccentric paths of the planets into conformity with the 'known' structure of the cosmos, the contemporary academic seeks to make coherent a world pre-given as the prerequisite for the self-identical subject. But the Copernican moment has long passed and the more direct and obvious approach is now to accept that the subject is non-identical and its world correspondingly fragmented. However unlikely such a conclusion might have appeared in the recent past, the absurdity now lies with outdated assumptions rather than faulty reasoning or deficient insight. The difficulty or oddity of an idea is not evidence of its incorrectness, or, to put the matter the other way around 'just because it's true doesn't mean it's plausible' (Marías 2006: 230).

However, even accepting that society undergoes a process of fragmentation, rather than simple differentiation, the overwhelming response has been to maintain the notion of the subject, both individual and collective, as the self-identity that remains more or less unchanged and aloof from the multiplicity of roles, positions, networks, and interactive and historical contexts through which it moves. This was and remains, the predominant view in European and North American sociology; a view that came to prominence in the work of Talcott Parsons in 1950s and 1960s but survived the demise of his particular brand of functionalism and flourished as an implicit assumption in much of the empirical research that, stressing social inequality and difference, supported alternative approaches.

In recent years, in reaction to what was, often wrongly, conceived as the passive role of the subject both in functionalism and structuralism, greater stress has been placed on agency in accounts of modern society. Increasingly self is viewed as a project; a trajectory through a variety of situations in which the subject is involved in different ways. Self is neither a fixed point of reference throughout these changes, nor the unfolding of authentic identity; it is, rather, a process of continuous recollection and narrative construction. Craig Ireland for example, points out that 'A consequence of modern temporality for strategies of self-formation ... has been the migration of a sense of self from a set of given attributes to a reflexively sustained project' (Ireland 2004: 128). And Giddens, in an influential work, argues that 'The reflexive project of the self, which consists in the sustaining of coherent, yet continuously revised, biographical narratives, takes place in the context of multiple choice as filtered through abstract systems' (Giddens 1991: 5). It is the relative detachment of self from *any* of its roles that leaves it free to create for itself a narrative of identity.

These views somewhat oddly juxtapose a coherent self with a fragmented, or at least highly differentiated, society. Self emerges in the interstitial freedom of a complex society and becomes meaningful to the extent that it has the resources to maintain a voluntaristic, episodic and biographically significant interrelation with a variety of social frameworks and institutions. This limits the self-project to the economically and educationally privileged. Further, it locates self in the meaningfulness of choice, rather than the commitment of decision. Self is neither fully a social, nor an existential, being. Certainly, it makes sense that self should be a self-project in advanced modernity. But it is less clear that the self-project can take the form of reflexive narrative, particularly if that project is founded in the oblivion of trauma.

The older work of George Herbert Mead, which was influential in the theoretical formulations of Talcott Parsons and, more generally, in making American Pragmatism accessible to sociologists, is still of considerable interest in this context. In his view self is a social relation of the most direct sort. It follows that 'The unity and structure of the complete self reflects the unity and structure of the social process as a whole; and each of the elementary selves of which it is composed reflects the unity and structure of one of the various aspects of that process in which the individual is implicated' (Mead 1967: 144). This might be described as the standard model of the social self in modern sociology. The assumption of unity and totality of the social process is an essential aspect of the experience of coherent selfhood. But such an experience is by no means universal, not uncommonly the fragmentation of experience provides the most compelling evidence for the fragmentation of society at every level; 'The phenomenon of dissociation of personality is caused by a breaking up of the complete, unitary self into the component selves of which it is composed and which respectively correspond to different aspects of the social process in which the person is involved and within which his complete or unitary self has arisen; these aspects being the different social groups to which he belongs within that process' (Mead 1967: 144). And for Mead the 'meaning' of self is not an internal narrative, or external value, but an aspect of social relations themselves; it is 'a development of something objectively there as a relation between certain phases of the social act; it is not a psychical addition to that act and it is not an "idea" as traditionally conceived' (Mead 1967: 76).

Why should the more fluid, diverse and differentiated structure of modern society give rise to liberated projects of self-identity rather than to 'dissociation of the personality?' And how can it be constituted as narrative when social narrative has been fragmented into an ever-growing number of incommensurable worlds?

Rather than view contemporary society as a continuation of modernity, it makes sense to grasp the modern as a developmental history of trauma, a growing consciousness of the foundational significance of the break. The postmodern is simply the consciousness of the break, as distinct from the self-consciousness of an identity liberated into the empty space of the post-traumatic void. The trauma is a shock, in the case of the modern the shock of war, the destruction of tradition, the mass destruction of disease; the forced movement of people into unfamiliar and insecure environments. The post-traumatic is a world without memory, or, rather, for which memory has to be invented. At the origins of self-identity, for the individual as for the collective, for history and for philosophy there is – oblivion. Fragmentation affects every dimension of social life. Institutional differentiation, spatial separation, distinctions of status and style of life, differences in culture, alternative forms of knowledge and belief characterize the development of modernity.

Given that experience is a social relation, as the social world fragments, the synthetic unity of experience also fragments. And this in two respects. First, the sense in which experience is ultimately coherent and 'all-of-a-piece', undergoes profound change. Different kinds of experience emerge which are not simply distinctions in content but in the constitution of what is taken to be real. What had been immediately and fully interconnected as aspects of the same reality become separated and form distinct regions or zones in which qualities of specific kinds make their appearance in terms of their own range of variation. The qualities that previously were held together as an object or thing now appear independently as discrete regions of the real. And, second, experience is wrenched apart from the experiencing subject. Experience becomes something manufactured and presented as consumable. Consequently the subject, from being constituted as the self-identical unity of experience in which qualitatively distinct experiences merged in a characteristic way, is fragmented and parcelled out into incomparable and incommensurate regions.

BOURGEOIS CULTURE AND THE TRANSITION TO POSTMODERNITY

The heroic struggle of self-identity to assimilate reality and impart to its world a coherent and transparent unity is over. Now the self-identical is not so much shattered as confined to occasional moments of sober reflection and serious endeavour, coming and going in an unpredictable way amidst the incomprehensible succession of forms. Society has not 'broken down;' it has been broken apart and reconstituted as everyday life; the ecstatic quotidian which is, at the same time, utterly banal (Gosetti-Ferencei 2008).

How did this happen? Modern society was created and became self-sustaining as the bourgeois world of modernity. Yet, the bourgeois world, in the end, fell apart. It was not overthrown or transformed from within. At the height of its political, economic and symbolic power, towards the end of the nineteenth century, bourgeois modernity underwent a profound crisis of confidence (Burrow 2000).

Why the bourgeois half-heartedness and final deflection from modernity; the falling back into anachronistic forms of self-identity – community, nation, race, gender, and so on? One reaction is simply to claim that we have never really become modern (Latour 1993) and indeed there is plenty of evidence of the 'survival' of premodern forms in contemporary life. But as a general thesis this hardly addresses the issue. Bourgeois culture is a definite falling back from the wholehearted embrace of the modern which can be observed in the early modern period. The bourgeois world was selective in its propagation of modernity, which it moulded to industrial capitalism. Even so, the extent to which the bourgeois world was permeated by premodern and no longer meaningful, far less valid, identity forms is astonishing.

Asceticism founded a culture of moderation, sobriety, and constraint. Even when this culture began to relax its grip the damage was done; the fundamental rule was moderation not truth. This form of asceticism has a deeper logic. Once faith is made a matter of conscience, an existential choice, modern culture generally can be made a market choice. Choices determined ultimately by satisfaction of inner wants. The absolute alien other of ultimacy and transcendental value was finally assimilated and transformed into a human condition of *comfort*. Ultimacy lost its exteriority, the encounter with a given and alien reality. The problem with bourgeois culture might be put as follows: the final defeat of transcendentalism and the rise of secularism, resulted in the creation of an inner psychic economy governed by a norm of mediocrity, philistinism, and comfort. Modest pleasure took precedence over truth. This is simply because the absolute was lost; bourgeois values, like any other, had a provisional validity adapted to present circumstances but should not be taken too seriously. Or, rather, all seriousness (and there was an abundance of that) was connected with moderate projects of worthy self improvement that stopped short of any principle.

Thus, the survival and eventual prospering of self-identities, premodern in form and content, is an anticipation of postmodernity. It was not that the bourgeois were committed to the reality of race or gender, nationhood, or community; they were well aware of their arbitrariness and saw through such conventions; but they remained possible because nothing was absolute – and for some groups in some places and times, such identities were attractive.

Bourgeois philistinism and half-heartedness goes some way in accounting for the curious anachronisms that abound in the institutional and cultural development of modern society. This view might be summed up as a bourgeois failure of nerve; a drawing back from the full implications of the revolution of modernity. Immanuel Kant's vision of Enlightenment is exemplary in this respect. On the one hand Kant proclaims Enlightenment in the most radical terms; it is to cast aside all traditional authority and rely wholly and solely on reason as a guide for the conduct of human affairs. On the other hand, if reason is to hold sway, human passions must be restrained by a voluntary act of surrender to given ethical demands. The modern arousal and positing of self, which is in principle absolutely free, is at once suppressed, not any longer by external authorities but by the emerging self-identical subject. In a yet more incisive and compelling version Sigmund Freud argued that the very possibility of self-enjoyment, of the experience of pleasure, requires the primary process undergoes repression; and this can only be an act of self-repression. Self-identity emerges only at the cost of its own freedom.

There is more here than any simple 'loss of nerve;' something more deeply paradoxical sets in train the continuous process of undoing that characterizes the history of modernity. The insights of Kant and Freud (and one might add here, Kierkegaard, Nietzsche, and Weber) cannot be written off as 'mere' psychology. As individual and collective are aspects of the same relations, the paradox of self-suppression applies equally and, indeed, with greater force to the collective history of modernity.

All versions of totality, *including* self-identical projects of nationhood, revolution, and cultural communication were conjured out of modern society as admired images of the Other. What modern society had as its own, rationality, commodity production, science, aesthetic detachment and so on, manifest continuous internal differentiation and fragmentation. Modern society founded itself in a free act of rejection and a break with the past. In founding itself as a new beginning free of primal origin (a story rather than a myth), modern society came to itself in projects of self-identity; in positing both being and being-in-its world.

Every self-project required for its completion an imaginary companion, projected ahead of itself, as a dialectical partner in a, frequently deadly, modern waltz. The Other played an extraordinarily contradictory role. On the one hand, the Other manifest what the self-identical was not, or no longer was, everything that the self-identical rejected, despised and expelled from the magic circle of its own culture. On the other hand, the Other was a tantalizing reminder of what the revolution of modernity had foregone. Sunk in superstition, at the mercy of a world it could not comprehend, the Other, nonetheless and in a still exemplary fashion manifest the virtue of totality. In liberating itself from the past the suspicion grew that modernity had liberated itself from *society*.

The project of self-identity foundered on paradox. The self-identical, individual or collective, was always less than itself, always incomplete, always restless and impatient; at best a tendency, a peculiar tension felt in waves of longing and recollection. Having abandoned the absolute and all authority modernity bravely faced up to its own world as something uncertain, changeable and temporary. However, rather than discover, reclusive but safe in the midst of the maelstrom of experience, secure, indubitable self-presence modernity revealed itself to be nothing other than chronic insecurity. The unprecedented combination of power and doubt – a fearless rejection of the past coupled with a fearful inability to create the future – generated a world of intense anxiety.

Modernity, itself the product of unacknowledged interconnections of societies and cultures, imposed itself on the world. Like science, capitalism was something of an unexpected and inexplicable success. The self-expanding character of modernity easily gives rise to an impression of firm intention, confidence, and optimism; but the anxious probing of sketchy and always provisional projects of self-identity oscillated between nostalgia for an imagined past that knew nothing of freedom, and strident assertions of superiority. The rest of the world became the desiderata of the west, just as the world became the desiderata of selfhood. And neither would settle into a satisfyingly coherent and transparent totality in which would be confirmed and experienced the unity of the self-identical. The unfolding drama of twentieth-century history, like the high energy collisions in a particle accelerator, split asunder the myth of the self-identical revealing a strange and unsuspected reality, rich in exotic phenomena, flaring into existence only to die away without trace; the postmodern is the realization of the *hubris* of modernity.

Now, finally, the urgent question arises; given the demise of self-identity as a project, what can be said about human experience in contemporary society? This cannot be posed as an alternative of some sort; a formulation, principle, or other kind of unity. It cannot be a self-identity other than the self-identical! The postmodern, contemporary society – the post-traumatic world, is fragmentary. This is not a whole broken into parts it is, rather, an uncombined discontinuity, which can only be the unbounded indeterminacy of everyday life.

Can fragmentation be described other than as breakdown, disintegration, and loss? What is the life of selfless-non-identity? Though not easy to describe, it can at least be indicated without difficulty; it is the unbounded indeterminacy of everyday life.

MOTIFS IN EVERYDAY LIFE

Where modernity constituted reality as self-identical experience, contemporary everyday life is the evanescence of varied existential motifs; it is the non-identical. This is the case even where unfounded, mythical and arbitrary forms are established as socially 'real'. The sense in which conventionalization is resistant to historical and conceptual insight and, even more significantly the extent to which these conventions persist in spite of their transparent arbitrariness and willful construction, is nonetheless wholly transformed by the emergence in contemporary society of non-identical motifs in everyday life. The new context of everyday life places all prior, modern self-identical forms 'in brackets'. That is, it has the effect of suspending judgement on their validity. Contemporary everyday life is an actual process of 'phenomenological reduction' in which experience is deconstructed and presented as separate fragments of life.

Everyday life is the unbounded and indeterminate arena in which all unrelated and non-identical events 'appear' and 'happen'. The 'everydayness' of the everyday consists in a characteristic quality of ordinariness and familiarity; but it is important also to take note of its simple formal meaning. It is the every day, the daily in its manifold variety. The everyday in a literal sense refers to a host of routine activities, private and public, carried out on a regular, if not actually daily, basis; such as eating, sleeping, working, commuting, shopping, and so on. More significantly the everyday is the inclusive arena in which occasional, incidental, and unusual events *also* take place. The *quality* of everydayness is ubiquitous; everything becomes banal by virtue of taking place in the framework of everyday life. It is not repetition, routinization, or the specific function of any activity that makes it everyday and therefore ordinary; it is ordinary, rather, by virtue of making its appearance in the midst of everyday life.

The disordered juxtaposition of recorded events in the diary supplants the developmental coherence of the autobiography as the 'authentic' voice of experience. The diary is the literary form of everydayness. Life is here reduced to a sequence of equivalent temporal divisions. The most significant contemporary documents are these records of everyday life: from Nikolai Gogol to Franz Kafka and Victor Klemperer and Mandalstam, whether factual or imaginary diaries seize on the empty formality of the calendar as an organizing device. The sequence of days provides a semblance of order in a world made incoherent by the non-identical and incomprehensible; war, loss, suffering and joy. The diary is a recording device; it eschews meaning, explanation, intention and self-hood. The diary models everyday life on the daily account book rather than the journal of an expedition. Everyday life is converted into a ledger of events; a record of transactions (Poovey 1998, 2008).

The newspaper goes even further in grasping the fragmentary as the real form of contemporary life. The daily news is laid out in poster form; ideally a single page in which items appear, interspersed with advertisements and notices, without regard to sequence or meaning; a random juxtaposition of unconnected items that readers scan as part of their daily routine of eating breakfast and going to work (Fritzsche 1998).

Here and now

As distinct from all forms of modern self-identity contemporary life is characterized by the here and now; it is immediate. Contemporary life is wholly in the present. Now we live 'for the moment' and are provided with innumerable ways of intensifying the instantaneous 'now' of something that is taking place. The excitement of roller-coaster rides, bungee jumping, being drunk, gambling, eroticism, sport, news, performances of all sorts, thunderstorms, beauty and all other 'saturated' phenomena is just that they overwhelm the living moment with content in such a way as to mark it as occurring 'right now' (Marion 2002; Gergen 2000). The intensification of the moment has the effect of distinguishing it sharply from a 'before' and 'after'. Thus, surprisingly, these events are readily forgotten. Far from being 'unforgettable' they enter memory in the attenuated form of 'having taken place' while preserving nothing of the moment itself. Hence their ceaseless repetition, their continuing novelty as the everyday mini-traumas in which is discovered the comfort of oblivion.

What is involved here is a distinctive and important transformation of the relationship of the experiencing subject to their experience. Where, for classical modernity, experience is experience of the world to which the subject is continually linked, in the excited moment of the present experience becomes an indicator of self-presence. The world, that is to say, is reduced to being a *desideratum* of the self-aware subject. The point of heightened momentary awareness is to furnish proof of self-presence. This is profoundly different to the structure of experience taken-for-granted by the most insightful of its investigators in the modern period. For Kant, as for Descartes, it made no sense to 'prove' self existence. The self was a precondition of any kind of experience and experience, while an unreliable guide to the nature of exterior reality, is always self-experience. But in the twentieth century people learned, above all, to doubt themselves, to want a world that proved they existed. But they were caught in a deeper paradox. The intensification of the moment, its artificial separation as pure immediacy, had the effect of dissolving selfhood into the irresistible transience of the 'now' (Friese 2001, 2002).

A number of important writers during the 1920s and 1930s emphasized the immediacy of contemporary culture and its unexpected consequences. Pre-eminently in the writings of Walter Benjamin and Ernst Bloch, both unorthodox Marxist philosophers with exceptionally wide-ranging interests in, and knowledge of, the literary, musical, and architectural genealogy of modernity, can be found rich 'thick descriptions' of the momentary.

And much earlier, in the middle of the nineteenth century, Kierkegaard fully explored the hidden difficulties in what he called 'aesthetic existence'; that is, life lived in the 'instant' (Ferguson 1995). The enthusiasm of the moment, which wholly absorbs and 'carries away' the subject, is not the instant of self-realization but the despairing evanescence of the subject. By identifying with the instant, the self locks itself into a vanishing moment and loses itself to an inaccessible past. The instant, by its artificial isolation from the flow of time, in fact cease to be a temporal relation at all and cannot be distinguished either by succession or duration; it is the eternal. At this point the entire project of modernity comes apart. Finally ridding itself of transcendental goals, values, and all forms of ultimacy the subject grasps itself as sheer immanence and disappears! Self is stranded. It cannot find a place outside of the immanent flux of actual events and if it identifies with that flux, is sucked into the 'obscurity of the lived moment' (Bloch 1999: 197).

In the practical compromise of everyday life, however, the pure immediacy of the 'here and now', is replaced by a vague and shifting 'present'. The pure forms immanent in the development of modernity, in the end, cannot support ordinary experience. Self-identity, in other words, depends not only on the fictional unity and totality of experience; it requires that the radical implications of modernity are softened and obscured. The paradox of modernity consists in suppressing the full consequences of the very self-identity that was originally seized as its essential character. Bourgeois philistinism is an expression of this paradox and not simply a failure to take its own values seriously. In this context it is possible to see that the unprincipled mediocrity of the present age arises from the human impossibility of living through the non-identity of sheer immanence. Self-identity taken seriously to its limit dissolves into the non-identical and negates modernity; self-identity taken *half*-seriously as conventional respectability, nationhood, narrative autobiography, good manners, a reasoned world-view filled with controllable objects, and so on, supports a particular and interested view of the modern.

The present, stretched beyond fleeting oblivion, nonetheless opens itself to distinctively postmodern motifs of non-identity. Everyday life is characterized by vague, indefinite, and continually changing *moods*, by liminal states including *illness*, by the newness of *fashion* and the pure objectivity of social *performance*; a world at once cosmopolitan and *banal*. In these varied states and unanticipated changes, subject and object are merged, the world is not held apart as if it were a picture and the alert, wide-awake, fully focused intentional social actor falls back into lethargic and drowsy inactivity, or is caught up in nebulous currents of excitement.

Mood

The present, albeit extended beyond the fleeting moment, is constituted in an essentially atemporal manner. Everyday life is *felt*. The daily greeting 'how are you?' always means 'how do you feel?' and the conventional reply 'fine', means 'I am in a good mood'. A good mood, as distinct from any specific gratification, pleasure, or satisfaction is now a measure of the good life. But it is precisely the characteristic of mood that temporality, identity and intentionality stand apart from it. One 'finds oneself' in a good mood, or in a bad or any other kind of mood. Mood cannot be the aim of an intention or deliberate action; we cannot simply decide to be cheerful, glum, anxious, excited, and so on. Our relation to the present and to the current state of our world, in so far as it may be characterized as *mood*, is then quite distinct from, for example, Max Weber's account of modernity which so forcefully brings out the significance of a calculative attitude.

Moods are feelings detached from actions and events. They are float-ing, decontextualized, and indefinite states of being. Mood is atmos-pheric, something 'in the air' or 'of the times'. Mood is a collective sentiment that comes and goes in waves and pulses. The detachment of mood from actuality is a feature of the contemporary dislocation of self-identity. Moods, that is to say, cannot be grasped as consequences of spe-cific causes, or as the meaningful content of experience. The question of mood is not what causes a mood, but how is it 'rationalized', that is, how is it imaginatively connected with the circumstances of everyday life. Mood is not the mechanical effect of a cause any more than the outcome of an intention. Robert Burton, for example, at the inception of modern society, insightfully defines the subject of his *Anatomy of Melancholy* as 'sad-ness without a cause'. And while it is tempting to find a 'real' cause for modern melancholy in the loss of community, homeliness, and 'ontolog-ical security', imagined (wrongly) to be characteristic of premodern soci-ety (Lepenies 1992; Giddens 1991), Burton's formulation remains faithful to the 'moodiness' of mood and captures the sense of its being something extraneous and imposed.

The peculiarity of the present is not just that its moods are distinctive and characteristically different to those that colour daily life in other soci-eties, but that moodiness is its primary relation to reality. Mood is not a vague, background to contemporary life; it *is* contemporary life. Life now is described predominantly by its mood; dull, boring, tedious, tense, anx-ious, mournful, despairing, triumphant; without recourse to events, expe-riences, goals, values, or psychic contents of any sort. Contemporary moodiness is the accompaniment to non-identity. This is not at all the same as loss of identity; here there is no identity to lose, be denied, or renounced. Moods are 'empty' states that, unlike sense impressions, or voluntary movement, have no propensity towards objectification or eventuate in action of some sort. Where sensing, reasoning, and acting are oriented to the world in terms of 'interest' the passions generally are related to the world in terms of 'openness' and to the inexplicable pulse of mood.

Where the active, identity-seeking dimension of life seeks coherence in terms of reason and self, mood surrenders to the non-identical, which finds its generic form in *boredom*.

The essential connection between boredom and modernity, at once evident and obscure, is the particular focus for one of Martin Heidegger's most important philosophical works. The first part of *The Fundamental*

Concepts of Metaphysics, which was conceived as the continuation of *Being and Time* and drafted in the late 1920s but not published until 1978, is devoted to an extraordinary discussion of boredom, which seeks to clarify the oscillation between lethargy and distraction as two seemingly distinctive but ultimately identical experiences of waste time. Heidegger presents boredom as a 'fundamental attunement' to reality and, given his previously elaborated analysis of human being as essentially historical (*Dasein*). It is the characteristic *mood* of contemporary life. Boredom is not, for Heidegger, an orientation or disposition that retains a voluntaristic element; it is not an attitude. He asserts boldly that it is the world that is boring and the experience of boredom has an essential validity for us. It is not that we turn our back on the world; in boredom, rather, the world withdraws from us and leaves us stranded in a void.

Heidegger distinguishes two common forms of boredom. The first he describes as 'becoming bored by something'. In an obscure way boredom arises *'from out of things themselves'* (Heidegger 1996: 83) and is revealed first of all to the extent that we continually seek to escape it. Above all we seek to 'pass the time'. But the object that is boring *does not concern* us and remains something to which we remain indifferent. Heidegger arrives at an initial, challenging formulation; 'Boredom is that which we seek to drive away by passing the time' (Heidegger 1996: 92–93).

He provides an example of waiting for a train. Waiting is not itself boredom; not every waiting is boring, it may be a condition of keen anticipation, suspenseful, tense, excited and so on. Rather, as Benjamin (1999: 105) also notes, 'We are bored when we don't know what we are waiting for'. Nor is boredom identical with impatient waiting; 'Our passing the time has this peculiar character of a fluttering unease that brings this impatience with it. For what happens in becoming bored is that our unease while having to wait does not allow us to find anything that could grip us, satisfy us or let us be patient' (Heidegger 1996: 94). When bored and seeking to pass the time; 'We do not look at anything in particular because nothing in particular offers itself to us. Indeed the inherent predicament of becoming bored is precisely that we cannot find anything in particular' (Heidegger 1996: 99). In this relation time is 'dragging' and oppressive, a dragging oppressiveness that keeps time apart from us and 'holds us in limbo'. Things are withdrawn from us part, seemingly, of a quite different stream of time that in which we have become stuck.

The second type of boredom is being bored *with* (not by) something. For example, an evening out may seem easy, pleasant and unoppressive.

There is no sense here of withdrawnness and its accompanying arousal of an effort to pass the time (Heidegger 1996: 111). Many conventionally pleasant activities, in fact, actually have the character of passing the time as their essence. In the second form nothing in particular bores us. This type of inconspicuous boredom, which is the most general form of distraction, has the character of 'letting oneself be swept along by whatever is transpiring there' (Heidegger 1996: 117). This 'whiling' away the time, casually 'going along' with events, in fact, leaves time 'standing'. In 'whiling' we close ourselves off from the 'unsettling and paralyzing sound' of time ticking away. The sheer transition of the now is extended, sealed off and eternalized. Nothing actually happens; there is a sense of pure duration without transition. And this standing time, for Heidegger, is a purely formal self-experience stripped of any particular content. Boredom, here, is 'self forming emptiness' (Heidegger 1996: 127); it's oneself that is bored and the incidental events become boring as the bored self touches them.

Heidegger's detailed investigation of these two common forms of boredom, insightful as it is, serves primarily as an introduction to his original and striking account of a third form; profound boredom. Here, '*indifference* yawns at us out of all things, an indifference whose grounds we do not know … a profound boredom draws back and forth like a silent fog in the abysses of *Dasein*'(Heidegger 1996: 77). Profound boredom is 'boring for one', rather than boring for me, or you, or us. There is a collective experience of boredom, a mood that settles over an entire period in an undisguised way and does not arise from a particular situation, or from within the self held in suspension. Here emptiness and being held in limbo are overwhelmingly forced upon one. Boredom here is a general indifference; it is a world for which '*everything is of equally great and equally little worth* … it takes us back to the point where all and everything appears indifferent to us' (Heidegger 1996: 137). Indifference 'enveloping beings *as a whole*', is, in fact, the only remaining form of wholeness and, as distinct from any notion of positively shared values or beliefs, might be viewed as the distinctive mode of negative integration that sustains contemporary society.

This is 'a telling refusal on the part of beings as a whole' and Heidegger is uncompromising in his insistence that it characterizes every aspect of contemporary experience; 'All beings withdrawn from us without exception in every respect (*Hinsicht*), everything we look at and the way in which we look at it; everything in retrospect (*Rücksicht*), all beings that we look back upon as having become and as past and the way we look back at them; all beings in every prospect (*Absicht*), everything we look at prospectively as future and the way we have thus regarded them prospectively. Everything – in every respect, in retrospect and prospect, beings simultaneously withdrawn' (Heidegger 1996: 145). It is from within the attunement of profound boredom that a '*single* and *unitary universal horizon of time*' (Heidegger 1996: 145), comes into view. Being left empty is nothing other than Being's refusal to be drawn into differentiated forms; or, positively, 'our *being entranced by the temporal horizon as such*' (Heidegger 1996: 147).

For Heidegger, as previously for Kierkegaard, human being is inherently interested in its world, so the experience of boredom seems fundamentally to contradict the very possibility of *Dasein*. Heidegger's radical solution is to shift the entire burden of Being into a region prior to all particularity. Boredom, like Pascal's 'wretchedness', is a trace or intuition of the withdrawn fullness of Being. Boredom is fascinating because its empty eternity, pale and insubstantial as it is, makes human spirit present in a more vivid way than is open to any interested experience. Profound boredom should not be mistaken for abstract, worldless, and indeterminate Being; it is an ordinary world filled with indifferent content (Visker 2005).

Heidegger's view of profound boredom revives and radicalizes a genealogy that serves to designate, for modernity, the borderland between humanity and spirit. And Heidegger is not alone. At the same time that he was formulating his thoughts on the withdrawnness of Being, Alberto Moravia's (2001) startling first novel, with the precisely forensic title *A Time of Indifference* was published in 1929; a theme to which he returned throughout his writing life. Unsurprising, then, that he should say; 'I recall having suffered always from boredom' (Moravia 1999: 5), a vague and indefinite state of mind he characterizes as 'lack of contact with external things' (Moravia 1999: 16).

And the Portuguese writer Fernando Pessoa (2002), who, like Heidegger, had learned everything from Kierkegaard, concurs. His *Book of Disquiet* revels in boredom as the most powerful spiritual solvent of modernity. Boredom is not just democratic in the sense that it is open to all, but, more significantly, it advances a radical equality in which every distinction is nullified and every object loses its value as a particular thing. Boredom is the truth of modern life; 'The tedium of the forever new, the tedium of discovering – behind the specious differences of things and ideas – the unrelenting sameness of everything ... the eternal concordance of life with itself ... all of it equally condemned to change (Pessoa 2002: 110). This is a strangely comforting, tensionless world; 'To suffer without suffering, to want without desire, to think without reason ... It's like being possessed by a negative demon, like being bewitched by nothing at all' (Pessoa 2002: 208).

Boredom is the infinitely plastic medium in which everything becomes possible; the empty coherence of the multiple realities of contemporary life. The radical discontinuity in experience that founded modernity and which is repeated with every novelty it ushers into existence, is assimilated without disturbance to a familiar world of enduring, banal objects through boredom; 'Boredom, extinction, is precisely a continuity in nothingness' (Kierkegaard 1980: 133).

Kierkegaard, not simply anticipating, but surpassing Heidegger, finds in boredom a veritable negative principle of modern society. It is more than withdrawnness and indifference; there is, rather, a genuinely negative relation to the world. Proceeding from 'the basic principle that all people are boring', Kierkegaard discovers a principle of existential movement; the exact point of his rejection of Hegel was just that it introduced such a principle into a system of philosophical abstraction. But a system is defined by formal relations and rules of transformation that are bound by the conservation of identities; only in living beings can movement occur, because existence is not something identical with itself. Boredom is in some respects like a philosophical system in its detachment of reality, in its eternity and disinterest in the world; but on closer inspection it is clear that boredom actually repels, it pushes back; 'This basic principle has to the highest degree the repelling force always required in the negative, which is actually the principle of motion. It is not merely repelling but infinitely repulsive ... It is very curious that boredom, which itself has such a calm and sedate nature, can have such a capacity to initiate motion' (Kierkegaard 1988: 285).

Kierkegaard links boredom and the culture of the present in the idea of 'demonic pantheism'. The spirit of modernity, thus, is profoundly negative; 'Pantheism ordinarily implies the qualification of fullness; with boredom it is the reverse: it is built upon emptiness, but for this very reason it is a pantheistic emptiness, but for this very reason it is a pantheistic qualification. Boredom rests upon the nothing that interlaces existence (*Tilvaerelsen*); its dizziness is infinite, like that which comes from looking down into a bottomless abyss ... demonically possessed by

boredom in an attempt to escape it, one works one's way into it'
(Kierkegaard 1988: 291).

Boredom is the resilience and continuity of the non-identical.
Contemporary society is 'held together' by boredom rather than shared
values, a dominant ideology, or the continuous exercise of force. The
cohesive unity-totality of self-identity finds itself at last, but in the
strangely inverted form of indifference. And where self-identity dissolves, attunement to reality must be to indifference and the banal world
of boredom; to a world within which no difference makes a difference.

Liminality

Moodiness is an interruption in boredom; difference without distinction,
difference within the ever-same. The non-identical is also and vividly
experienced as an interrupted or *liminal* state of withdrawal from ordinary
life (Turner 1969). In a less obvious way, *liminality* has itself been wholly
assimilated to the routines of everyday life and has become indistinguishable from its changing moodiness. The exemplary case of illness yields
rich descriptive material testifying to the actual suffering of non-identity.
Interestingly, in an extreme case of 'saving the phenomenon', this literature is often construed as illness *narratives*; a formal approach that effectively imposes upon it the alien form of self-identity.

The significance of illness for contemporary life is difficult to overesti-
mate. Illness is ubiquitous and, as historic hardship and basic insecurity
for large numbers of people in advanced societies gives way to anxieties
of different sorts, illness not only continues to threaten life and happiness, it appears in ever new and more menacing forms. New illnesses,
some themselves the corporealizations of profound negative moods in
contemporary everyday life such as stress, fatigue and panic, emerge in
contemporary everyday life; postmodern illnesses for the present age
(Rabinbach 1990; Morris 1998; Showalter 1997).

In a more general sense illness has become the metaphor of normality
as distinct from the condition of abnormality (Sontag 2002; Broyard
1992). This was foreseen by Nietzsche and a widely held view by the end
of the nineteenth century. The human motor was running down, degeneration was the inescapable somatic outcome of the decline of western
civilization (Nordau 1993). These cultural assessments of illness were
given fresh biological credibility in studies of both organic and psychological conditions in which the 'disease process' was no different to the

healthy process and the distinction of outcome was an arbitrary judgement; 'If we acknowledge the fact that disease remains a kind of biological norm, this means that the pathological state cannot be called abnormal
in an absolute sense, but abnormal in relation to a well-defined situation.
Inversely, being healthy and being normal are not altogether equivalent
since the pathological is one kind of normal. Being healthy means being
not only normal in a given situation but also normative in this and other
eventual situations. What characterizes health is the possibility of transcending the norm, which defines the momentary normal, the possibility
of tolerating infractions of the habitual norm and instituting new norms
in new situations' (Canguilhem 1989: 196–197).

   Illness begins in a general feeling of unease rather than with any specific
symptom. There is something wrong *with the world*; 'Illness is, in the last
analysis, not the established result which scientific medicine declares as illness but, rather, the experience of the person suffering it … Illness, then, is
in general experienced by the person who is ill as a disturbance which can no
longer be ignored. The recognition that something is lacking is connected
with the idea of balance … illness represents a fall from a self-sustaining
equilibrium into a state of unbalance (Gadamer 1995: 55). Illness manifests
itself first as hesitancy, withdrawal and a reluctance to step out into the
world. But this condition, initially felt as temporary, readily becomes a permanent mode of being. The Epicurean of modern illness, Franz Kafka,
embraces this state and makes it normative for contemporary life:

> … for about ten years I have had this ever growing feeling of not being in per-
> fect health: the sense of well-being that comes with good health, the sense
> of well-being created by a body that responds in every way, a body that func-
> tions even without constant attention and care, this sense of well-being
> which in most people is the source of constant cheerfulness and above all
> unselfconsciousness – this sense of well-being I lack. And I lack it in every,
> indeed in every single manifestation of life. And this defect is not due to any
> specific illness I might have had; on the contrary, apart from children's com-
> plaints I have never really been ill enough to stay in bed, perhaps not even ill
> at all, in any case I cannot remember any such illness.
>
> (Kafka 1978: 378)

Kafka gains an important insight not only into his own fascination with
illness but into its general significance for contemporary everyday life;

> … ever since my childhood a minor, fleeting illness has always been a much
> coveted but rarely achieved pleasure. It breaks the inexorable passage of

time and bestows on this worn-out, dragged-along being that one is a minor rebirth, which I am now really beginning to crave

(Kafka 1978: 260).

And, furthermore, illness becomes an 'attunement' to contemporary reality, a kind of sensitivity to relational and shared moods

... recently you have had headaches, sore throats, states of languor and all these repeatedly and actually without a break ... I am as much involved in your suffering as you are. I don't exactly get a sore throat every time you have one, but when I hear about it, or suspect it, even only fear it, I suffer from it no less than you, in my own way. And I suffer even more from your exhaustion and more still from your headaches. And if you take some aspirin, then I too feel physically sick. All last night, that is from 3.30 to 7.30 and into the early part of the morning, I felt a strange kind of pressure inside myself such as I never remember before in the thirty years of my life; it emanated neither from the stomach, nor from the heart, nor from the lungs, but perhaps from all three together. It subsided in daylight. If you took some aspirin yesterday, then I am sure it was due to that; if not, to the previous aspirins.

(Kafka 1978: 223–224)

Novalis, as in so much else, anticipates the contemporary significance of illness. The vulnerability of illness and which in a general way is indicated by illness, is the proper condition of contemporary life. As distinct from bourgeois self-enclosure, illness places oneself in others' hands; 'Through imperfection one becomes open to the influence of *others* ... In *illness* only *others ought* and *can* help us' (Novalis 1997: 107). Illness is nothing less than the 'Dissolution of the difference between life and death' (Novalis 1997: 114) and, in that sense, a triumph over a mistaken conception of both. Illness is a contemporary way of life, not a temporary interruption in normality; 'Illnesses, particularly long-lasting ones, are years of apprenticeship in the art of life and the shaping of the mind. One must seek to use them through daily observations' (Novalis 1997: 163).

Illness is significant as the experience of a break that becomes more than a liminal interruption and is an important 'proof' of self-presence. In illness the body is returned to a palpable reality and, at the same time, the horizon of time and space shrinks to the immediate here and now (Van den Berg 1972). Illness is important because it is the last corner of authority the self can claim over its own experience; an existential compromise between modern self-identity and postmodern non-identity. But this compromise moves inexorably towards the contemporary fascination with feeling. Illness is now important, not as a heightened and vivid experience of corporeal self-embodiment, but as embodied feeling. Illness becomes an encounter with something more real than the self; and transforms the body from being a vehicle of self-identity to being the site of an encounter with something alien.

Ontological playfulness

Yet distinctions do matter; the muffled indifference of a world filled with non-identical but equally indifferent objects comes to life in its own way through ceaseless ontological variation. Things are just as they appear, there is no underlying, overarching, or ultimate reality, but they appear in many different ways. The fragmentation of experience, in one sense, enriches the field of possible appearances. Giddens has described the modern project of self-identity in terms of ontological *insecurity*; as distinct from the premodern enclosed community in which identity was ascribed, known, and fixed, the modern self is set loose in a world of divergent and conflicting relations in which nothing is fully known, or fixed. The trajectory of the self through the shifting relations and regions of modern life gives rise to new possibilities of self-realization, agency and the experience of autonomy. But with these possibilities come persistent self-doubt, anxiety, and the heavy responsibility of self-development. However, in spite of the psychological insecurity common in contemporary everyday life, it is clearly the case that *ontological* shifts of a somewhat different sort play an increasingly significant role in the construction of reality.

The deconstruction of experience is more than the loss of a sense of coherence and community, or the replacement of fixed and bounded relationships with mobile and shifting attachments; it means, above all, that the same events, objects, forms, and relations are given in a number of different ways. The object that is sensed is, in a different way, remembered, viewed as an image, described to a friend and imagined in the future and so on.

A characteristic of contemporary culture is the way in which the same event or object is given in a variety of ways simultaneously. At a live event, a big concert or sporting event for example, the audience watch images on a large screen as well as on the stage or field, then watch replays interspersed with instructions and advertisements. At these same events many people take photographs or film actions and send it to friends. In Japan, when the first radiant burst of cherry blossoms appear many people watch the tiny image in the back of their digital camera to make sure they have the best 'view' to transmit to their friends or relatives who cannot be there to see it 'live'.

The complex, overlapping and ultimately independent modalities of appearance, rather than being focused on a single event or object in which they are synthesized as the 'reality' of the object or event itself, increasingly lead separate lives, according to their own conventions related to other images and objects given in the same manner. The memories of being bombed, rescued from a fire, and visiting Florence, for example, are related together as particular kinds of recollections, but each memory is disconnected from its circumstances and appears singly as an unexplained, ghostly image. Photographs are collected and sorted by date, like a diary; 'remembering' become a particular kind of awareness rather than a mechanism for constituting the past.

The many worlds of contemporary experience are not new. Multiplicity and plurality have been a hallmark of modernity since its inception. The plurality of selves, corresponding to these worlds, was made central to the psychological and philosophical reconstruction of experience over a hundred years in the writings of William James. And the possibility of multiple personality and radical forms of mental dissociation was a key topic for medical and other researchers in the latter part of the nineteenth century (Hacking 1998). But where such states had been regarded as abnormal and the occasion for new exotic illnesses such as hysteria, they have since become commonplace and normal. We have learned to live with multiplicity. Ontological playfulness has replaced ontological insecurity as the dominant mood of indeterminacy.

And where until much more recently all multiplicity was nonetheless founded on an original, primal, and taken-for-granted world in relation to which every other was a variant, deviation, copy, or altered form, it is now much less clear that any world can successfully sustain a claim to being *the* reality. It was 'taken-for-granted' by Edmund Husserl, the founder of modern phenomenological philosophy that the spatio-temporal, empirical world of perceptually constructed objects was 'reality', for most people, most of the time. In fact, the difficulty in understanding phenomenology as a philosophical method was primarily a matter of overcoming the obstacle of this deeply rooted assumption. And when phenomenology entered American sociology through the writings of Albert Schutz and his students, the primacy of the shared, inter-subjective world of perceptual objects was similarly assumed (Schutz 1962; Berger and Luckmann 1967).

The dominance of the sensory-perceptual world has come to an end. Now it is less obvious that the sensory world, in any case, constitutes a unity. Not only do sense impressions break apart from feelings, will, value, and so on, but vision is no longer essentially connected with hearing, or either with taste. The senses break apart and like memories, are arranged in relation to the same kind of sense data rather than related together in the substantial unity of an object. Sensing, as a result, has little to do with the world of objects, which now have their being, so to speak, as the neutral material required by the process itself. Sensing, like remembering, becomes a self-aware process rather than a means of self-identification. Sensing is a process in which the subject becomes aware of sensing, as distinct from the object sensed. Of course, it was always possible for people to become aware in this second-order, reflective way; but in contemporary society it becomes the primary mode of awareness.

Now 'experiences' finds its meaning as a proof and test of the existence of the subject. Sensing, remembering, acting, and so on have become so many ways in which we become aware of a receptive and active subject. But the need for such proof arises just because 'experience' as a self-identical, coherent unity-totality has undergone radical fragmentation. What arises is not the self-identical subject-object of experience, but disconnected, discontinuous, and incommensurable pulses of sensation, feeling, tendencies to movement, memories, and so on. Subjectivity is dispersed in these distinct regions and fields of awareness.

More remarkable still and the genuinely original aspect of the post-modern, is the new relation of experiential and existential worlds to each other. In an extraordinary way distinct and incompatible worlds coexist in tolerant disregard of one another, like Leibnizian *monads*. This much, of course, is implicit in William James's conception of the multiple self and is inherent in the approach of symbolic interactionism that developed in relation to his work. What emerged more slowly was the radical sense that such worlds were not more or less optional social roles, variant and inessential from the point of view of a self unambiguously founded in the primary, taken-for-granted world of experience, but constituted in themselves the only kinds of experiences there could be. Such a view animates Walter Benjamin's heroic attempt to catalogue the available fragments of contemporary experience (Frisby 1989: 187–265). The fragment is a genuine world, even when minimally constituted and displaying little content, it exists for the subject as a distinctive kind of awareness.

Different ontological regions, awareness of distinctive qualities, separate self-referential worlds, jostle together in the unbounded indeterminacy of contemporary everyday life. Fragments are not ordered and organized in everyday life, like objects in a space, or specimens in a museum. Above all they are not interchangeable and commensurable; they do not enter into processes of exchange and they are not mediated by a universal equivalent, or by reason, or value. This means that separate worlds of contemporary life cannot be grasped as available choices in an economic or market sense. Fragments are not ends and are not the objects of purposive action. We cannot plan to fall in love, become angry, or change our mood. We might wish we could shake ourselves free of boredom, or turn on happiness like a tap; but we cannot. We are overwhelmed by the most profound changes in feeling and awareness. Bewildered we try to cope. Throughout the period of bourgeois modernity we coped by processes of rationalization; imposing meaning on appearance and awareness, interpreting feelings as more or less appropriate reactions to specific circumstances, and by reducing the plurality of worlds to a paramount reality decorated with a penumbra of imagined variations. But now everything dissolves into indeterminacy; into everyday life for which everything is possible.

It might seem that ontological playfulness, the wonderland of selfless non-identity, has rather a limited bearing on the lives of most people for whom it is simply not the case that everything is possible. A paramount reality and its harsh resistance to playfulness seem unambiguously to dominate the lives of the vast majority of people in contemporary society. But this would be to misjudge the situation. The harshness of work, the greater harshness of unemployment, squalid housing conditions, poor education and so on, are not obstacles to the continuous fragmentation of contemporary life. Ontological variation is not a contemporary consumer luxury, or the doubtful privilege of a cultural *avant garde*, it is simply the way we live now. Fantasy, memory, imagination, desire, excitement, depression, boredom and anxiety are real for everyone; and have been transformed into the modalities of discrete forms of life.

More significantly, however, the situation itself is misleading. Ontological playfulness is a way of describing contemporary everyday life that is focused on *one* of its possibilities; the possibility of the fragment, which is something new and distinctive in the construction of the present. Older forms of life and experience, however, do not simply disappear as something new emerges. *Those* worlds persist; indeed, they are essential to the unbounded character of everyday life, which is simply the ceaseless appearing of all possible forms. In contemporary society, that is to say, it is possible, even unavoidable, to live through identities that 'belong' to contexts and systems of meaning that arose in the past. The self-identical, singular world of high modernity has not been eclipsed and hardly even displaced, by the fall into postmodernity. *That* world also coexists with the multiple realities of the postmodern. By the same token premodern, ancient, archaic, oriental, and cosmopolitan identities are regenerated and rediscovered. It is possible to adopt the values of the medieval monk and live through the symbolic hierarchy of his cosmos. Equally, Buddhism or Confucian secularism can appeal as plausible world-views or attractive 'life-styles'. And as these worlds are discontinuous and incommensurable surrender to one does not negate future openness to others. This is quite unprecedented. Society hitherto was constituted in an exclusive fashion. *Its* world was *the* world. Now reality is constructed in an inclusive fashion; *all* realities are accommodated as possibilities, including all those worlds for which such prodigality is inconceivable. Thus, *within* the unbounded indeterminacy of everyday life can be found innumerable positions, points of view, forms of life and so on, that are self-enclosed, clearly bounded and wholly determined. The selfless non-identity of contemporary life contains and, indeed, is almost entirely filled, with self-identical forms each of which insist upon their priority or exclusiveness with respect to characterizing reality.

But in this moment everything is changed. Every world is shifted into the subjunctive mood and, thus, becomes one of an unknown number of alternatives. The cohesive unity of the modern rational world-view is effective only for the subject *in* that world. Sooner or later, however, the subject finds itself in another world, equally real, equally convincing, and wholly different. The peculiarity of the postmodern lies simply in its acknowledgement of *all* possibilities. Like a cubist painting it juxtaposes radically different points of view without feeling any need to synthesize and smooth over apparently contradictory images.

The spirit of playfulness that, in spite of the appalling history of the twentieth century, continues to animate contemporary culture, it is inherent in the process of fragmentation. The connection was intuitively grasped by the first theorists of the fragment, Novalis and Friedrich Schlegel, for whom play was the effortless, world-creating discourse of the ancient gods rediscovered in modern childhood (Spariosu 1997). Activity free from need and necessity, unlimited and unrestrained, displayed the charm of eternity and became the model of contemporary everyday life. The freedom of play was wholly other than the self; it brought forth a plurality of other worlds and without alienating consequences for the simple reason that the self was not invested in any of them, it did not need to be because these worlds carried their own warrant of reality. Play is performative rather than expressive.

Performativity

The continuous flow of human subjectivity is no longer necessarily experienced as the meaningful interiority of 'events' in the exterior world. The two frequently draw apart, contradict one another, and move in opposed directions. The disjunction between inner experience and the meaningful course of events is increasingly obvious; to such an extent, indeed, that it now requires a different language to describe and grasp its content. Neither any longer is constituted as a world of sense; a world that makes sense. The worldness of experience fragments into a series of discrete performances.

In the contemporary non-identical field of awareness body and self become disjointed, incommensurate, and disproportionate. For such a world social relations are not established and sustained on the basis of mutual interest, expressive meaning, or mutual sympathy. Human subjects are engaged together in performative acts; that is in 'pure' actions without reference to any transcendental value, inner meaningfulness, or bodily expressiveness. Performative acts 'speak for themselves' in the sense that they 'do' something irrespective of and indifferent to, intentions, wishes, or desires of the actors. Performance is committed role distance; socialization without internalization (Turner 1974, 1982, 1988).

Like music, or modern dance, everyday performances are 'out there'. Neither self nor other, performance does not require an accompanying self-consciousness. Subjectivity, rather, picks its way through everyday performances (Schechner 2003). Occasionally identifying with some aspect of performance as a role, at other times encountering self-actions as distant and strange, everyday life presents ever-changing *tableaux vivants* that invite and tolerate an extraordinary variety of interpretations, including the view that it is independent of any interpretation; 'performance consciousness is subjunctive, full of alternatives and potentiality' (Schechner 1985: 6).

The myth of self-identity is challenged by the practice of theatricality. The modern world is, indeed, a stage upon which everyone is forced to perform (Agnew 1986; Egginton 2002). But no one has a script; everyday life is a continuous improvisation in which, like children's play, people are 'caught up'.

Performativity is a discovery of the subaltern and product of *ressentiment*; forced to suppress subjectivity and see the world as something utterly objective.

In fact there are original insights into this notion of performance in Mead and other pragmatists, who for philosophical reasons, reduced or eliminated the role of consciousness in understanding action. The conventions of everyday life exist 'in between' and not in the expressive or meaningful consciousness of individuals. This is also the lesson of the linguists following Saussure (Sapir 1949; Whorf 1956). Language is certainly meaningful, but is not a neutral modality of communication. Derrida and others have stressed the independence of language from the flow of subjective life and the communicative intentionality of the subject (Derrida 1973; Butler 1997). Additionally, following the analytic philosophy of J. L. Austin (1976) they have stressed performativity of language itself; notably, for example, in the act of naming. The comparison with music is helpful. Music is 'pure sensuousness' outside the body; expression but not expressive of the performer, listener, or composer.

Theatricality and the notion of performativity become available as models of everyday life only because the theatre emerged as a distinct institution separate from the ordinary context of daily activities. This did not happen in Japan where different performance forms remained contextualized and, in the modern period, retained their contextual meaning in a theatrical setting. The differentiation of theatre in the west is peculiar because it constitutes itself from the beginning as a picture, rather than part of society. Performance is ubiquitous and does not require an audience. Even within formal theatrical presentations the audience is detached and present as if by accident to observe the unfolding scene. In Japan the rise of everydayness and the centrality of performance in the organization of life coincide (Inoura and Kawatake 2006). Japanese modernity is popular culture regulated as a performance art and predates the establishment of the state or the nation.

The Japanese performance arts of the early modern period were varied and drew on a number of premodern models. They developed significantly to extend traditional forms to non-elite audiences and new urban classes. A new repertoire of drama emerged that found its content, as well as its audience, in the new urban world itself. The theatre presented *another* version of everyday life, particularly in the *bunraku*, puppet theatre, of Chikamatsu, as distinct from modern western theatre of the non-everyday.

The performance of everyday life in contemporary western society is, therefore, distinct from its counterpart in Japan. In Japan the everyday is continuously developed throughout the modern period as its primary mode of organization. Performance is organized from the outset to establish 'Japaneseness' in ordinary life. In modern western society ordering principles were taken out of everyday life, centralized in rational and authoritative institutions and structures. In relation to these structures everyday life formed and developed both as a counter-culture and, more significantly, as an 'underground' practice. Everyday life, simple by escaping the rationalizing tendencies of modern fragmented discourses, was always on the verge of transgression.

In de Certeau's work (1998) the separateness and non-identical fluidity of the everyday is a key theme. The everyday is a level beneath the realm captured in the transcendental discourses of modernity. Certeau peers microscopically into the Brownian motion of everyday life; a chaotic jumble of fragmented and free improvisation. His is a quantum view of the everyday. His starting point for a 'theory' of the practice of everyday life is Wittgenstein's view of ordinary language; informal, inconsistent, contradictory and possible only on the basis of implicit assumptions. This draws attention to the ceaseless creativity of everyday *practices*, which are always creative improvisations. Everyday life remains 'the great unknown' (de Certeau 1998: 9) always 'what is most difficult to discover' (Blanchot 1992: 238). The everyday is constructed by people who are 'poets of their own acts' (de Certeau 1998: xx). But, in spite of this, the 'invisible everyday' is also a 'silent and repetitive system of servitude' (de Certeau 1998: 171).

Reading is paradigmatic of this creative operation, a process that aims primarily at consumption; 'In reality, the activity of reading has on the contrary all the characteristics of a silent production: the drift across the page, the metamorphosis of the text effected by the wandering eye of the reader, the improvisation and expectation of meanings inferred from a few words, leaps over written spaces in an ephemeral dance ... this production is also an "invention" of memory' (de Certeau 1984: xxi).

> In reality, a rationalized, centralized, spectacular and clamorous production is confronted by an entirely different kind of production called "consumption" and characterized by its ruses, its fragmentation (the result of the circumstances), its poaching, its clandestine nature, its tireless but quiet activity, in short by its quasi-invisibility, since it shows itself not in its own products (where would it place them?) but in an art of using those imposed on it.
>
> (de Certeau 1998: 31)

The performance of everyday life is the continuous creation of the fragment; a *bricolage* of the disjointed.

Familiarity

A particularly important ontological variant is familiarity. Everyday life, in one respect, is given as the absolutely familiar. Everything appearing in this modality has the quality of familiarity in an essential way. And, just as memory is given 'as if' from the past, the familiar is given 'as if' it were already known. The familiar is the antithesis of the encounter; it is, to paraphrase Marx 'the self in a selfless world'. For contemporary life everything is repetition, the uncanny, and *déjà vu*. The most striking instances of familiarization in contemporary life are the phenomena of fashion and the banal.

Fashion

The phenomenon of fashion arose in modern society in connection first, with the ending of sumptuary regulation and, second, the emergence of a new understanding and valuation of change.

In medieval western society clothing styles and materials was regulated by sumptuary laws. The nobility wore entitled to wear rich silks and brocades. Other orders in society were forbidden to do so, whether or not they could afford to acquire such expensive fabrics. Modern society opened clothing to the market and the emerging system of class stratification was reflected in, no longer obligatory but price sensitive, dress styles. In modern society identity is exteriorized as *appearance*; this is important in a society where a high proportion of interaction takes place amongst strangers. These distinctions are sustained, therefore, not only by differences in wealth, but also rationalized in terms of appropriateness for different social categories. Notably age and gender, as well as occupational groups are more distinctive differentiated in terms of appearance than class. This is characteristic of the development of modern society; while distinctions founded on 'natural' identity are, in principle, swept aside, in practice they re-emerge as the consequence of apparently spontaneous market choices. Modern society, that is to say, displays distinctive, socially differentiated styles of appearance. However each style is subject to a new regime of fashion; to continuous change.

Fashion is characteristic of many aspects of everyday life, but has its primary locus in the ceaseless modulation of clothing styles. In contemporary society this process becomes transparent. It is not only the sociologist that notices 'not the slightest reason can be found for its creations from the standpoint of an objective, aesthetic or other expediency … Judging from the ugly and repugnant things that are sometimes worn, it would seem as though fashion were desirous of exhibiting its power by getting us to adopt the most atrocious things for its sake alone' (Simmel 1997: 189). The conventionalisation of identity and absolute freedom of selfhood are disconnected from each other as well as from social processes of a totalising sort. The fragmentation of society makes itself felt ultimately in transparency of identity and the arbitrariness and ever-changing character of appearance. Identity then comes to appearance uniquely in unstable and inauthentic fashion. Identity dissolves into sheer transition and, to that extent, finds its adequate form in fashion. This gives rise to the pseudo passion of contemporary life and the obliteration of the distinction between excitement and boredom; the running together of all feeling in a general indifference.

On the one hand, 'the more nervous the age, the more rapidly its fashions change' (Simmel 1997: 192), dissolving selfhood in continuous transition. On the other hand, however, 'The fashion system, particularly fashion journalism, constantly freezes the flow of everyday practices of dress and orders it into distinct entities of past, present and future … The self, while experiencing an undifferentiated internal time, is also forever being 'caught', frozen, temporally fixed by fashion' (Entwistle 2000: 32). Fashion is the metronome with which we keep pace to stay in the present.

More significantly, still, fashion is a process of familiarization with arbitrariness and with change. It makes the novel not only longed for and highly valued (Lipovetsky 2002: 45–46) but unthreatening. Every growth of a fashion drives it to its doom, because it thereby cancels out its distinctiveness ... the charm of newness and simultaneously of transitoriness. Fashion's question is not that of being, but rather is simultaneously being and non-being; it always stands on the watershed of the past and the future and, as a result, conveys to us, at least while it is at its height, a stronger sense of the present than do most other phenomena (Simmel 1997: 192). Fashion instantly transforms novelty into something already familiar and known and normalizes a process of continuous innovation. Thus, while fashion is a general process in which people are carried along, its 'attunement' to reality is always in terms of being 'cool'. Fashion is an implausible amalgamation of involvement and detachment; a kind of excited disenchantment.

Banality

Avital Ronell, echoing an essay by the great Austrian novelist Robert Musil, remarks that stupidity 'the indelible tag of modernity' is 'our symptom'. The inexhaustible patience of stupidity rivals boredom as an abyss of selfless non-identity. It is utterly banal; 'Extreme yet ordinary, the forces of stupidity press forward a mirage of aggression, a front without limits' (Ronell 2002: 15). Stupidity is invulnerable to enlightenment, the stark continuity of a break in consciousness. Stupidity is the pure form of banality, a world of the commonplace for which anything is not simply possible, but every possibility is ordinary.

The modern *fashion* for evil displayed in the hideous catwalk of modern warfare, genocide and mass destruction reduces everything human to the utterly banal (Eksteins 1990; Arendt 1994). And contemporary everyday life, the life of familiar and fashionable variety, accommodates the inhuman along with the human. Torture coexists with wringing endorsements of human rights, starvation with superabundance and anxiety with boredom. It is not that everything falls into a vague and indistinct condition in which everything seems to be the same, though such a condition is also characteristic of contemporary life (Zerubavel 1991) but, rather, that the starkest distinctions ultimately do not *matter*. This is a world for which, in its most advanced and progressive cities 'mental institutions, prisons and courtrooms became part of everyday life' (Ugresic 2005: 13) and where

'Death went hand in hand with day-to-day detritus ... evil was as banal as the everyday artifact and had no special status' (Ugresic 2005: 59). The banal is deadeningly familiar; 'There was a war going on in the world, dear God; and war was a raging madness, isn't that so? And yet the world could be so peaceful and still, so replete with slowly dragging time and boredom' (Szep 1994: 9).

There is nothing puzzling about the banal; it is simply the unlimited inclusiveness of everydayness; 'Everything in this life is really terrifyingly simple. Nothing simpler than the way a new and initially strange situation becomes mundane and the destruction of that new and as it turned out, terribly fragile everyday state of affairs is even simpler than that' (Kross 2003: 59).

For the everyday world goodness, equally, is reduced to banality (Terestchenko 2007; Scott 2007). And it is within the banal that the virtue of goodness can be restored. In an important passage, Nietzsche commends the everyday virtue of benevolence, rather than beliefs, ultimate values, truth and everything 'higher' in civilization, as the sustaining heart of a genuinely human culture:

> I mean those expressions of friendly sentiment in social interaction, that smile of the eyes, that shaking of hands, that comfortable pleasure with which almost all human actions are ordinarily entwined ... Good-naturedness, friendliness, politeness of the heart, are the ever-flowing streams of the unegotistical drive and have worked more powerfully in building culture than those much more famed expressions of it that we call sympathy, compassion and sacrifice.
>
> (Nietzsche 1986: 49)

Translation

If self-identity is fragmented how can social life more generally be described? The process of transforming, assimilating, comparing, contrasting, gaining insight, assigning equivalence, recognition, and repetition, all of which figure as variant forms of grasping contemporary realities, are also modes of translation. For the modern west translation, first of all, has a mathematical meaning as change of location under fixed coordinates; that is the movement of an object without alteration to its size, shape, or orientation. Translation also refers to the movement from one official position to another, equivalent position; as in the translation of a bishop to a different see. Linguistically translation is a change of language under fixed terms of reference and meaning. Translation, in other terms, assigns new words without alteration in the meaning to which they refer; translation is a practical example of the distinction between sense and reference. An identical meaning is capable of being differently encoded.

In a more radical sense, however, other cultures constitute the process of translation in distinctive ways. In Japan, thus, translation is not effected through narrative selfhood and the stability of inner meaning, but through the accumulation of cultural performances. There are issues of translation, in other words, not only *between* cultures and *within* cultures but over the process of translation as such. Translation is not only a matter of finding an adequate expression for a foreign term or relation; what constitutes translation is itself equivocal. It is in this sense that Walter Benjamin insisted that translation 'is a form of its own' (Benjamin 2004: 258).

One model of translation is silent and inward reading; a subjectively meaningful intention is actualized in the medium of an expressive semiotic system; the system is transformed according to specific rules of equivalence and the result assimilated by a parallel and equivalent subject. Translation is a formal matter of determining equivalence between two or more systems of signs. Another model of translation, however, abandons communicative intent as its grounding necessity and possibility and takes intersubjectivity to be both the mode and substance of translation. Here the subject is not independent of the system of signs, nor is the system of signs a pure communicative device, rather both are caught up in continual reciprocal interaction. Benjamin expresses this idea by drawing attention to the paradoxical character of translation the 'essential quality (of which) is not communication or the imparting of information. Yet any translation that intends to perform a transmitting function cannot transmit anything but communication – hence, something inessential' (Benjamin 2004: 253). Translation, therefore, is 'only a somewhat provisional way of coming to terms with the foreignness of languages' (Benjamin 2004: 257).

The interrelating of Japanese and European modernity, historically as well as conceptually, involves a radical type of translation. Meaningful elements from one field of signification are transformed into performative elements in another and vice versa. Of course there is a species kind of Orientalism at work here; in characterizing the Japanese cultural field as 'performative' rather than 'meaningful' some pejorative valuation might be suggested, though it is not obvious which is to be regarded as superior. It is not suggested that performativity is the only significant mode of acculturation in Japan; rather that performativity has become a dominant mode of reality construction, as compared to Europe, for which subjectivity has been normative. Of course, both modes exist in both fields; Japanese and European are used here as shorthand referents for specific (dominant and orthodox) forms of reality construction in Europe and Japan respectively. It is worth noting, however, the extraordinary hybridity that characterizes the Japanese spoken and written language (Gottlieb 2005). There are an extraordinary number of untranslated loanwords, particularly from Chinese and English and many English language terms introduced into Japan after the Meiji Restoration were translated into new institutional contexts that defined their performative standards rather than conceptual meanings (Howland 1996, 2002).

A consideration of translation in this way also raises substantive historical issues that are at the heart of the classical sociological account of modernity. The process of translation challenges the self-understanding of modern European society. The need for translation arises from an *encounter* of some kind; obdurate otherness breaks into the continuity of a familiar world. At the same time the unfamiliar is embraced as potentially intelligible; otherness is effaced by translation. In the emergence of European modernity might be described as the simultaneous expansion and specification of the field of translation. On the one hand, the spatial extension of European societies resulted in significant encounters with distant and in some cases previously unknown societies (Todorov 1999; Pagden 1994; Fernández-Armesto 2006). And, on the other hand, humanity alone was translatable. Non-human orders of reality, most notably nature and God, along with most of the human world of the past were not intelligible as other they were incomprehensibly *alien* (Theunissen 1984); that is, comes to mark a particular kind of difference, one founded, not on the particulars of shared experience, but on the supposition that the world, for self and other, is alike in being constituted *as* human experience.

This makes translation into and out of a European perspective asymmetric. From a modern European perspective the *other* is transformed into *another self* before it is united with the subject (translated) in an inclusive world of meaning. This excludes from what we call Japan anything that in a radical sense is alien and meaningless. Japan has to be grasped as like Europe in the crucial respect of constituting itself as a historical subject before it can be translated and become familiar. However, if 'Japan', in a Japanese perspective, is constituted as an inclusive reality that encompasses what European modernity made inaccessible to *its* immediate experience and could only *represent* through abstractions (Nature, God, the Past), then *its* translation of European modernity could be effected through direct participation in its developed forms. Indeed, it could participate also in just those forms European modernity had discarded.

In the first perspective translation is a purely technical manipulation of a neutral symbolic medium which acts as the mediator between two self-identical subjects and, ideally, both the translation process and the strictly equivalent symbolic media it interrelates disappear; what is crucial is the transmission of meaning from one subject to another. In the second perspective translation is the immediate experience of the other as part of a single reality. In both perspectives, as *communication* or as *assimilation*, distinctive techniques of inclusion grasp the other as a moment of the self, but for each, to the extent that these (pre)translations were effective, the self-understanding of the culture of the translator, is undermined.

In a curious way, translating the other is possible only by a prior negation of the otherness that made it necessary in the first place. Translation is a betrayal of the other; like a neurotic symptom that by indirect means draws attention precisely to the event it seeks directly to efface, translation presupposes the very difference its practice denies. Translation supposes identity and presupposes alterity; it is the performance of everyday life in a world without self or identity.

In the west postmodernity is the break that was modernity taken into itself – fragmentation and discontinuity. In Japan modernity was not a break, but an accumulation and juxtaposition. The character of indifference in Japan is achieved by emptying the self, not by reducing difference to zero. In Japan the even temper of everyday life accommodates infinite difference by expanding its collection of stuff to infinity. Modern Japan is the infinite collection; in which everything is different. In the west the jostling monads collide and break open.

INTERRUPTION 6: FICTION

The author sifted through some old family photographs. He did not recognize himself. A school photograph showed a group of fifteen boys aged about thirteen. With some difficulty, and prompted by a visitor with whom he had attended the school, names were attached to all but one of the group. By this process of elimination he arrived at the conclusion that the hunched, nervous looking figure on the left of the second row was, in fact, him at that age. But there was no moment of recognition, no ability to recall the day, or put himself in the place of the pictured figure and feel he was 'there'. In fact he failed to recognize all but three of the group; they simply did not 'match' his recollection of their features, though he recognized the names his friend attached to them. He had not seen any of these people since he had left the school after little more than a year.

This was not a lapse of memory so much as a failure of imagination; and one easy enough to diagnose. The author had been very unhappy at that time and did not want to recall anything from that period in his life. But what he did recall of the period, in spite of his best efforts to bury the past, was a bitter residue of fear that he could trace through subsequent uncomfortable experiences, culminating in a recent stressful period at work. The mood and feeling of the period, but none of the physical details and events, was somehow preserved and, unwanted, visited him on an unpredictable but not infrequent schedule.

The small failure of self-recognition was of no consequence. It was connected, however, with a larger difficulty amounting to a 'crisis of identity' in relation to his work as an author. Commissioned to write a brief introductory text entitled *Self-Identity and Everyday Life* he found himself, long after the manuscript had been due for submission, still unable to compose his thoughts in a satisfactory way. The powerful inhibition he felt in relation to writing must be connected, he surmised, with the difficult and turbulent period also associated with the photographic image he had viewed as a stranger. This, after all, made perfect sense. The sense of vulnerability and apprehension he felt every time he sat down to work, the reluctance to commit his half-formed thoughts to the screen, and his resistance to reading over and revising any of the drafts and notes he had managed sporadically to accumulate all stemmed from the period of his first identity crisis. Writing about identity had re-activated, as it were, all the uncertainties of his teenage years. Those long moments of self doubt, unremarkable and undramatic as they had been, were felt with sufficient intensity to motivate a highly successful process of suppression. Youthful timidity implausibly linked with devouring spiritual longing, had long since been overlaid with sober, realizable personal goals and a successful, unspectacular professional career.

The project, accepted on a whim, quickly undermined his carefully nurtured defenses. He felt exposed and lost. He tried hard to work out what he really thought about the issues involved, read haphazardly and with frantic endeavour anything that might prove insightful. Everything was insightful, and nothing was insightful enough. The smallest detail posed insurmountable difficulties. He worried his colleagues (like a an uncontrolled dog worries sheep) over outlines, chapter plans, vague ideas of all sorts, hoping to find in their encouragement the strength he needed, and lacked in himself, to complete the task. Then he tried just to forget it for a while, went on holidays, and devoted himself with more than usual enthusiasm to teaching.

Then he had a good idea. Some years before he had attended an evening class in Italian with a view to learning sufficient of the language to feel comfortable travelling to the many beautiful towns he wished to visit. He found foreign languages difficult to learn and was painfully embarrassed at speaking even simple sentences and phrases he knew to be full of childish errors. He approached his Italian class in a positive frame of mind. He put behind him the failures of the past. But the method used by the teacher was new to him, and terrifying. The class was conducted exclusively in Italian and consisted primarily in the teacher speaking for a few minutes, providing simple descriptions of himself, objects in the room, everyday routines, and so on; then he would ask questions, answers to which had been provided in what he had said. The procedure was effective and enjoyable for everyone except the author; who froze in stony silence whenever he was asked a question. After three weeks he realized what was wrong. He could easily have answered any of the questions the teacher addressed to his classmates; but as soon as he said 'Harvie . . .' panic set in and the hapless student gasped for air. The solution lay in assuming a false identity! The following week the author read out a carefully prepared statement in Italian, requesting that from now on everyone should refer to him as Giordano; for the purposes of the class he was to be considered a reincarnation of Giordano Bruno, burned at the stake as a heretic in 1600, and one of the author's cultural heroes.

It worked. He did not learn much Italian, but he enjoyed the class, and what he did learn he could speak, and thereafter enjoyed many visits to Italy. Now he would identify himself with a contemporary social theorist and cultural critic that he most admired. He need only address himself as 'Michel' (Foucault, Serres, de Certeau, it hardly mattered which), and pages of startling prose and penetrating insight would flow.

Alas, it did not work, For Michel or Jacques, Jean-Luc, Pierre, Walter, Ernst, Norbert or any, less illustrious and closer to home, that he tried. He was not so easily fooled this time.

In despair he went to Greece and imagined himself retired. Heaven.

Past caring he hit on a desperate remedy. Summoning all his resolve he convinced himself he was Harvie Ferguson, author of several sociological works that had been completed, if not easily, then at least more or less on time. It worked; that was the author, he remembered, who was sensible enough never to identify himself with his work, conscientiously researched the topic, and never asked himself what he 'really' thought about anything. In the end, it was, after all, just a job.

Fiction is what did not happen; it is the imaginary. Fiction is the literature of the non-identical. Self-identity cannot be narrated. Self-identity is not a story; it is a fiction. Fiction is literature of self-identity. Fiction is the literature of the identical and the non-identical; it posits the identity of identity and the non-identical.

Where narrative begins with actual events and forms them into something coherent and meaningful in terms of its directionality, duration, succession, expressiveness, character, and so on, fiction is break. The literary revolution of modernity, one need only think of Proust, Joyce, or Faulkner, even where they took a singular life as its subject matter wholly transformed the meaningful world of the *Bildungsroman*.

Fiction is about – nothing. It begins elsewhere; and just because reality is now elsewhere. It is not an ill-judged escape attempt from the real, but a determined pursuit of spirit as it rushes into oblivion. It is fiction that sustains our sense of reality, and it is only by fictionalizing, that is through the rupture of the non-identical, that we can generate a bubble of self-identity within which everything appears with thing-like solidity and continuity. Not narrating events that have already occurred, but imagining them afresh is what counts. Empathy, not sympathy, is affective, and the empathic is really imaging oneself as another; not imagining the other as the self, not taking the place of the other, but allowing the other to invade and occupy the self. Self becomes exterior, strange, and bewildering. Self and identity part company; body has dissolved into fluidity and sensitivity; identities merge and become vague; self falls back into the inexperiencable 'I', the pure transition of the now.

The question of identity, consequently, changes. It is no longer a question of 'Who are we?' or even 'Who are we like?' but, 'Who is having this experience?' Experience now becomes an event that takes place elsewhere. The 'I/we' is no longer the experiencing subject. How, then, can we grasp ourselves when all identities fade or become ambiguous, and self protects its freedom by a draconian act of self-alienation? Not, certainly, as an explanatory 'cause' of our own actions or of events in the world, and not, any longer, as a meaningful narrative, a trajectory of the subject rich in intention. We can grasp ourselves, and what remains of our world, only by following the 'I' into the curious plenitude of nihilism; that is we live, when we live at all, fictively. And fictions, the non-identical, are marked simply by the label 'real.' Only fictions have the possibility of being real and everyday life is the home of fictions

Self-identity is an assertion of the non-identical; and the experience of the non-identical rouses self to life. Self-identity is not an entity and cannot reach completion. It is the open, the non-identity of self with itself; the continuous difference of living being. There can be no conclusion to a reflection on self-identity, any more than the project of self-identity can reach completion. This is not a text that moves from introduction to conclusion, or even beginning to end; but from begin to begin. The liveliness of life continually demands another beginning. For the digital age the trick is simply to fall in with the algorithm of everyday life:

Begin.

Start

REFERENCES

Abe, K. (2002) *The Box Man*, New York: Vintage.

Abe, K. (2006) *The Face of Another*, Harmondsworth: Penguin.

Abu-Lughod, J.L. (1989) *Before European Hegemony: The World System A.D. 1250–1350*, New York and Oxford: Oxford University Press.

Agamben, G. (2004) *The Open: Man and Animal*, Stanford: Stanford University Press.

Agamben, G. (2007) *Profanations*, Cambridge MA: Zone Books.

Agnew, J-C. (1986) *Worlds Apart: The Market and the Theatre in Anglo-American Thought 1550–1750*, Cambridge MA: Cambridge University Press.

Ameriks, K. (2000) *Kant and the Fate of Autonomy*, Cambridge MA: Cambridge University Press.

Anderson, B. (1991) *Imagined Communities*, London: Verso.

Ankersmit, F.R. (2005) *Sublime Historical Experience*, Stanford: Stanford University Press.

Anzieu, D. (1989) *The Skin Ego* (transl. Chris Turner), New Haven: Yale University Press.

Appadurai, A. (1986) *The Social Life of Things*, Cambridge: Cambridge University Press.

Arendt, H. (1994) *Eichmann in Jerusalem: A Report on the Banality of Evil*, London: Penguin.

Ariès, P. (1996) *Centuries of Childhood* (transl. Robert Baldick), London: Pimlico.

Arnason, J.P., Eisenstadt, S.N. and Witrock, B. (eds) (2005) *Axial Civilizations and World History*, Leiden: Brill.

Auslander, L. (1996) *Taste and Power: Furnishing Modern France*, Berkeley: University of California Press.

Austin, J.L. (1976) *How To Do Things With Words*, Oxford: Oxford University Press.

Bakhtin, M. (1968) *Rabelais and His World* (transl. Hélène Iswolsky), Cambridge MA: MIT Press.

Bataille, G. (1994) *Eroticism*, London: Marion Boyars.

Baudrillard, J. (2004) *Fragments*, London: Verso.

Beard, G. (1881) *American Nervousness: Its Causes and Consequences*, New York: Putnam.

Beauvoir, S. de (1976) *Old Age*, Harmondsworth: Penguin.

Becker, M.B. (1988) *Civility and Society in Western Europe 1300–1600*, Bloomington: Indiana University Press.

Beech, G.T., Bourin, M. and Chareille, P. (2002) *Personal Names: Studies of Medieval European Social Identity and Familial Structures*, Kalamazoo MI: Western Michigan University Press.

Bendix, R. (1960) *Max Weber: An Intellectual Portrait*, London: Heinemann.

Benjamin, W. (2004) *Walter Benjamin: Selected Writings Volume 1, 1913–1926* Marcus Bullock and Michael W. Jennings (ed.) Cambridge MA: Harvard University Press.

Benveniste, E. (1964) *Indo-European Language and Society* (transl. Elizabeth Palmer), London: Faber and Faber.

Berger, P. and Luckmann, T. (1967) *The Social Construction of Reality*, London: Allen Lane.

Berque, A. (1997) *Japan: Nature and Artifice* (transl. Ros Schwartz), Yelvertoft Manor, Northamptonshire: Pilkington Press.

Berry, M.E. (2006) *Japan in Print: Information and Nation in the Early Modern Period*, Berkeley: University of California Press.

Blanchot, M. (1992) *The Infinite Conversation* (transl. Susan Hanson), Minneapolis: University of Minnesota Press.

Bloch, E. (1999) *Literary Essays*, Stanford: Stanford University Press.

Bloch, M. (1989) *Feudal Society* 2 vols (transl. L.A. Manyon), London: Routledge.

Blumenberg, H. (1983) *Legitimacy of the Modern Age* (transl. Robert M. Wallace), Cambridge MA: MIT Press.

Blussé, L., Smits, I. and Remmelinks, W. (2000) *Bridging the Divide: 400 Years the Netherlands-Japan*, The Netherlands: Hotei Publishing.

Borkenau, F. (1981) *End and Beginning: On the Generations of Culture and the Origins of the West*, New York: Columbia University Press.

Braudel, F. (1974) *Capitalism and Material Life 1400–1800* (transl. Miriam Kochan), London: Fontana.

Braudel, F. (1981) *The Structures of Everyday Life* (transl. Siân Reynolds), London: Collins.

Braudel, F. (1995) *A History of Civilizations* (transl. Richard Mayne), New York: Penguin.

Brown, P. (1988) *Body and Society: Men, Women, and Sexual Renunciation in Early Christianity*, New York: Columbia University Press.

Broyard, A. (1992) *Intoxicated By My Illness*, New York: Clarkson Potter.

Brubaker, R. (1984) *The Limits of Rationality*, London: Allen and Unwin.

Bruck, G. vom and Bodenhorn, B. (2006) *The Anthropology of Names and Naming*, Cambridge: Cambridge University Press.

Bryson, N. (1990) *Looking at the Overlooked*, London: Reaktion Books.

Bumke, J. (1991) *Courtly Culture: Literature and Society in the High Middle Ages*, Berkeley: California University Press.

Burckhardt, J. (1990) *The Civilization of the Renaissance in Italy* (transl. S.G.C. Middlemore), Harmondsworth: Penguin.

Burrow, J.W. (1966) *Evolution and Society*, Cambridge: Cambridge University Press.

Burrow, J.W. (2000) *The Crisis of Reason: European Thought 1848–1914*, New Haven: Yale University Press.

Butler, J. (1997) *The Psychic Life of Power: Theories in Subjection*, Stanford: Stanford University Press.

Butler, J. (2005) *Giving an Account of Oneself*, New York: Fordham University Press.

Buxton, R. (1999) *From Myth to Reason?: Studies in the Development of Greek Thought*, Oxford: Clarendon Press.

Bynum, C.W. (2005) *Metamorphosis and Identity*, New York: Zone.

Canguilhem, G. (1989) *The Normal and The Pathological* (transl. Carolyn R. Fawcett), New York: Zone.

Carrithers, M., Collins, S. and Lukes, S. Eds. (1985) *The Category of the Person: Anthropology, Philosophy, History*, Cambridge: Cambridge University Press.

Caruth, C. (1995) *Unclaimed Experience: Trauma, Narrative and History*, Baltimore: The Johns Hopkins University Press.

Caruth, C. (1996) *Trauma: Explorations in Memory*, Baltimore: The Johns Hopkins University Press.

Castells, M. (1997) *The Power of Identity*, Oxford: Blackwell.

Certeau, M. de (1984) *The Practice of Everyday Life* (transl. Steven Rendall), Berkeley: University of California Press.

Certeau, M., de Giard, L. and Mayol, P. (1998) *The Practice of Everyday Life Volume 2: Living and Cooking* (transl. Timothy J. Tamasik), Minneapolis: University of Minnesota Press.

Chatterjee, P. (1993) *The Nation and its Fragments*, Princeton NJ: Princeton University Press.

Childe, V.G. (1964/1951) *Man Makes Himself*, Harmondsworth: Penguin.

Chrétien, J-L. (1996) *De la fatigue*, Paris: Editions de Minuit.

Clarke, B. and Henderson, L.D. (2002) *From Energy to Information,* Stanford: Stanford University Press.

Coetzee, J.M. (1999) *The Lives of Animals,* Stanford: Stanford University Press.

Cohen, J.J. (2003) *Medieval Identity Machines,* Minneapolis: Minnesota University Press.

Cole, S.A. (2001) *Suspect Identities: A History of Fingerprinting and Criminal Identification,* Cambridge MA: Harvard University Press.

Collingwood, R.G. (1994) *The Idea of History,* New York: Oxford University Press.

Corbin, A., Courtine, J.J. and Vigarello, G. (2006) *Histoire du Corps,* Paris: Seuill.

Crossley, P.K. (2008) *What is Global History?,* Cambridge MA: Polity Press.

Deleuze, G. and Guattari F. (1983) *Anti-Oedipus: Capitalism and Schizophrenia,* Minneapolis: Minnesota University Press.

Derrida, J. (1973) *Speech and Phenomena,* Evanston IL: Northwestern University Press.

Derrida, J. (1995) *On The Name,* Stanford: Stanford University Press.

Derrida, J. (2008) *Psyche: Inventions of the Other Volume 1,* Stanford: Stanford University Press.

Detienne, M. (2007) *The Greeks and Us,* Malden MA: Polity.

Dilthey, W. (1988) *Introduction to the Human Sciences* (transl. Ramon J. Betanzos), London: Harvester Wheatsheaf.

Dilthey, W. (1996) *Poetry and Experience,* Princeton NJ: Princeton University Press.

Douglas, M. (1978) *Natural Symbols,* Harmondsworth: Penguin.

Duarra, P. (1995) *Rescuing History from the Nation,* Chicago: University of Chicago Press.

Duby, G. (1980) *The Three Orders: Feudal Society Imagined,* Chicago: University of Chicago Press.

Duby, G. and Ariès, P. (eds) (1985–87) *A History of Private Life,* Cambridge MA: Harvard University Press.

Duby, G. Ed. (1992–94) *A History of Women in the West* 5 vols., Cambridge MA: Harvard University Press.

Durkheim, É. (1984) *The Division of Labour in Society* (transl. W.D. Hall), London: Palgrave Macmillan.

Durkheim, É. (1995) *The Elementary Forms of Religious Life* (transl. Karen E. Fields), New York: Free Press.

Durkheim, É. (2002) *Suicide* 2nd edn., London: Routledge.

Egginton, W. (2002) *How the World Became a Stage: Presence, Theatricality, and the Question of Modernity,* Albany: SUNY Press.

Eisenstadt, S.M. (1986) *The Origins and Diversity of Axial Age Civilizations,* Albany: SUNY Press.

Eisenstadt, S.M. (1996) *Japanese Civilization: A Comparative View*, Chicago: University of Chicago Press.

Eisenstein, E.L. (1983) *The Printing Revolution in Early Modern Europe*, Cambridge: Cambridge University Press.

Eksteins, M. (1990) *Rites of Spring: The Great War and the Birth of the Modern World*, New York: Anchor.

Eliade, M. (1959) *The Sacred and The Profane: The Nature of Religion* (transl. Willard R. Trask), New York: Harcourt, Brace and World.

Elias N. (1982) *The History of Manners*, New York: Panthenon.

Elias, N. (1998) *The Norbert Elias Reader* Johan Goudsblom and Stephen Mennel (eds), Oxford: Blackwell.

Elias, N. (2000/1939) *The Civilizing Process: Sociogenetic and Psychogenetic Investigations*, Oxford: Blackwell.

Entwistle, J. (2000) *The Fashioned Body: Fashion, Dress and Modern Social Theory*, Cambridge: Polity.

Faure, B. (2003) *Double Exposure: Cutting Across Buddhist and Western Discourses* (transl. Janet Lloyd), Stanford: Stanford University Press.

Febvre, L. (1973) *A New Kind of History: From the Writings of Febvre* (transl. K. Folca), London: Routledge and Kegan Paul.

Feher, M. Ed. (1989) *Fragments for a History of the Human Body* 3 vols, New York: Zone.

Ferguson, H. (1995) *Melancholy and the Critique of Modernity*, London: Routledge.

Ferguson, H. (1997) 'Me and My Shadows: On the Accumulation of Body-Images in Western Society Part Two – Corporeal Forms of Modernity', *Body and Society*, 4(3), 1–29.

Ferguson, H. (2000) *Driscoll's Folly*, Xlibris.com.

Ferguson, H. (2006) *Phenomenological Sociology: Experience and Insight in Modern Society*, London: Sage.

Fernández-Armesto, F. (2002) *Food: A History*, London: Pan.

Fernández-Armesto, F. (2006) *Pathfinders: A Global History of Exploration*, Oxford: Oxford University Press.

Fichte, J.G. (2008) *The Science of Knowledge*, Cambridge: Cambridge University Press.

Flandrin, J.L. and Montanari, M. (eds) (1999) *Food: A Culinary History from Antiquity to the Present*, New York: Columbia University Press.

Foucault, M. (1977) *Discipline and Punish: the Birth of the Prison* (transl. Alan Sheridan), London: Allen Lane the Penguin Press.

Foucault, M. (2005) *The Hermeneutics of the Subject*, London: Palgrave Macmillan.

Fowler, E. (1988) *The Rhetoric of Confession*, Berkeley: University of California Press.

Fraser, N., Honnet, A., Golb, J. and Wilke, C. (2003) *Redistribution or Recognition?: A Political-Philosophical Exchange,* London: Verso.

Freud, S. (1990) *Case Histories* 2 vols, Harmondsworth: Penguin.

Freud, S. (1991) *On Sexuality: Three Essays on the Theory of Sexuality and Other Works,* Harmondsworth: Penguin.

Friese, H. Ed. (2001) *The Moment: Time and Rupture in Modern Thought,* Liverpool: Liverpool University Press.

Friese, H. Ed. (2002) *Identities: Time, Difference, and Boundaries,* New York: Berghahn Books.

Frisby, D. (1989) *Fragments of Modernity,* Cambridge: Polity.

Fritzsche, P. (1998) *Reading Berlin 1900,* Cambridge MA: Harvard University Press.

Fujii, J.A. (1993) *Complicit Fictions: The Subject in the Modern Japanese Prose Narrative,* Berkeley: University of California Press.

Fujita, T. (1996) *Splendid Monarchy: Power and Pageantry in Modern Japan,* Berkeley: University of California Press.

Gadamer, H-G. (1995) *The Enigma of Health* (transl. Nick Walker and Jason Geiger), Stanford: Stanford University Press.

Gaita, R. (2004) *The Philosopher's Dog,* London: Routledge.

Garon, S. (1997) *Molding Japanese Minds: The State in Everyday Life,* Princeton NJ: Princeton University Press.

Geary, P.J. (2003) *The Myth of Nations,* Princeton NJ: Princeton University Press.

Genette, G. (1997) *Paratexts: Thresholds of Interpretation* (transl. Jane E. Lewin), Cambridge: Cambridge University Press.

Gergen, K.J. (2000) *The Saturated Self: Dilemmas of Identity in Contemporary Life,* New York: Basic Books.

Giddens, A. (1991) *Modernity and Self-Identity,* Cambridge: Polity.

Giddens, A. (1995) *The Transformation of Intimacy,* Cambridge: Polity.

Giedion, S. (1948) *Mechanization Takes Command,* New York: Oxford University Press.

Gilmore, L. (2001) *The Limits of Autobiography: Trauma and Testimony,* Ithaca: Cornell University Press.

Gilson, E. (1990) *The Spirit of Medieval Philosophy,* Notre Dame IND: Notre Dame University Press.

Ginzburg, L. (1991) *On Psychological Prose* (transl. Judson Rosengrant), Princeton NJ: Princeton University Press.

Girard, R. (2005) *Violence and the Sacred,* London: Continuum.

Glete, J. (2002) *War and the State in Modern Europe,* London: Routledge.

Gluck, C. (1985) *Japan's Modern Myths,* Princeton NJ: Princeton University Press.

Goffman, E. (1959) *The Presentation of Self in Everyday Life,* New York: Doubleday.

Goffman, E. (1973) *Interaction Ritual,* Harmondsworth: Penguin.

Goldmann, L. (1964) *The Hidden God,* London: Routledge.

Goody, J. (1996) *The East in the West,* Cambridge: Cambridge University Press.

Goody, J. (2004) *Capitalism and Modernity,* Malden MA and Cambridge: Polity.

Goody, J. (2006) *The Theft of History,* Cambridge: Cambridge University Press.

Gosetti-Ferencei, J.A. (2008) *The Ecstatic Quotidian: Phenomenological Sightings in Modern Art and Literature,* University Park PA: Pennsylvania University Press.

Gottlieb, N. (2005) *Language and Society in Japan,* Cambridge: Cambridge University Press.

Gray, J. (2002) *Straw Dogs: Thoughts on Humans and Other Animals,* London: Granta.

Greenblatt, S. (1980) *Renaissance Self-Fashioning,* Chicago: Chicago University Press.

Greenfeld, L. (1993) *Nationalism: Five Roads to Modernity,* Cambridge MA: Harvard University Press.

Groebner, V. (2007) *Who Are You?: Identification, Deception and Surveillance in Early Modern Europe* (transl. Mark Kybury and John Peck), New York: Zone Books.

Grosz, E. (1994) *Volatile Bodies,* Bloomington: Indiana University Press.

Gurevich, A.J. (1985) *Categories of Medieval Culture,* London: Routledge.

Gusdorf, G. (1948) *La découverte de soi,* Paris: Presses Universitaires de France.

Gusdorf, G. (1993) *Le romantisme* 2 vols, Paris: Payot.

Habermas, J. (1989) *The Structural Transformation of the Public Sphere* (transl. Thomas Burger), Cambridge: Polity.

Hacking, I. (1998) *Rewriting the Soul: Multiple Personality and the Sciences of Memory,* Princeton NJ: Princeton University Press.

Hadot, P. (1995) *Philosophy as a Way of Life,* Oxford: Blackwell.

Hall, D.L. and Ames, R.T. (1995) *Anticipating China: Thinking through the Narratives of Chinese and Western Culture,* Albany: SUNY Press.

Hall, D.L. and Ames, R.T. (1998) *Thinking from the Han: Self, Truth, and Transcendence in Chinese and Western Culture,* Albany: SUNY Press.

Halsey, A.H. (2004) *A History of British Sociology,* New York: Oxford University Press.

Hankiss, E. (2001) *Fears and Symbols; Understanding the Role of Fear in Western Civilization,* Budapest: Central European University Press.

Hardacre, H. (1989) *Shinto and the State, 1868–1988,* Princeton NJ: Princeton University Press.

Harman, G. (2002) *Tool-Being: Heidegger and the Metaphysics of Objects,* Chicago: Open Court.

Harré, R. (1998) *The Singular Self: An Introduction to the Psychology of Person-hood*, London: Sage.

Hegel, G.W.F. (1977) *Phenomenology of Spirit* (transl. A.V. Miller), Oxford: The Clarendon Press.

Heidegger, M. (1996) *The Fundamental Concepts of Metaphysics* (transl. William H. McNeill and Nicholas Walker), Bloomington: Indiana University Press.

Heller, T.C., Sosna, M. and Wellbery, D.E. (1986) *Reconstructing Individualism: Autonomy, Individuality, and the Self in Western Thought*, Stanford: Stanford University Press.

Hendry, J. (1993) *Wrapping Culture: Politeness, Presentation, and Power in Japan and Other Societies*, Oxford: Clarendon Press.

Herder, J.G. von (1992) *Johann Gottfried Herder: Selected Early Works* Karl Menges (ed.), University Park PA: Pennsylvania University Press.

Herrin, J. (1989) *The Formation of Christendom*, London: Fontana.

Highmore, B. (ed.) (2002) *The Everyday Life Reader*, London: Routledge.

Hobsbawm, E. (1992) *Nationals and Nationalism Since 1780*, Cambridge: Cambridge University Press.

Hobsbawm, E. and Ranger, T. (1992) *The Invention of Tradition*, Cambridge: Cambridge University Press.

Hodgson, M.G.S. (1974) *The Venture of Islam* 3 vols, Chicago: University of Chicago Press.

Honneth, A. (1996) *The Struggle for Recognition*, Cambridge: Polity.

Howland, D.R. (1996) *Borders of Chinese Civilization*, Durham: Duke University Press.

Howland, D.R. (2002) *Translating the West: Language and Political Reason in Nineteenth-Century Japan*, Honolulu: University of Hawaii Press.

Huber, T.M. (1981) *The Revolutionary Origins of Modern Japan*, Stanford: Stanford University Press.

Husserl, E. (1990) *Ideas Pertaining to A Pure Phenomenology and to a Phenomenological Philosophy Book Two* (transl. F. Kersten), Dordrecht: Kluwer.

Husserl, E. (2003/1891) *The Philosophy of Arithmetic* (transl. Dallas Willard), Dordrecht: Kluwer.

Ikegami, E. (1995) *The Taming of the Samurai*, Cambridge MA: Harvard University Press.

Ikegami, E. (2007) *The Bonds of Civility*, Cambridge: Cambridge University Press.

Inoura, Y. and Kawatake, T. (2006) *The Traditional Theatre of Japan*, Warren CT: Floating World Editions.

Ireland, C. (2004) *The Subaltern Appeal to Experience*, Montreal: McGill-Queen's University Press.

Iser, W. (1993) *The Fictive and the Imaginary*, Baltimore MD: The Johns Hopkins University Press.

Jay, M. (2005) *Songs of Experience: Modern American and European Variations on a Universal Theme*, Berkeley: University of California Press.

Jensen, M. (1995) *The Making of Modern Japan*, Cambridge MA: Harvard University Press.

Joas, H. (1993) *Pragmatism and Sociology*, Chicago: Chicago University Press.

Johns A. (1998) *The Nature of the Book*, Chicago: University of Chicago Press.

Jütte, R. (2004) *A History of the Senses* (transl. James Lynn), Cambridge MA: Polity.

Jullien, F. (1999) *The Propensity of Things: Towards a History of Efficacy in China* (transl. Janet Lloyd), New York: Zone.

Jullien, F. (2004) *Detour and Access: Strategies of meaning in China and Greece* (transl. Sophie Hawkes), New York: Zone.

Jullien, F. (2007) *Vital Nourishment: Departing from Happiness* (transl. Arthur Goldhammer), New York: Zone.

Kafka, F. (1978) *Letters to Felice*, Harmondsworth: Penguin.

Kafka, F. (1999) *Metamorphosis and Other Stories*, Harmondsworth: Penguin.

Kalberg, S. (1994) *Max Weber's Comparative-Historical Sociology*, Cambridge MA: Polity.

Kasulis, T.P. (2004) *Shinto: The Way Home*, Honolulu: University of Hawaii Press.

Kern, S. (1990) *The Culture of Space and Time, 1880–1918*, Cambridge MA: Harvard University Press.

Kierkegaard, S. (1980) *The Concept of Anxiety* (transl. Reidar Thomte), Princeton NJ: Princeton University Press.

Kierkegaard, S. (1988) *Either/Or: A Fragment of Life* 2 Vols (transl. Howard V. Hong and Edna H. Hong), Princeton NJ: Princeton University Press.

Kim, R.E. (1998) *Lost Names*, Berkeley: University of California Press.

Kleinschmidt, H. (2000) *Understanding the Middle Ages*, Woodbridge: The Boydell Press.

Koselleck, R. (1985) *Futures Past: On the Semantics of Historical Time* (transl. Keith Tribe), Cambridge MA: MIT Press.

Koyré, A. (1978) *Galileo Studies*, Atlantic Highlands NJ: Harvester and Humanities Press.

Kripke, S.A. (1980) *Naming and Necessity*, Oxford: Blackwell.

Kross, J. (2003) *Treading Air* (transl. Eric Dickens), London: Harvill Press.

Kuper, A. (1988) *The Invention of Primitive Society: Transformation of an Illusion*, London: Routledge.

Lambropoulos, V. (1993) *The Rise of Eurocentrism*, Princeton NJ: Princeton University Press.

Latour, B. (1993) *We Have Never been Modern* (transl. Catherine Porter), Cambridge MA: Harvard University Press.

Latour, B. (2004) *Politics of Nature* (transl. Catherine Porter), Cambridge MA: Harvard University Press.

Le Goff, J. (1980) *Time, Work, and Culture in the Middle Ages*, Chicago: University of Chicago Press.

Lebra, T.S. (2005) *Self in Cultural Logic*, Honolulu: University of Hawaii Press.

Lefebvre, H. (2008) *Critique of Everyday Life* 3 Vols (transl. John Moore and Gregory Elliott), London: Verso.

Lepenies, W. (1992) *Melancholy and Society* (transl. Jeremy Gaines and Doris Jones), Cambridge MA: Harvard University Press.

Levathes, L. (1994) *When China Ruled the Seas*, New York: Oxford University Press.

Levi-Strauss, C. (1966) *The Savage Mind*, London: Weidenfeld and Nicolson.

Lewis, M.W. and Wigen, K.E. (1997) *The Myth of Continents: A Critique of Metageography*, Berkeley: University of California Press.

Leys, R. (2000) *Trauma: A Genealogy*, Chicago: University of Chicago Press.

Lipovetsky, G. (2002) *Empire of Fashion: Dressing Modern Democracy* (transl. Catherine Porter), Princeton NJ: Princeton University Press.

Lloyd, G.E.R. (1996) *Adversaries and Authorities: Investigations into Ancient Greek and Chinese Science*, Cambridge: Cambridge University Press.

Lloyd, G.E.R. (2002) *The Ambitions of Curiosity: Understanding the World in Ancient Greece and China*, Cambridge: Cambridge University Press.

Lloyd, G.E.R. (2005) *Delusions of Invulnerability: Wisdom and Morality in Ancient Greece, China, and Today*, London: Duckworth.

Löwith, K. (1964) *From Hegel to Nietzsche: The Revolution in Nineteenth Century Thought*, London: Constable.

Lüdtke, A. (1995) *The History of Everyday Life: Reconstructing Historical Experiences and Ways of Life* (transl. William Templer), Princeton NJ: Princeton University Press.

Luhmann, N. (1998) *Love as Passion: The Codification of Intimacy* (transl. Jeremy Gaines and Doris L. Jones), Stanford: Stanford University Press.

Lukes, S. (1973) *Individualism*, Oxford: Blackwell.

Maalouf, A. (2000) *On Identity* (transl. Barbara Bray), London: Harvill Press.

Marías, J. (2006) *Your Face Tomorrow: Fever and Spear* (transl. Margaret Jull Costa), New York: Vintage.

Marin, L. (1988) *Portrait of the King* (transl. Martha M. Houle), London: Macmillan.

Marion, J-L. (2002) *In Excess: Studies in Saturated Phenomena*, New York: Fordham University Press.

Martin, R. and Barresi, J. (2006) *The Rise and Fall of the Soul and Self*, New York: Columbia University Press.

Matsunosuke, N. (1997) *Edo Culture: Daily Life and Diversions in Urban Japan, 1600–1868*, Honolulu: University of Hawaii Press.

Mattelart, A. (1994) *Mapping World Communication* (transl. Susan Emanuel and James A. Cohen), Minneapolis: Minnesota University Press.

Mauss, M. (1952) *The Gift: Forms and Functions of Exchange in Archaic Society*, London: Cohen and West.

Mauss, M. (1979) *Sociology and Psychology: Essays* (transl. B. Brewster), London: Routledge and Kegan Paul.

McClain, J.L., Merriman, J.M. and Kaoru, U. (1994) *Edo and Paris: Urban Life and the State in the Early Modern Era*, Ithaca: Cornell University Press.

Mead, G.H. (1967) *Mind, Self, and Society*, Chicago: University of Chicago Press.

Mennell, S. (1985) *All Manners of Food*, Oxford: Blackwell.

Merleau-Ponty, M. (1962) *The Phenomenology of Perception* (transl. Colin Smith), London: Routledge.

Meyerson, É. (1930) *Identity and Reality* (transl. Kate Loewenberg), London: Allen and Unwin.

Montaigne, M. de (1991) *The Complete Essays* (transl. M.A. Screech), London: Allen Lane the Penguin Press.

Montgomery, S.L. (2000) *Science in Translation*, Chicago: University of Chicago Press.

Moravia, A. (1999) *Boredom* (transl. Angus Davidson), New York: New York Review Books.

Moravia, A. (2001) *A Time of Indifference* (transl. Tami Calliope), South Royalton, Vermont: Steerforth Press.

Morris, D.B. (1998) *Illness and Culture in the Postmodern Age*, Berkeley: University of California Press.

Nagatomo, S. (1992) *Attunement through the Body*, Albany: SUNY Press.

Nancy, J-L. (2002) *The Restlessness of the Negative*, Minneapolis: University of Minnesota Press.

Nancy, J-L. (2007) *The Invention of the World or Globalization* (transl. Francois Raffoulis and David Pettigrew), New York: SUNY Press.

Nelson, J.K. (2000) *Enduring Identities: The Guise of Shinto in Contemporary Japan*, Honolulu: University of Hawaii Press.

Newton, Sir I. (1999) *The Principia: Mathematical Principles of Natural Philosophy* (transl. I. Bernard Cohen and Anne Whitman), Berkeley: University of California Press.

Nietzsche, F. (1986) *Human, All Too Human* (transl. Erich Heller), Cambridge: Cambridge University Press.

Nietzsche, F. (1999) *The Birth of Tragedy and Other Writings* (transl. Ronald Speirs), New York: Cambridge University Press.

Nietzsche, F. (2008) *On the Genealogy of Morals*, Oxford: Oxford University Press.

Nock, A.D. (1933) *Conversion*, Oxford: Clarendon Press.

Nora, P. (1996–1998) *Realms of Memory* 3 Vols, New York: Columbia University Press.

Nordau, M.S. (1993) *Degeneration*, Lincoln NE: University of Nebraska Press.

Novalis (Friedrich von Hardenberg) (1997) *Novalis: Philosophical Writings* Margaret Mahony Stoljar (ed.), Albany: SUNY Press.

O'Hear, A. (1996) *Verstehen and Humane Understanding*, Cambridge: Cambridge University Press.

Oelschlaeger, M. (1993) *The Idea of Wilderness: From Prehistory to the Age of Ecology*, New Haven: Yale University Press.

Ohnuki-Tierney, E. (1993) *Rice as Self: Japanese Identities Through Time*, Princeton NJ: Princeton University Press.

Ohnuki-Tierney, E. (2002) *Kamikaze, Cherry Blossom and Nationalisms: The Militarization of Aesthetics*, Chicago: University of Chicago Press.

Ortolani, B. (1995) *The Japanese Theatre*, Princeton NJ: Princeton University Press.

Pagden, A. (1994) *European Encounters with the New World*, New Haven NJ: Yale University Press.

Parsons, T. (1952) *The Social System*, London: Routledge.

Pastoureau, M. (2004) *Une histoire symbolique du Moyen Age occidentale*, Paris: Seuil.

Pessoa, F. (2002) *The Book of Disquiet* (transl. Richard Zenith), London: Penguin.

Pirenne, H. (1939) *Mohammed and Charlemagne* (transl. Bernard Miall), London: Allen and Unwin.

Plutschow, H. (1995) *Japan's Name Culture*, Folkestone: Japan Library.

Poggi, G. (1978) *The Development of the Modern State*, London: Hutchinson.

Poggi, G. (1990) *The State: Its Nature, Development and Prospects*, Cambridge: Polity.

Pohier, J. (1985) *God: In Fragments* (transl. J.S. Bowden), London: SCM.

Pomeranz, K. (2000) *The Great Divergence*, Princeton NJ: Princeton University Press.

Poovey, M. (1998) *A History of the Modern Fact*, Chicago: University of Chicago Press.

Poovey, M. (2008) *Genres of the Credit Economy*, Chicago: University of Chicago Press.

Porter, R. (1999) *The Greatest Benefit to Mankind: A Medical History of Humanity from Antiquity to the Present*, London: Fontana.

Pseudo-Dionysius the Areopagite (1940) *The Divine Names; and the Mystical Theology* (transl. C.E. Rolt), London: SPCK.

Rabinbach, A. (1990) *The Human Motor: Energy, Fatigue, and the Origins of Modernity*, Berkeley: University of California Press.

Reader, I. and Tanabe, G.J. (1998) *Practically Religious: Worldly Benefits and the Common Religion of Japan*, Honolulu: University of Hawaii Press.

Reddy, W.M. (2001) *The Navigation of Feeling: A Framework for the History of Emotions*, Cambridge: Cambridge University Press.

Reiss, T.J. (2002) *Against Autonomy: Global Dialectics of Cultural Exchange*, Stanford: Stanford University Press.

Richards, J.F. (2003) *The Unending Frontier: An Environmental History of the Early Modern World*, Berkeley: University of California Press.

Richards, R.J. (2002) *The Romantic Conception of Life*, Chicago: University of Chicago Press.

Ricoeur, P. (1990, 1994, 2004) *Time and Narrative* 3 vols., Chicago, University of Chicago Press.

Ricoeur, P. (1992) *Oneself as Another* (transl. Kathleen Blamey), Chicago: University of Chicago Press.

Ricoeur, P. (1966) *Freedom and Nature: The Voluntary and the Involuntary* (transl. Erazim V. Kohák), Evanston Il: Northwestern University Press.

Roche, D. (1996) *The Culture of Clothing* (transl. Jean Birrell), Cambridge: Cambridge University Press.

Rohde, E. (1925) *Psyche: The Cult of Souls and Belief in Immortality Among the Greeks*, London: K. Paul, Trench and Trubner.

Ronell, A. (2002) *Stupidity*, Urbana: University of Illinois Press.

Rose, N. (1999) *Governing the Soul: The Shaping of the Private Self*, London: Free Association Books.

Rosenberger, N.R. (1992) *The Japanese Sense of Self*, Cambridge: Cambridge University Press.

Saenger, P. (1997) *Space Between Words: The Origins of Silent Reading*, Stanford: Stanford University Press.

Said, E.W. (1978) *Orientalism*, Harmondsworth: Penguin.

Sand, J. (2003) *House and Home in Modern Japan*, Cambridge MA: Harvard University Press.

Santner, E.L. (2006) *On Creaturely Life*, Chicago: The University of Chicago Press.

Sapir, E. (1949) *Selected Writings in Language, Culture, and Personality*, Berkeley: University of California Press.

Saramago, J. (1999) *All The Names*, London: Harvill Press.

Sarti, R. (2002) *Europe at Home: Family and Material Culture 1500–1800* (transl. Allan Cameron), New Haven: Yale University Press.

Schechner, R. (1985) *Between Theatre and Anthropology*, Philadelphia: University of Philadelphia Press.

Schechner, R. (2003) *Performance Theory*, London: Routledge.

Schilder, P. (1935) *The Image and Appearance of the Human Body*, London: K. Paul, Trench, and Trubner.

Schlegel, F. von (1971) *Lucinde and Fragments*, Peter Firchow (ed.), Minneapolis: University of Minnesota Press.

Schluchter, W. (1996) *Paradoxes of Modernity: Culture and Conduct in the Theory of Max Weber*, Stanford: Stanford University Press.

Schneewind, J.B. (1998) *The Invention of Autonomy*, New York: Cambridge University Press.

Schutz, A. (1962–66) *Collected Papers* 3 Vols, The Hague: Nijhoff.

Schutz, A. (1967) *The Phenomenology of the Social World*, Evanston Ill: Northwestern University Press.

Schwartz, B.I. (1985) *The World of Thought in Ancient China*, Cambridge MA: Harvard University Press.

Scott, C.E. (2007) *Living with Indifference*, Bloomington: Indiana University Press.

Sennett, R. (2004) *Respect: The Formation of Character in an Age of Inequality*, Harmondsworth: Penguin.

Serres, M. (2004) *The Parasite* (transl. Lawrence R. Schehr), Minneapolis: University of Minnesota Press.

Shankman, S. and Durrant, S.W. (2002) *Early China/Ancient Greece: Thinking through Comparisons*, Albany: SUNY Press.

Sheringham, M. (2006) *Everyday Life: Theories and Practices from Surrealism to the Present*, New York: Oxford University Press.

Showalter, E. (1997) *Hystories: Hysterical Epidemics and Modern Culture*, London: Picador.

Siegel, J. (2005) *The Idea of the Self*, Cambridge: Cambridge University Press.

Simmel, G. (1997) *Simmel on Culture* David Frisby and Mike Featherstone (eds), London: Sage.

Smith, M.M. (2007) *Sensing the Past*, Berkeley: University of California Press.

Smith, P. (1994) *Possessing Nature: Museums, Collecting, and Scientific Culture in Early Modern Italy*, Berkeley: University of California Press.

Smith-Bannister, S. (1997) *Names and Naming Patterns in England 1538–1700*, Oxford: Clarendon Press.

Sontag, S. (2002) *Illness as Metaphor*, Harmondsworth: Penguin.

Sorabji, R. (2000) *Emotion and Peace of Mind*, Oxford: Clarendon Press.

Spariosu, M. (1997) *Wreath of Wild Olive: Play, Liminality, and the Study of Literature*, Albany: SUNY Press.

Starobinski, J. (1988) *Jean-Jacques Rousseau: Transparency and Obstruction* (transl. Arthur Goldhammer), Chicago: University of Chicago Press

Steadman, J.M. (1970) *The Myth of Asia*, London: Methuen.

Stearns, P.N. (Ed.) (2006) *A Day in the Life: Studying Daily Life through History*, Westport CT: Greenwood Press.

Suzuki, T. (1996) *Narrating the Self: Fictions of Japanese modernity*, Stanford: Stanford University Press.

Szep, E. (1994) *The Smell of Humans* (transl. John Batki), Budapest: Central European University Press.

Taylor, C. (1989) *Sources of the Modern Self: Making of the Modern Identity*, Cambridge: Cambridge University Press.

Taylor, C. (2004) *Modern Social Imaginaries*, Durham NC: Duke University Press.

Te Brake, W. (1998) *Shaping History: Ordinary People in European Politics, 1500–1700*, Berkeley: University of California Press.

Terestchenko, M. (2007) *Un si fragile vernis d'humanité: Banalité du mal, banalité du bien*, Paris: La Découverte .

Theunissen, M. (1984) *The Other: Studies in the Social Ontology of Husserl, Heidegger, Sartre, and Buber*, Cambridge MA: MIT Press.

Todorov, T. (1999) *The Conquest of America: The Question of the Other*, Norman, Oklahoma: University of Oklahoma Press.

Tönnies, F. (1955) *Community and Association* (transl. Charles P. Loomis), London: Routledge.

Totman, C. (2000) *A History of Japan*, Malden MA: Blackwell.

Turner, V.W. (1969) *The Ritual Process: Structure and Anti-Structure*, London: Routledge.

Turner, V.W. (1974) *Dramas, Fields, and Metaphors: Symbolic Action in Human Society*, Ithaca: Cornell University Press.

Turner, V.W. (1982) *From Ritual to Theatre: The Human Seriousness of Play*, New York: Performing Arts Journal Publications.

Turner, V.W. (1988) *The Anthropology of Performance*, New York: PAJ Publications.

Ugresic, D. (2005) *The Ministry of Pain*, London: Saqi Books.

Unger, R.M. (1975) *Knowledge and Politics*, New York: The Free Press.

Unger, R.M. (1984) *Passion – An Essay on Personality*, New York: Free Press.

Van den Berg, J.H. (1972) *Psychology of the Sickbed*, Pittsburgh: Duquesne University Press.

Vernant, J-P. (1991) *Mortals and Immortals: Collected Essays*, Princeton NJ: Princeton University Press.

Vico, G. (1984) *The New Science of Giambattista Vico* (transl. M.H. Fisch and T.G. Bergin), Ithaca: Cornell University Press.

Vinen, R. (2002) *A History in Fragments: Europe in the Twentieth Century*, London: Abacus.

Visker, R. (2005) *The Inhuman Condition: Looking for Difference after Levinas and Heidegger*, Dordrecht: Kluwer.

Voegelin, E. (2000) *Order and History: The Ecumenic Age*, Baton Rouge: University of Missouri Press.

Washburn, D. (1995) *The Dilemma of the Modern in Japanese Fiction*, New Haven: Yale University Press.

Washburn, D. (2007) *Translating Mount Fuji: Modern Japanese Fiction and the Ethics of Identity*, New York: Columbia University Press.

Weber, M. (1947) *From Max Weber: Essays in Sociology*, Hans Gerth and C. Wright Mills (eds), London: Routledge.

Weber, M. (1965) *The Sociology of Religion* (transl. Ephraim Fischoff), London: Methuen.

Weber, M. (1975) *Roscher and Knies: The Logical Problems of Historical Economics*, New York: The Free Press.

Weber, M. (1979) *Economy and Society* 2 vols, Berkeley: University of California Press.

Weber, M. (2001) *The Protestant Ethic and the Spirit of Capitalism*, London: Routledge.

Whorf, B.L (1956) *Language, Thought, and Reality*, Cambridge MA: MIT Press.

Wilson, S. (1998) *The Means of Naming*, London: UCL Press.

Wittgenstein, L. (1968) *Philosophical Investigations*, Cambridge: Cambridge University Press.

Wright Mills, C. (2000) *The Sociological Imagination*, New York: Oxford University Press.

Yates, F. (1966) *The Art of Memory*, London: Routledge.

Yuasa, Y. (1987) *The Body: Towards and Eastern Mind-Body Theory* (transl. Nagatomo Shigenori and T.P. Kasulis), Albany: SUNY Press.

Zammito, J.H. (2002) *Kant, Herder and the Birth of Anthropology*, Chicago: University of Chicago Press.

Zaretsky, E. (1976) *Capitalism, the Family, and Personal Life*, London: Pluto Press.

Zeldin, T. (1995) *An Intimate History of Humanity*, New York: Vintage.

Zerubavel, E. (1991) *The Fine Line: Making Distinctions in Everyday Life*, Chicago: University of Chicago Press.

Žižeck, S. (2006) *The Parallax View*, Cambridge MA: MIT Press.

INDEX